SHAKESPEARE RESTORED

AMS PRESS
NEW YORK

Reprinted from the edition of 1726, LONDON
First AMS EDITION published 1970
Manufactured in the United States of America

International Standard Book Number: 0–404–06364–0

Library of Congress Number: 70–131499

AMS PRESS INC.
NEW YORK, N.Y. 10003

SHAKESPEARE reſtored:

OR, A

SPECIMEN

OF THE

Many ERRORS,

AS WELL

Committed, as *Unamended*, by Mr. *POPE*

In his Late

EDITION of this POET.

DESIGNED

Not only to correct the ſaid EDITION, but to reſtore the True READING of *SHAKESPEARE* in all the *Editions* ever yet publiſh'd.

By Mr. THEOBALD.

-------------- Laniatum Corpore toto
DEIPHOBUM *vidi & lacerum crudeliter Ora,*
Ora, manuſque ambas, -------- VIRG.

LONDON:

Printed for R. FRANCKLIN under *Tom's*, J. WOODMAN and D. LYON under *Will's*, *Covent-Garden*, and C. DAVIS in *Hatton-Garden*.

M.DCC.XXVI.

TO

JOHN RICH Eſq;

SIR,

IT may ſeem a little particular, that, when I am attempting to reſtore SHAKESPEARE, I ſhould addreſs that Work to One, who has gone a great Way towards ſhutting him out of Doors; that is, towards baniſhing him the Benefit of the Stage, and confining us to read him in the Cloſet. Let me ſtand excuſed from intending any perſonal Accuſation here; for it is not You, indeed, but that Affection, with which *Entertain-*

ments of a *different Species* are pursued, has done this; and therefore I would fain transfer the Fault from You to the Town. Let us lay it upon the Times, as we are pleas'd to do some of our Sins upon Fate and Providence. Or, perhaps, the very Frame of our Nature is concern'd; and the Dissecters of an *Eye* and *Ear* can tell us to what Membranes, or Organs, we owe the Communication of *Pleasures*, in which the *rational Soul* has no Share. So shall we be able to account both for the Reception of GROTESQUE and OPERA.

IF PANTOMIMING be a Debauchery of the Stage, it is a Vice which is so becoming in the Excellence of Your own Performance, that I can scarce find in my Heart to be the first to wish it cur'd. Yet, as it is fabled of ACHILLES's *Spear*, that it had a Virtue to heal the Wounds it made; so we may prophesy, one Time or other, that the *Rust* of PANTOMIMES will be a *Salve* for the Recovery of DRAMATIC *Poetry.*

I AM juſtified in this Addreſs by another Conſideration, which is, That however you may have been a Sinner againſt SHAKESPEARE, you are not an impenitent one. And as King *Henry* IV. erected a Chapel to expiate the Injuries which he had done to his Predeceſſor, King *Richard*; ſo, the Town at leaſt ſay, you intend to appeaſe the *Manes* of our POET by *erecting* a MONUMENT to him. Go on in that pious, that reputable Intention; and, while the Taſte of the Publick demands it of you, continue to ſacrifice freſh *Pantomimes* to his Memory; when their Palates alter, convince them that You are provided to entertain them with an Elegance ſuitable to their Expectations.

BUT I am fall'n into a Strain which I had no Thoughts of purſuing, when I firſt ſate down to write this Epiſtle. The great OTWAY dedicated

one

one of his Plays to his Bookseller, as a Receipt for the *Copy-Money*; and I meant this merely (*si parva licet componere magnis*) as an Acknowledgment of some Obligations receiv'd, which you will not expect me to specify in Print. I design'd it to carry the Sentiments of *Friendship* and *Gratitude*; but, where it falls short in those Points, let it make Amends by this Profession, that You are always entitled, to the utmost of my poor Power, to demand all the Service of,

SIR,

Your most Obliged, and

Faithful Humble Servant,

March 18. 1725.

LEWIS THEOBALD.

SHAKESPEARE reſtor'd:

OR, A

SPECIMEN of ERRORS, &c

INTRODUCTION.

I HAVE very often declar'd, and that in a number of Companies, that what thro' the *Indolence*, what thro' the *Ignorance* of his EDITORS, we have ſcarce any Book in the *Engliſh* Tongue more fertile of Errors, than the Plays of *SHAKESPEARE*. And, I believe, whenever I have fall'n on this Subject, I have not fail'd to expreſs my Wiſh, that ſome fine *Genius*, equal to the taſk, would befriend the Memory of this immortal Poet, and contribute to the Pleaſure of the preſent and of future Times, in retrieving, as far as poſſible, the *original Purity* of his *Text*, and rooting out that vaſt Crop of *Errors*, which has almoſt choak'd up his *Beauties*.

 It

It was no ſmall Satisfaction therefore to me, when I firſt heard Mr. *Pope* had taken upon him the Publication of *Shakespeare*. I very reaſonably expected, from his known Talents and Abilities, from his uncommon Sagacity and Diſcernment, and from his unwearied Diligence and Care of informing himſelf by an happy and extenſive Converſation, we ſhould have had our Author come out as perfect, as the want of *Manuſcripts* and *original Copies* could give us a Poſſibility of hoping. I may dare to ſay, a great Number of *Shakespeare*'s Admirers, and of Mr. *Pope*'s too, (both which I ſincerely declare myſelf,) concurred in this Expectation: For there is a certain *curioſa fælicitas*, as was ſaid of an eminent *Roman* Poet, in that Gentleman's Way of working, which, we preſum'd, would have laid itſelf out largely in ſuch a Province; and that he would not have ſate down contented with performing, as he calls it himſelf, the *dull Duty* of an Editor only. *Shakespeare*'s *Works* have always appear'd to me like what he makes his *Hamlet* compare the World to, an *unweeded Garden grown to Seed:* And I am ſorry there is ſtill reaſon to complain, the *Weeds* in him are ſo very ſparingly thin'd, that, not to ſpeak out of compaſs, a thouſand *rank* and *unſightly* ones are left to ſtare us in the Face, and clog the Delight of the expected Proſpect.

It muſt neceſſarily happen, that where the Aſſiſtance of *Manuſcripts* is wanting to ſet an Author's Meaning right, and reſcue him from thoſe Errors which have been tranſmitted down thro' a Series of incorrect Editions, and a long Intervention of Time, many Paſſages muſt be deſperate, and paſt a Cure, and their true Senſe irretrievable, either to Care, or the Sagacity of Conjecture.

And there is one Unhappineſs too, which generally attends the *Republication* of *Engliſh* Books, which is, That being the Property of ſome Perſons *in Trade*, who, too often, know nothing more of their Copy than that there is a *Demand* for *reprinting* it; and who are, withal, Perſons of ſuch *commendable* Frugality, that they think every Farthing which is given for the Labour of *Reviſe*, to be ſo much Money given away for nothing: The *Preſs* is ſet to work from a *printed* Precedent, and ſo the

more

more the Editions of any Book multiply, the more the Errors multiply too, and propagate out of their own Species. " *Of* " *this* (to borrow the Words and Obſervation of my ingenious " Friend, * Mr. *SEWEL*;) Shakeſpeare *is a very remarkable In-* " *ſtance, who has been handed down, from Age to Age, very incor-* " *rect, his Errors increaſing by Time, and being almoſt conſtantly* " *republiſh'd to his Diſgrace. Whatever were the Faults of this* " *great Poet, the Printers have been hitherto as careful to multiply* " *them, as if they had been real Beauties; thinking, perhaps, with* " *the* Indians, *that the disfiguring a good Face with Scars of arti-* " *ficial Brutes, had improv'd the Form and Dignity of the Per-* " *ſon.*"

THIS, indeed, has not been altogether the Caſe in the late Edition of *SHAKESPEARE*: The BOOKSELLER, who *farms* a Right to *ſome* part of this Author, and *claims* a Right to *ſome other* part of him, has ſo far *miſunderſtood* himſelf, (I mean, in Contradiction to the *Rule* of *Trade*,) as to be at the Expence of having his AUTHOR *reviſed*; and therefore we promiſed ourſelves, this WORK would be compleat.

I HAVE ſo great an Eſteem for Mr. *POPE*, and ſo high an Opinion of his Genius and Excellencies, that I beg to be excuſed from the leaſt Intention of derogating from his Merits, in this Attempt to reſtore the true Reading of *SHAKESPEARE*. Tho' I confeſs a Veneration, almoſt riſing to Idolatry, for the Writings of this inimitable Poet, I would be very loth even to do *him* Juſtice at the Expence of *that other* Gentleman's Character. But, I am perſuaded, I ſhall ſtand as free from ſuch a Charge in the *Execution* of this Deſign, as, I am ſure, I am in the *Intention* of it; for I am aſſuming a Taſk here, which this learned *Editor* ſeems purpoſely (I was going to ſay, with too nice a Scruple) to have declined.

To explain myſelf, I muſt be obliged to make a ſhort Quotation from Mr. *POPE*, in his Preface to *SHAKESPEARE*: " *In* " *what I have done*, ſays he, *I have rather given a Proof of my* " *Willingneſs and Deſire, than of my Ability to do him Juſtice. I*

* *In his Preface to the Seventh Volume of the Works of* SHAKESPEARE, *in* Quarto.

" *have diſcharg'd the dull Duty of an* Editor, *to my beſt Judgment,* " *with more Labour than I expect Thanks, with a* religious Abhor- " rence *of all* Innovation, *and without any Indulgence to my pri-* " *vate Senſe or Conjecture.*" I cannot help thinking this Gentleman's *Modeſty* in this Point too *nice* and *blameable*; and that what he is pleaſed to call a *religious Abhorrence* of *Innovation,* is downright *Superſtition:* Neither can I be of Opinion, that the Writings of *SHAKESPEARE* are ſo *venerable,* as that we ſhould be excommunicated from good Senſe, for daring to *innovate properly*; or that we ought to be as cautious of altering *their* Text, as we would That of the *ſacred Writings.* And yet even They, we ſee, have admitted of ſome Thouſands of *various Readings*; and would have a great many more, had not Dr. *BENTLEY* ſome particular Reaſons for not proſecuting his Undertaking upon the *New Teſtament,* as he propos'd.

CERTAINLY, that Phyſician would be reckon'd a very unſerviceable Member in the Republick, as well as a bad Friend to himſelf, who would not venture to preſcribe to a Patient, becauſe not abſolutely ſure to cure his Diſtemper: As, on the other hand, he would be accounted a Man of very indifferent Morals, if he raſhly tamper'd with the Health and Conſtitution of his Fellow-Creature, and was bold to try Concluſions only for private Information. The ſame Thing may be ſaid with regard to *Attempts* upon *Books:* We ſhould ſhew very little Honeſty, or Wiſdom, to play the Tyrants with any Author's Text; to raze, alter, innovate, and overturn, at all Adventures, and to the utter Detriment of his Senſe and Meaning: But to be ſo very reſerv'd and cautious, as to interpoſe no Relief or Conjecture, where it manifeſtly labours and cries out for Aſſiſtance, ſeems almoſt as abſurd as the Indolence of that good honeſt *Prieſt,* who had for thirty Years together miſtakingly, in his Breviary, read *Mumpſimus* for *Sumpſimus*; and being told of his Blunder, and ſollicited to correct it, *The Alteration may be juſt,* ſaid he; *but, however, I'll not change my old* MUMPSIMUS *for your new* SUMPSIMUS.

FOR

For my own part, I don't know whether I am miſtaken in Judgment, but I have always thought, that whenever a *Gentleman* and a *Scholar* turns *Editor* of any Book, he at the ſame Time commences *Critick* upon his *Author*; and that wherever he finds the Reading ſuſpected, manifeſtly corrupted, deficient in Senſe, and unintelligible, he ought to exert every Power and Faculty of the Mind to ſupply ſuch a Defect, to give Light and reſtore Senſe to the Paſſage, and, by a reaſonable Emendation, to make that ſatisfactory and conſiſtent with the Context, which before was ſo abſurd, unintelligible, and intricate.

This is a *Task*, which, as I above intimated, Mr. *Pope* has *purpoſely diſclaim'd*, and which I (by what Fatality, or with what Event, I know not;) have taken upon my ſelf to proſecute. I am not inſenſible under what Diſadvantages I muſt ſet out upon ſuch a Work, and againſt ſuch an Antagoniſt; ----- *impar congreſſus* Achilli: But as I have laid it down as a Rule to myſelf not to be arbitrary, fantaſtical, or wanton, in my Conjectures upon our Author, I ſhall venture to aim at ſome little Share of Reputation, in endeavouring to reſtore Senſe to Paſſages in which no Senſe has hitherto been found; or, failing in that Hope, muſt ſubmit to incur, which I ſhould be very unwilling to do, the Cenſure of a raſh and vain Pretender.

As *Shakespeare* ſtands, or at leaſt ought to ſtand, in the Nature of a Claſſic Writer, and, indeed, he is corrupt enough to paſs for one of the oldeſt Stamp, every one, who has a Talent and Ability this Way, is at liberty to make his Comments and Emendations upon him. This is a Palm, which (as *Terence* ſaid, of writing Comedies) is in common to every poetical Contender:

--------- *In medio omnibus*
Palmam eſſe poſitam, qui artem tractant muſicam.

And he, who has the Luck to be allowed any Merit in it, does not only do a Service to the Poet, but to his Country and its Language. This Author is grown ſo univerſal a Book, that there are very few Studies, or Collections of Books, tho' ſmall, amongſt which

which it does not hold a Place: And there is ſcarce a Poet, that our *Engliſh* Tongue boaſts of, who is more the Subject of the Ladies Reading. But with what Pleaſure can they read Paſſages, which the Incorrectneſs of the Editions will not ſuffer them to underſtand? No Vein of Pedantry, or Oſtentation of uſeleſs Criticiſm, incited me to this Work: It is a Sacrifice to the Pleaſure of SHAKESPEARE's Admirers in general; and ſhould it fail of all the Succeſs which I wiſh, it may chance to work this good Effect, That many will be tempted to read this Poet with a more diligent Eye than hitherto: The Conſequence of which will be, that better Criticks will make their own Obſervations, with more Strength than I can pretend; and this Specimen prove only an Invitation to lead them into nobler Corrections. If, however, till that happens, where SHAKESPEARE has yet, thro' all his Editions, labour'd under flat Nonſenſe, and invincible Darkneſs, I can, by the Addition or Alteration of a ſingle letter, or two, give him both Senſe and Sentiment, who will be ſo unkind to ſay, this is a trifling or unwarrantable Attempt? Or, rather, if I may dare to flatter myſelf ſo far, what true Lover of this Poet, who ſhall find him ſo eaſily cur'd, will not owe his Thanks for a Paſſage retriev'd from Obſcurity, and no Meaning? and ſay, SHAKESPEARE muſt certainly have wrote ſo------? But I remember a Line in *Horace*, which ought to ſtop me ſhort, and give me ſome Fears:

Quid dignum tanto feret hic promiſſor hiatu?

I am running too largely in debt, upon Promiſe, to my Readers, and they are calling for Payment in ſome Specimens of my Performance.

I am ſorry that the Uſe and Intention of this Undertaking ties me down to the Neceſſity of one unpleaſant Office, That of ſetting right the Faults in Pointing, and thoſe meerly literal, committed by the Printer, and continued by too negligent a Reviſal. This is the Drudgery of Correction, in which I could wiſh to have been ſpar'd, there being no Pleaſure in the Execution of it, nor any Merit, but that of dull Diligence, when executed.

cuted. But, *unpleaſant* as it is, even this Part muſt be diſpens'd with; and all that I can do, to eaſe myſelf or Readers in it, is to mark theſe minute Corrections with all poſſible Brevity, and proceed to more important Matter.

I CAN ſcarce ſuſpect it will be thought, if I begin my Animadverſions upon the Tragedy of *HAMLET*, that I have been partial to myſelf in picking out this Play, as one more fertile in Errors than any of the reſt: On the contrary, I choſe it for Reaſons quite oppoſite. It is, perhaps, the beſt known, and one of the moſt favourite Plays of our Author: For theſe thirty Years laſt paſt, I believe, not a Seaſon has elaps'd, in which it has not been perform'd on the Stage more than once; and, conſequently, we might preſume it the moſt purg'd and free from Faults and Obſcurity. Yet give me Leave to ſay, what I am ready to prove, it is not without very groſs Corruptions. Nor does it ſtand by itſelf for Faults in Mr. POPE's Edition: No, it is a Specimen only of the epidemical Corruption, if I may be allowed to uſe that Phraſe, which runs thro' all the Work: And I cannot help ſaying of it, as *Æneas* does of the *Greeks* Treachery upon the Inſtance of *Sinon*'s,

----------- *Crimine ab uno*
Diſce omnes: ------------

IF *HAMLET* has its Faults, ſo has every other of the Plays; and I therefore only offer it as a Precedent of the ſame Errors, which, every body will be convinced before I have done, poſſeſs every Volume and every Play in this Impreſſion.

BUT to proceed from Aſſertion to Experiment: In order to which I ſhall conſtantly be obliged, that the Emendations may ſtand in a fairer Light, to quote the Paſſages as they are read, with ſome part of their Context, in Mr. POPE's Edition; and likewiſe to prefix a ſhort Account of the Buſineſs and Circumſtances of the Scenes from which the faulty Paſſages are drawn; that the Readers may be inform'd at a ſingle View, and judge of the Strength and Reaſon of the Emendation, without a Reference to the Plays themſelves for that purpoſe. But this will

will be in no kind neceſſary, where Faults of the Preſs are only to be corrected: Where the Pointing is wrong, perhaps, That may not be alone the Fault of the Printer; and therefore I may ſometimes think myſelf obliged to aſſign a Reaſon for my altering it.

As every Author is beſt expounded and explain'd in *One* Place, by his own Uſage and Manner of Expreſſion in *Others*; wherever our Poet receives an Alteration in his Text from any of my *Corrections* or *Conjectures*, I have throughout endeavour'd to ſupport what I offer by *parallel Paſſages*, and *Authorities* from himſelf: Which, as it will be my beſt Juſtification, where my Attempts are ſeconded with the Concurrence of my Readers; ſo, it will be my beſt Excuſe for thoſe *Innovations*, in which I am not ſo happy to have them think with me.

I HAVE likewiſe all along, for the greater Eaſe and Pleaſure of the Readers, diſtinguiſh'd the Nature of my Corrections by a ſhort marginal Note to each of them, *viz. Falſe Pointing*, *Falſe Print*, *Various Reading*, *Paſſage omitted*, *Conjectural Emendation*, *Emendation*, and the like; ſo that every body will at once be appriz'd what Subject-matter to expect from every reſpective Diviſion.

THE

THE

Examination *and* Correction

OF THE

TRAGEDY of *HAMLET*.

I. Act 1. Scene 1. Page 346.

Various Reading.

WHEN yon same star, that's westward from the pole,
Had made his course t'illume *that part of heav'n*
Where now it burns, -----

SOME of the old Editions read, *t'illumine*; which seems to be the truest deriv'd Word, (from *illumino* in the *Latin*,) and is the Word used by our Author in another Place.

TWO GENTLEMEN of *VERONA*, pag. 195.

If I be not by her fair Influence
Foster'd, illumin'd,

In another of his Plays, our Poet has extended this Word to *illuminate.*

JULIUS CÆSAR, *pag.* 234.

> -------- *What Trash is* Rome?
> *What Rubbish, and what Offal? when it serves*
> *For the base Matter to* illuminate
> *So vile a Thing as* Cæsar?

And I almost think, Mr. POPE was of the Opinion that *illumine*, rather than *illume*, in this Place of *Hamlet*, is the right Word; since he, in another of the Tragedies, has wrote *relumine*, tho' one of the old Editions there have it *relume.*

OTHELLO, *pag.* 578.

> *I know not where is that* Promethean *Heat,*
> *That can thy Light* relumine. ------

But may it not be objected, that if we should read,

> *Had made his Course* t'illumine *that Part of Heav'n*, &c.

this Additional *Syllable* spoils the Scanning of the Verse? In a Word, too nice a Regard must not be had to the Numbers of *SHAKESPEARE:* Nor needs the Redundance of a *Syllable* here be any Objection; for nothing is more usual with our Poet than to make a *Dactyl*, or allow a supernumerary *Syllable*, which is sunk and melted in the Pronunciation. It were most easy to produce above a thousand Instances of this Custom in him; but unnecessary, because they lie open to the Observation of every discerning Reader.

II. Ibid.

II. Ibid. Page 347.

So frown'd he once, when in an angry Parle [,] *False Pointing.*
He ſmote the ſledded Polack *on the Ice.*

All the old Editions, which I have ſeen, read it rightly without the ſecond *Comma*;

So frown'd he once, when in an angry Parle
He ſmote &c.

III. Ibid. Page 350.

Shall I ſtrike [ ] *it with my Partizan?* *Various Reading.*

The Verſification manifeſtly halts here, without any Neceſſity. The ſecond Edition in *Folio*, printed in 1632, and which is one of thoſe that Mr. POPE profeſſes to have collated, makes out the Numbers of this Line by reading,

Shall I ſtrike at *it with my Partizan?*

IV. Ibid. Page 350.

------- *I have heard,* *False Pointing.*
The cock [ ] *that is the trumpet to the morn,*
Doth with his lofty and ſhrill-ſounding Throat &c.

It ought to be pointed, as it is in the Quarto Edition, of 1637; (of which I ſhall have Occaſion to ſpeak anon.)

------- *I have heard,*
The Cock, that is the Trumpet to the Morn,
Doth &c.

V. Ibid. Page 351.

False Pointing.

But look, the morn in ruſſet mantle clad [,]
Walks o'er the dew &c.

Here again, either the ſecond *Comma* muſt be entirely taken away, or this Paſſage muſt be ſtopp'd thus;

But look, --- the Morn, in ruſſet Mantle clad,
Walks o'er the Dew &c.

VI. Act 1. Scene 2. Page 352.

False Pointing, and Conjectural Emendation.

CLAUDIUS, King of *Denmark*, his Queen, *Hamlet*, and Courtiers, coming upon the Stage, the King makes a Speech, apologizing, and giving Reaſons, for his haſty Marriage with his Brother's Widow. He then proceeds to acquaint them, that *Fortinbras* of *Norway*, ſuppoſing the State of *Denmark* to be much weaken'd and disjointed by the Death of the late King, had demanded, with Threats of Invaſion, certain Lands loſt by his Father to the ſaid late *Daniſh* King; and that therefore he (*Claudius*, the now King) had wrote Letters to the old King of *Norway*, deſiring him to ſuppreſs his Nephew *Fortinbras*'s unjuſt Procedure in that Affair. This is the Buſineſs and Import of the Speech; let us now ſee how it ſtands in the Edition.

--------- *Nor have we herein barr'd*
Your better wiſdoms, which have freely gone
With this affair along [,] (*for all, our thanks.*)
Now follows [,] *that you know* [ ] *young* Fortinbras,
Holding a mean ſuppoſal of our worth;
Or thinking by our late dear brother's death
Our ſtate to be disjoint and out of frame [,]
COLLEAGUED with this dream of his advantage [;]
He hath not fail'd to peſter us with meſſage, &c.

Tho'

Tho' all the printed Copies, that ever I have ſeen, concur in reading *Colleagued* in this Place, I cannot but think it carries a harſh and intricate Senſe, and does not ſo aptly fall in with the Context. This makes me ſuſpect it corrupted from a Word very near it, both in Sound and Writing, and which carries a much more plauſible Meaning, as well as connects better both with what precedes and follows. 'Tis true, *Colleagued* ſignifies *joined with, putting himſelf on the Side,* or *Faction of,* &c. and therefore it is not to be utterly diſallowed in Senſe. But if we can only, with the Alteration of a Letter or two, ſubſtitute another Word that gives a ſtronger and more proper Image, and connects better with the Reaſoning of the Paſſage; I hope, I ſhall be allowed to offer it, at leaſt, as a Conjecture, if not as a Correction. Suppoſe therefore that *SHAKESPEARE* might write it thus;

--------- Nor have We herein barr'd
Your better Wiſdoms, which have freely gone
With this Affair along: (For all, our Thanks.)
Now follows that you know, Young Fortinbras,
Holding a weak Suppoſal of our Worth;
Or thinking, by our late dear Brother's Death,
Our State to be disjoint, and out of Frame;
* *COLLOGUED with this Dream of his Advantage,*
He hath not fail'd to peſter us with Meſſage, &c.

Here you have a Reaſon for the Young Man's Opinion, and Proceeding, and for his Inſolence in making the Demand on *Denmark, viz.* he being *flattered, impoſed on, cajol'd,* by the Dream of his Advantage. However, if the Readers are inclined to imbrace the firſt Reading, I am willing to retract Mine, or at leaſt keep it to my ſelf, which I propoſed but as a Gueſs. The Correction

* **Collogue,** *Blanditiis tentare, parùm deflexo ſenſu, à* Lat. *Colloqui; vel ſi à* Germanicâ *Origine deducere malis, à* Teut. **Koſen,** *garrire, &* **Lugen;** Belg. **Logen,** *Mentiri: q. d.* **Koſlogen** *eliſô propter Euphoniam ſ: q. d. blandis Mendaciis imponere.*

SKINNER's Lexic. Etymolog.

Correction of the next Passage shall be founded on something more than Conjecture.

VII. Ibid.

False Pointing.

> -------- *We have here writ*
> *To* Norway, *uncle of young* Fortinbras,
> *Who* [ ] *impotent and bed-rid, scarcely hears*
> *Of this his nephew's purpose, to suppress*
> *His further gate herein* [. *I*] *n that the levies,*
> *The lists, and full proportions are all made*
> *Out of his Subjects* [;]

That is, We have writ to the Old King to stop his Nephew's Expedition, because his Army is compos'd all out of the old King's Subjects. But this Passage is so pointed, that, by the Reasoning being disjoined from the Sentence of which it ought to be a Part, the Sense is so much weaken'd, that it is almost lost. Restore it therefore, as some of the Editions lead the Way;

> -------- *We have here writ*
> *To* Norway, *Uncle of young* Fortinbras,
> *Who, impotent and bed-rid, scarcely hears*
> *Of this his Nephew's Purpose, to suppress*
> *His further Gate herein; in that the Levies,*
> *The Lists, and full Proportions, are all made*
> *Out of his Subjects:*

VIII. Ibid.

Conjectural Emendation.

> -------- *and we here dispatch*
> *You, good* Cornelius, *and you* Voltimand,
> *FOR bearers of this greeting* &c.

The

The Word, FOR, here ſeems to be meerly ſupplimental, and introduced to keep the Verſe from halting; beſides that, *to diſpatch* for *Bearers*, is a bald and poor Expreſſion. It certainly will be more in the Stile of Majeſty, if we may ſuppoſe the Poet wrote;

> --------- *and we here diſpatch*
> *You, good* Cornelius, *and You*, Voltimand,
> *OUR Bearers of this Greeting* &c.

This Speaking in the plural Number connects exactly with the Beginning of the Sentence laſt quoted, We *have here writ*, and We *here diſpatch You, and You*, Our *Bearers of this Greeting to old* Norway. Beſides, the Miſtake of *for* inſtead of *our* is ſo eaſy, that, in the ſecond *Folio* Edition, it has happen'd again in this very Act in another Paſſage; and the plain Senſe has led the later Editions to corect it.

> Haml. *Never to ſpeak of This that you have ſeen,*
> *Swear by my Sword.*
> Ghoſt. *Swear.*
> Haml. Hic, & ubique? *Then we'll ſhift FOR Ground.*

IX. Ibid.

> *Giving to you no further perſonal power*
> *OF TREATY with the King*, &c.

Various Reading.

This is a Reading adopted, and of a modern Stamp, as I take it; either from Want of Underſtanding the Poet's genuine Words, or on a Suppoſition of their being too ſtiff and obſolete. All my old Copies have it, as I think it ought to be reſtor'd,

> *Giving to you no further perſonal Pow'r*
> *TO BUSINESS with the King*, &c.

i. e.

i. e. to *negotiate*, or *transact* with him. It is a Licence in our Poet, of his own Authority, to coin new *Verbs* both out of *Substantives* and *Adjectives*; and it is, as we may call it, one of the *Quidlibet audendi's* very familiar with him. I'll throw in a few Instances of the like kind, and it were very easy, with little Pains, to produce a Croud more.

(1.) TEMPEST, *pag.* 32.

Proofs of Substantives *made* Verbs.

The Setting of thine Eye and Cheek proclaim
A Matter from Thee, and a Birth indeed,
Which [a] throes *thee much to yield.*

[a] *Throes* signify a Woman's Pains in Child-bearing; and he here uses the Word for *pains thee*, or *gives thee those Pains.*

(2.) So again, *pag.* 54.

-------- *And the Thunder,*
That deep and dreadful Organ-Pipe, pronounc'd
The Name of Prosper; *it did* [b] base *my Trespass*, &c.

[b] it did play a terrible Base to it; resounded hoarsely in a Base-Tone.

(3.) MIDSUMMER NIGHT'S DREAM, *pag.* 138.

And as Imagination [c] bodies *forth*
The Forms of Things unknown, the Poet's Pen
Turns them to Shape, &c.

[c] gives them Bodies.

(4.) TWO GENTLEMEN of VERONA, *pag.* 213.

Recking as little what betideth me,
As much I wish all Good [d] befortune *you.*

[d] fall to you by good Fortune.

(5.) MEASURE for MEASURE, *pag.* 370.

Lord Angelo [e] dukes *it well in his Absence*, &c.

[e] acts, represents, the Duke.

(6.) And

(6.) And again, *pag.* 371.

Either this is Envy in You, Folly, or Miſtaking: the very Stream of his Life, and the Buſineſs he hath [f] helm'd, &c.

[f] manag'd; ſteer'd, as at the Helm.

(7.) MERCHANT of *VENICE*, *pag.* 20.

Give him Direction for this merry Bond,
And I will go and [g] purſe *the Ducats ſtrait*, &c.

[g] put them in a Purſe.

(8.) KING *LEAR*, *pag.* 49.

-------- *I could as well be brought*
To [h] knee *his Throne, and, 'Squire-like, Penſion beg*, &c.

[h] bend the Knee to.

(9.) Second Part of *HENRY* IV. *pag.* 352.

And therefore will he wipe his Tables clean,
And keep no Tell-tale to his Memory,
That may repeat and [i] hiſtory *his Loſs*, &c.

[i] tell the Hiſtory of.

(10.) *HENRY* V. *pag.* 418.

------- *Why! what read you there,*
That hath ſo [k] cowarded *and chas'd your Blood*
Out of Appearance?

[k] frighted, made a Coward of.

(11.) *HENRY* VIII. *pag.* 444.

------- *And his own Letter,*
(The Honourable Board of Council out,)
Muſt fetch in Him he [l] papers.

[l] marks down on Paper.

(12.) *TIMON* of *ATHENS*, *pag.* 7.

------- His large Fortune,
Upon his good and gracious Nature hanging,
Subdues and [a] properties *to his Love and Tendance*
All Sorts of Hearts.

[a] makes them his own; gives him a Property in them.

(13.) So *CORIOLANUS*, *pag.* 128.

------- That to's Pow'r he would
Have made them Mules, ſilenc'd their Pleaders, and
[a] Diſproperty'd *their Freedoms.*

[a] took away the Property of.

(14.) And again, *pag.* 200.

Now, by the jealous Queen of Heaven, that Kiſs
I carried from thee, Dear; and my true Lip
Hath [a] virgin'd *it e'er ſince.*

[a] kept it as chaſtely as a Virgin.

(15.) *MACBETH*, *pag.* 547.

--------- I've ſeen
Hours dreadful, and Things ſtrange; but this ſore Night
Hath [p] trifled *former Knowings.*

[p] made Trifles of.

(16.) *ANTHONY* and *CLEOPATRA*, *pag.* 402.

---------- Eros,
Would'ſt thou be [a] window'd *in great* Rome, &c.

[a] plac'd in a Window.

(17.)

(17.) *OTHELLO, pag.* 501.

------- *He hath atchiev'd a Maid*
That [r] paragons *Description and wild Fame.*

[r] out-goes, sets a Paragon, or Pattern to.

(18.) *TROILUS, pag.* 24.

And with ridiculous and awkard Action
(Which, Slanderer! he Imitation calls;)
He [s] pageants *us.*

[s] plays us over, shews us as in a Pageant.

I am afraid of growing too luxuriant in Examples of this Sort, or I could stretch out the Catalogue of them to a great Extent. I shall only shew by a few Instances that it is as familiar with him to make *Verbs* out of *Adjectives*, and so shall return to *HAMLET*.

(1.) WINTER'S TALE, *pag.* 594.

Proofs of Adjectives *made* Verbs.

------ *Which had been done,*
But that the good Mind of Camillo [a] tardied
My swift Command.

[a] stopp'd, made slow, or tardy.

(2.) CYMBELINE, *pag.* 213.

------- *You married ones,*
If each of you would take this Course, how many
Must murther Wives much better than themselves
For [b] wrying *but a little?*

[b] going awry.

(3.) *TROILUS, pag.* 111.

Hark! how Troy *roars, how* Hecuba *cries out,*
How poor Andromache [e] shrills *her Dolour forth.*

[e] screams shrilly.

(4.) *JULIUS CÆSAR, pag.* 288.

And Nature must obey Necessity,
Which we will [d] niggard *with a little Rest.*

[d] We will make but short Rest, be Niggards of it.

(5.) *TITUS ANDRONICUS, pag.* 433.

Patient *your self, Madam, and pardon me.*

make your self patient.

(6.) *ANTHONY* and *CLEOPATRA, pag.* 322.

-------- *And all this*
(It wounds thine Honour that I speak it now,)
Was born so like a Soldier, that thy Cheek
So much as [f] lank'd *not.*

[f] grew lank, or lean.

(7.) And, again, *pag.* 337.

Age cannot wither her, nor Custom [g] stale
Her infinite Variety.

[g] make stale.

X. Ibid.

Various Reading

Volt. *In that, and all Things, will we shew our Duty.*
King. *We doubt IN nothing,* &c.

All

All the Editions, that I have ſeen, read, I think, more rightly,

We doubt IT nothing.

i. e. We in no wiſe doubt, but you will.

XI. Ibid. Page 354.

But yo umuſt know, your father loſt a father,
That father [ ] *his*, &c.

Various Reading.

All the Editions, that I have met with, old and modern, (and ſo, I know, the Players to this Day conſtantly repeat it,) read,

But you muſt know, your Father loſt a Father,
That Father loſt, loſt *his*; ----

The Reduplication of the Word *loſt* here gives an Energy and an Elegance, which is much eaſier to be conceiv'd, than explain'd in Terms. Every Reader of this Poet, however, muſt have obſerv'd how frequent it is with him to uſe this Figure, (which the Rhetoricians have call'd *Anadiploſis*;) where he intends either to *aſſert* or *deny, augment* or *diminiſh*, or add a Degree of *Vehemence* to his Expreſſion. Of this Uſage, were it neceſſary, I could bring a great Number of Examples; but the Inſtances, that I can at preſent remember in him, which ſeem moſt to reſemble this before us, are the following.

(1.) *OTHELLO, pag.* 483.

--- *The Duke does greet you, General,*
And he requires your haſt, poſt-haſt *Appearance*
Ev'n on the Inſtant.

(2.) Firſt Part of *HENRY* IV. *pag.* 239.

And That would nothing *ſet my Teeth on Edge,*
Nothing *ſo much as mincing Poetry.*

(3.)

(3.) And *Romeo, pag.* 272.

Fain *would I dwell on Forme,* fain, fain *deny*
What I have spoke.

(4) So *Timon* of *Athens, pag.* 58.

------ *Who* dares, *who* dares,
In Purity of Manhood, stand upright,
And say, This Man's a Flaterer?

(5.) And so *Macbeth, pag.* 581.

I know him now. Good God betimes remove
The Means, *the* Means, *that make us Strangers.*

XII. Ibid.

False Pointing.

As any the must *vulgar thing to Sense.*

Correct it,

As any the most vulgar Thing &c.

XIII. Ibid. Page 355.

False Pointing.

And the king's rowse the heav'n shall bruit again [ ]
Respeaking earthly Thunder.

Read it with a *Comma;*

And the King's Rowse the Heav'n shall bruit again,
Respeaking earthly Thunder.

XIV.

XIV. Act 1. Scene 3. Page 355.

The King, Queen, and Court, quitting the Stage, *HAMLET* remains, and makes a Soliloquy; beginning with this double Wish, either that his too solid Flesh would melt away into a Dew, *Conjectural* Emendation

> *Or, that the Everlasting had not fixt*
> *His CANNON 'gainst Self-slaughter.* ---

There is a various Reading upon this Passage, as Mr. POPE might have observ'd, which, in my Opinion, merits a Consideration, and, possibly, may give us the Poet's own Words. If he wrote it as it now stands, his Thought is, *Or that the* Almighty *had not planted his* Artillery, *his* Resentment, *or* Arms of Vengeance *against* Self-murther: But the Quarto Edition, publish'd in 1703. (which, indeed, has no other Authority, than its professing to be printed from the *Original Copy*;) and the Impression of *HAMLET* set out by Mr. *Hughs*, Both read,

> *Or that the Everlasting had not fixt*
> *His CANON 'gainst Self-slaughter.*

i. e. That he had not restrain'd *Suicide* by his *express Law*, and *peremptory Prohibition.* It is a Word that *SHAKESPEARE* has used in some others of his Plays; and the Mistake of the Printers is so very easy, betwixt a double and a single *n*, in *Cannon* and *Canon*, that it has actually happen'd elsewhere in our Author upon both these very Words.

CORIOLANUS, *pag.* 148.

> ------ *Shall remain?*
> *Hear you this* Triton *of the Minnows? mark you*
> *His absolute* Shall?

Comin. *'Twas from the CANON.*

i. e.

i. e. *from the Mouth of the Law*, as Mr. POPE rightly understands it; tho' the ſecond Folio Edition has it corruptly, *'Twas from the* Cannon. So again, on the other hand, twice in the ſecond *Act* of King *JOHN*, the ſecond Folio Edition has it;

The Canons *have their Bowels full of Wrath*, &c.

And afterwards,

Their batt'ring Canon, *charged to the Mouths*, &c.

Tho' 'tis manifeſt, in both Places, it ought to be *Cannon*, with a double *n*. I cannot help throwing in one Inſtance more, becauſe the Error has not only obtained in the old and common Modern Editions, but has likewiſe got a new Sanction in Mr. *POPE*'s Edition.

TIMON, *pag.* 59.

Religious CANNONS, civil Laws are cruel,
Then what ſhould War be?

The Propagation of this Fault is manifeſtly owing to the Negligence of Reviſal; and all future Impreſſions muſt correct it, --- *Religious* Canons, *&c.* But to paſs from theſe Miſtakes of the *Preſs*, there is another Paſſage in King *JOHN*, where the Poet uſes the Word *Canon* to ſignify Decree or Ordinance, *pag.* 129.

The CANON of the Law is laid on him, &c.

So in *CORIOLANUS*, *pag.* 119, 120.

-------- Where I find him, were it
At home, upon my Brother's Guard, even there
Againſt the hoſpitable CANON would I
Waſh my fierce hand in's heart.

But beſides that the Poet frequently employs the Terme, I have two or three Reaſons more which induce me to think, that, in this Place of *HAMLET*, he intended the *Injunction*, rather than the

the *Artillery* of Heaven. In the firſt Place, I much doubt the Propriety of the Phraſe, *fixing Cannon,* to carry the Meaning here ſuppoſed. The Military Expreſſion, which imports what would be neceſſary to the Senſe of the Poet's Thought, is, *mounting* or *planting Cannon:* And whenever Cannon is ſaid to be *fix'd,* it is when the Enemy become Maſters of it, and nail it down. In the next Place, to *fix* a *Canon* or *Law,* is the Terme of the *Civilians* peculiar to this Buſineſs. This *Virgil* had in his Mind, when he wrote, *Æneid* VI.

------- Leges *fixit* pretio, atque *refixit.*

And it was the conſtant Cuſtom of the *Romans* to ſay, upon this Occaſion, *figere legem*; as the *Greeks,* before them, uſed the *Synonymous* Term, παραπῆξαι. But my laſt Reaſon, and which ſways moſt with me, is from the Poet's own Turn and Caſt of Thought: For, as he has done in a great many more Inſtances, it is the very Sentiment which he falls into in another of his Plays, tho' he has cloath'd it in different Expreſſions.

CYMBELINE, pag. 178.

-------- *'Gainſt Self-ſlaughter*
There is a PROHIBITION ſo divine,
That cravens my weak Hand.

XV. Ibid.

After *HAMLET* has finiſh'd the two before mentioned Wiſhes, He falls into this Deſcant on the Groſſneſs of the World, and on his Mother's haſty Marriage with his Uncle. *Falſe Pointing, and various Reading.*

How weary, ſtale, flat, and unprofitable [ ]
Seem to me all the uſes of this world [?]
Fie on't! oh fie! 'tis an unweeded Garden [ ]
That grows to Seed; things rank, and groſs in nature [ ]
Poſſeſs it meerly [ ] that it ſhould come thus [.]
But two months dead! &c.

E Beſides

Besides that the *Hemistich* --- *that it should come thus,* --- is very mean and bald, as well as very indifferent *English*; I think, the Editor ought to have taken Notice, that there is a various Reading of old Date; which I verily believe to be the true One, because it makes the Passage much more elegant, and connective with what follows. The whole Passage should be pointed, and stand thus;

How weary, stale, flat, and unprofitable,
Seem to me all the Uses of this World!
Fie on't! oh, fie! 'Tis an unweeded Garden,
That grows to Seed: Things rank, and gross in Nature,
Possess it meerly. --- That it should come to this! ---
But Two Months dead! &c.

This is an Exclamation that our Poet makes his *Lear*, when in the Height of Agony for his Daughter's Ingratitude to him, stopping short his Passion, break into:

LEAR, pag. 27.

--------- *Old fond Eyes,*
Beweep her once again, I'll pluck you out,
And cast you, with the Waters that you lose,
To temper Clay. --- *Ha!* --- Is it come to this?

So likewise *Cleopatra,* when *Anthony* is rating and taxing her with Incontinence, for suffering *Cæsar's* Agent to kiss her hand, surprized at the Extremity of his Jealousy, cries out, *pag.* 381.

-------- *Oh! Is't come to this?*

So *HAMLET*, here, having made his general Reflexions upon the Grossness of the World, breaks into an *Interjection* of Surprize at once, and turns his Thoughts in particular upon his Mother's Conduct with Regard to her second Marriage: And so proceeds gradually to the Consideration of her late Husband's

Tenderness

Tenderneſs to her, and a Compariſon betwixt him and her preſent Conſort.

XVI. Ibid.

So excellent a king, that was, to this,
Hyperion to a Satyr: *So loving to my Mother,*
That he permitted not *the winds of Heav'n*
Viſit her face too roughly,

Emendation.

Here, again, is a Paſſage in which we have a *ſophiſticated* Reading, copied from the Players in ſome of the Modern Editions, for Want of underſtanding the Poet, whoſe Text is corrupt in the old Impreſſions: All of which, that I have had the Fortune to ſee, read,

- - - - - - - - - *So loving to my Mother,*
That he might not BETEENE *the Winds of Heav'n*
Viſit her Face too roughly.

'Tis true, there is no ſuch Word in *Engliſh*, that I know of, as *beteene*; and yet I am verily perſwaded, our Author's Words were ſo very like it, that it is only a Corruption from the Miſtake of a ſingle Letter, and two Words getting too cloſe together. See, how eaſy a Change reſtores you the Poet's own Words and Meaning.

- - - - - - - - - *So loving to my Mother,*
That he might not LET E'EN *the Winds of Heav'n*
Viſit her Face too roughly.

XVII. Ibid.

- - - - - - - - - *Married with mine Uncle,*
My father's brother; [ ] *no more like my Father,*
Than I to Hercules.

Various Reading.

Thus

Thus Mr. POPE reads it, with a nice Regard to the Numbers; not considering how perpetually the Poet, as I before remark'd, melts a Syllable in Pronunciation. The Generality, if not All, of the Editions have it with an emphatical *Disjunctive* in the Middle of the Reflexion.

> --------- *Married with mine Uncle,*
> *My Father's Brother:* --- but *no more like my Father,*
> *Than I to* Hercules.

XVIII. Act I. Scene 4. Page 358.

False Printing.

> -------- *Two-nights together* &c.

Correct, with all the Editions,

> -------- *Two Nights together* &c.

There is no more Reason for the *Hyphen* here, than there would be a little lower at this Verse,

> *And I with them the third Night held* &c.

XIX. Ibid.

Various Reading.

> Haml. *Indeed,* [ ] *Sirs, but This troubles me.*

The second Folio Edition (as Mr. POPE might have observ'd, who in so many Passages has a particular Regard to the Numbers,) makes a full Verse of this;

> Indeed, Indeed, *Sirs, but This troubles me.*

Which *Reduplication* of the Word seems to give a much stronger *Emphasis* to *Hamlet*'s Concern.

XX. Ibid.

XX. Ibid. Page 359.

False Printing.

Haml. *His Beard was grisly?*
Hor. *It was, as I have seen it in his Life,*
A sable-silver'd.

Here again, with the old Editions, the *Hyphen* ought to be remov'd, and we must read,

A Sable silver'd.

i. e. *a black*, (*subintellig.* Beard; and the *Adjective* is put like a *Substantive*,) grown white, or silver'd over with Age.

XXI. Act 1. Scene 5. Page 360, 1.

False Pointing.

-------- *but you must fear* [ ]
His greatness weigh'd, his will is not his own.

As this is pointed, the Sense is absolutely maim'd; *for Greatness* appears the *Accusative Case* to the *Verb* fear: Whereas, in the Poet's Meaning, it is an *Ablative absolute.* Read it therefore,

-------- *but you must fear,*
His Greatness weigh'd, his Will is not his own.

That is, his Greatness being weigh'd or consider'd by you, you must have this Fear, that his Will is not in his own Power, but subject to the State.

XXII. Ibid. Page 361.

Conjectural Emendation.

------- *for on his Choice depends*
The SANCTITY *and Health of the whole State.*

I do not well understand the Force, or Reason, of the Word *Sanctity* in this Place. Does it mean the Sacredness and Reverence

rence due to Majesty? They could not so well suffer by *HAMLET*'s Choice of a Wife; but the Health, or Preservation, of the State might, in some Degree, be concerned by it. The *Quarto* Edition of 1637 has a Various Reading, which I find Mr. *Hughs* has espoused in his Impression of this Play, *viz.* The *Safety and Health* &c. The Meaning, 'tis true, of the Poet is here implied, tho' not express'd in his own Termes; but the *Versification* is miserably crippled by it. To depart therefore not above a Letter or two from the present Reading for the Poet's own Word, as I conceive; suppose, he might have wrote,

> ------ *for on his Choice depends*
> *The* SANITY, *and Health, of the whole State.*

i. e. The *Welfare, Preservation* &c. The Word *Sanity* might not be so well known to the first Editors, as the other; as therefore suspecting it a Mistake of their Copy, they, with the more Readiness, might substitute *Sanctity* in its Room. Not but this very Term occurs again afterwards in the *second Act* of this Play. And that *Sanity* and *Health*, put together, may not be thought a Tautology to be question'd in our Author, in the next Passage, where I find it, it is likewise joined with a *Synonymous* Word of its own Efficacy and Signification.

HAMLET, page. 386.

> *How pregnant, sometimes, his Replies are?*
> *A Happiness that often Madness hits on,*
> *Which* SANITY *and Reason could not be*
> *So prosp'rously deliver'd of.*

For by *Sanity* here is meant not the Health of Body, but Soundness of Understanding. Now, to shew how natural it is for the *Press* to make a Mistake betwixt Words so like one another, as *Sanctity* and *Sanity*: It happens that the *Quarto* Edition of *HAMLET*, which I above mentioned, printed in 1703. reads the very Passage, last quoted, in this corrupt Manner: ---- *How pregnant sometimes his Replies are! A Happiness that often Madness hits on, which*

which Reaſon and Sanctity *could not ſo happily be deliver'd of.* Here *Sanctity*, as in the other Paſſage, is erroneouſly ſubſtituted in the Place of *Sanity*. And to deal freely, I have ſuſpected that the ſame literal Slip upon this Word has been made in another Paſſage of our Poet: I ſay, it has been a *Suſpicion* of mine; for I urge it no farther than as ſuch, and with the utmoſt *Diffidence*. However, I ſhall give it here, as Occaſion offers, and ſubmit it to the Deciſion of better Judgments. The Place is in *Macbeth*, *pag*. 580. where *Malcolme*, *Macduff*, and an *Engliſh* Phyſician, are talking of the extraordinary Gift to King *Edward* the Confeſſor, of curing by his Touch poor Souls that could find no Relief from the Aid of Phyſick, in that Diſtemper which ſucceeding Times have call'd the *King's Evil*. The Words are theſe:

Malc. ------- *Comes the King forth to Day?*
Doctor. *Ay, Sir; There are a Crew of wretched Souls*
That ſtay his Cure; their Malady convinces
The great Aſſay of Art. But at his Touch,
Such SANCTITY *hath Heaven given his Hand,*
They preſently amend.

I do not enirely object to this Reading that has the Warrant of all the Copies on its Side; nor am I at a Loſs, I think, to underſtand its Meaning. *Edward* the Confeſſor was a Man of ſingular Holineſs, for which Heaven bleſs'd him with that miraculous Power of curing by a Touch. But did the *Sanctity* of his Hand do theſe Cures? Or was it an *healing* Property imparted by Heaven, in Reward of his rare Piety? Certainly, the latter: And This has induc'd me to ſuſpect that our Poet wrote;

--------- *But at his Touch,*
Such SANITY *hath Heaven giv'n his Hand,*
They preſently amend.

i. e. *Such a Quality and Power of making whole all whom he touches.* This Conjecture, perhaps, will receive ſome Strength from certain Expreſſions in the Reply of *Malcolme* to this Account of the Doctor.

A

> *A most miraculous Work in this good King;*
> *Which often since my here-remain in* England,
> *I've seen him do.* How he sollicits heav'n,
> Himself best knows; *but strangely-visited People,*
> *All swoln and ulc'rous, pitiful to the Eye,*
> *The meer Despair of Surgery, he* cures;
> *Hanging a Golden Stamp upon their Necks,*
> *Put on with holy Prayers: And, 'tis spoken,*
> *To the succeeding Royalty he leaves*
> *The* healing *Benediction* ------

I shall leave it here naked, without any reinforcing, to be embraced, or rejected, at every Reader's Pleasure: Being resolved not to draw upon my self the Odium of imposing what I professed to offer but as a Guess; or the Chance of being laughed at for too fondly maintaining what may happen to be repugnant to every good Judge's Sense and Understanding.

XXIII. Act I. Scene 6. Page 362.

Conjectural Emendation, *from a Various Reading.*

> *Yet here,* Laertes*!* get *aboard for shame* [,]
> *The wind sits in the shoulder of your Sail,*
> *And you are staid for* [ ] *there* [.] *My Blessing with you*;

Here again the *Editor* seems in the first Verse to have a nice Regard to the Numbers. In all the old Editions, that I have seen, the first Verse is;

> *Yet here,* Laertes*!* Aboard, aboard, *for Shame*;

But the Variation is of no Moment. But then, in the third Line, why is not --- *And you are staid for* --- as good, and as full Sense as --- *And you are staid for* there? This *Adverb* in the Close seems a dragging and an idle *Expletive*; and of no Use but to support the Measure of the Verse. But if we come to point this Passage right, and to the Poet's Intention in it, we shall find it neither unnecessary, nor improper, in its Place. In the Speech

Speech immediately preceding this, *Laertes* taxes himſelf for ſtaying too long: but ſeeing his Father approach, he is willing to ſtay for a Second Bleſſing, and kneels down to that End.

Laer. *I ſtay too long; --- But here my Father comes:*
A double Bleſſing is a double Grace;
Occaſion ſmiles upon a ſecond Leave. [Kneeling.

Polonius gives him his Bleſſing accordingly; and therefore it ought to be read, (as I perceive my Two *Quarto* Editions of 1637, and 1703, have it;) in Support of my Conjecture.

Yet here, Laertes! Aboard, aboard, *for Shame:*
The Wind ſits in the Shoulder of your Sail,
And you are ſtaid for. --- There, --- *my Bleſſing with you;*
[Laying his Hand on *Laertes*'s Head.

XXIV. Ibid. Page 363.

Omiſſion *ſupply'd.*

What is't, Ophelia, *he* [ ] *ſaid to you?*

All my Editions have it, more numerouſly;

What is't, Ophelia, *he hath ſaid to you?*

XXV. Ibid. Page 363.

Various Reading, and Conjectural Emendation.

--- *Tender your ſelf more dearly;*
Or (*not to crack the wind of the poor phraſe*)
WRONGING *it thus, you'll tender me a fool*

The ſecond *Folio* Edition and Mr. *Hughs*'s read, --- *Roaming* it thus, --- Which Word, indeed, as our *Etymologiſts* explain it, metaphorically takes in our Poet's Meaning: and in ſuch Senſe is frequently uſed by him in ſeveral others of his Plays. But as, *Wronging* it, has the Authority of ſeveral old Books, we may correct the Paſſage with much leſs Variation from the preſent Text, thus:

------- *Tender your ſelf more dearly;*
Or, (*not to crack the Wind of the poor Phraſe,*)
RANGING *it thus, you'll tender me a Fool.*

i. e. You, behaving yourſelf with ſo much Careleſſneſs and Liberty, will bring me into Contempt for not taking ſtricter Care of your Conduct.

XXVI. Act. 1. Scene 6. Page 364.

Conjectural Emendation.

OPHELIA having received the Addreſſes of *HAMLET*, *Polonius*, her Father, takes her to Task for Indiſcretion in too lightly giving an Ear to the Prince's Proteſtations. He tells her, that *HAMLET* may walk with a greater Latitude, than her Honour and Reputation will admit her to imitate: And beſides that, being in the Heat of Youth, and profeſſing himſelf a Lover, his Soul was prodigal to lend his Tongue Vows; which *Polonius* cautions her to look upon not as the real Sentiments of his Heart, but as Baits to betray her Virtue. Upon which he counſels her thus:

-------- *In few,* Ophelia,
Do not believe his vows; for they are brokers,
Not of that die which their inveſtments ſhew
But meer implorers of unholy ſuits,
Breathing like ſanctified and pious BONDS,
The better to beguile. ------

Thus indeed all the Impreſſions, which have ever come in my Way, read this Paſſage; even that Edition of *HAMLET*, reviſed by the late accurate Mr. *John Hughs*. I muſt own, I have always ſtumbled at it; and been ſurprized how Men of Genius and Learning could let it paſs without ſome Suſpicion. What Ideas can we form to our ſelves of a *breathing* BOND, or of its being *ſanctified* and *pious*? Surely, ſo abſurd a Thought could ſcarce come from *SHAKESPEARE*. The only tolerable Way of reconciling it to a Meaning without a Change, is to ſuppoſe that the Poet intends by the Word BONDS, *Verbal Obligations*, *Proteſtations*; and then, indeed, theſe Bonds may, in ſome Senſe, be ſaid to have *Breath*: But this is to make him guilty of overſtraining the Word and Alluſion; and it will hardly bear

bear that Interpretation, at leaſt, not without much Obſcurity. As he, juſt before, is calling amorous Vows, *Brokers*, and *Implorers* of *unholy Suits*; I think, a Continuation of the plain and natural Senſe directs us to an eaſy *Emendation*, which makes the whole Thought of a Piece, and gives it a Turn not unworthy of our Poet. I am, therefore, very willing to ſuſpect it came from his Pen thus, tho' none of his *Editors* have ever been aware of it;

--------- In few, Ophelia,
Do not believe his Vows; for they are Brokers,
Not of that Dye which their Inveſtments ſhew,
But meer Implorers of unholy Suits,
Breathing like ſanctified and pious BAWDS,
The better to beguile.

It is uſual with our Poet, as his *Critical* Readers muſt have obſerved, to give thoſe infamous Creatures the Style and Title of *Brokers*; of which it may not be amiſs to ſubjoin a few Examples. In his *two Gentlemen of Verona, page,* 161. *Lucetta,* the Servant of *Julia,* having received a Love-Letter to her Miſtreſs as in her Name, *Julia,* who has a Mind to ſhew a Diſlike of this Proceeding in her Maid, thus repremands her.

Now, by my Modeſty, a goodly BROKER!
Dare you preſume to harbour wanton Lines?
To whiſper and conſpire againſt my Youth?
Now, truſt me, 'tis an Office of great Worth;
And you an Officer fit for the Place.

Where it is plain that *Broker* is uſed but as a more modeſt Word for *Bawd*; and the Buſineſs of ſuch a One is deſcrib'd in the Lines that follow it.

So likewiſe in *All's well that ends well,* pag. 420. *Helena,* diſcourſing with the Widow her Hoſteſs, concerning Count *Roſſillion*'s Conduct; and the Widow intimating that her Daughter

Diana might have an Affair with him, if ſhe pleas'd; *Helena* ſays that, It may be, the amorous Count ſollicits her in the unlawful Purpoſe: To which the Widow replies,

> - - - - - - - - - *He does indeed,*
> *And* brokes *with all that can in ſuch a Suit*
> *Corrupt the tender Honour of a Maid.*

Where *brokes*, or *brokers*, evidently implies --- *tampers with*, *treats with*, as with *Bawds*.

So likewiſe in King JOHN, page 142. *Falconbridge* deſcanting on Commodity and Self-Intereſt, and how all Ranks and Degrees of Perſons were ſubſervient to it, and, as it were, ſeduc'd and betray'd to forſake Virtue thro' its Inſtigations, uſes theſe Expreſſions:

> *That* BROKER, *that ſtill breaks the Pate of Faith,*
> *That daily Break-Vow, He that wins of all,*
> *Of Kings, of Beggars, Old Men, Young Men, Maids;*
> Who having no external Thing to loſe
> But the Word *Maid*, cheats the poor Maid of That, &c.

And, afterwards, a little lower he ſubjoins,

> *This* BAWD, *this* BROKER, &c.

BESIDES, what ſtrengthens my Suſpicion, and makes this Emendation the more neceſſary and probable, is, the Words with which the Poet winds up his Thought, *the better to beguile*. Every Body, I believe, is ſatisfied that it is the Cuſtom of *Bawds* to put on an Air and Form of *Sanctity*, to betray the Virtues of Young Ladies; by drawing them firſt into a kind Opinion of them, from their *exterior* and *diſſembled* Goodneſs. And *Bawds* in their Office of Treachery are likewiſe properly *Brokers*; and the *Implorers*, and Promoters, of unholy (that is, *unchaſte*) Suits; and ſo a Chain of the ſame *Metaphors* is continued to the End.

XXVII.

XXVII.

WE come now to a *degraded* Paſſage, as Mr. POPE ſtiles it; that is, One not receiv'd into the Text, but plac'd (as ſuſpected, and too bad to belong to SHAKESPEARE;) at the Bottom of his Page. I muſt tranſcribe the whole Paſſage, tho' long, before I attempt to ſet it right; becauſe it happens to labour under *falſe Spelling, falſe Pointing, falſe Reading, falſe Concord,* and *flat Nonſenſe.* Mr. POPE introduces the Verſes with this ſhort Note. [* *Theſe* 21 *Lines following are in the* firſt *Edition, but* ſince *left out, perhaps being thought too verboſe.*] Since *left out?* --- I have a *Quarto* Edition, which, I ſuppoſe, Mr. POPE never ſaw; (printed by *R. Young* and *John Smethwicke,* in the Year 1637.) where they are not *left out*; but inſerted with an Addition, which, tho' very corruptly printed, when amended, I doubt not will appear to be of our Author's own Writing: And they are again inſerted in the other *Quarto* Edition publiſh'd in 1703, and in the HAMLET reviſed by Mr. *Hughs.* So that they have not been *left out,* altogether, from the Time of the *firſt* Publication. But to the Lines; --- Emendations.

HAMLET, holding the Watch with *Horatio,* in Order to ſee his Father's Apparition, a Noiſe of Warlike Muſick is heard: Which *Horatio* deſirous to know the Meaning of, HAMLET tells him, that the King ſat up to drink, and whenever he took his Draught, the Kettle-Drum and Trumpet proclaim'd the Triumph of his Pledge. *Horatio* aſking, whether it was a Cuſtom; HAMLET replies, Yes; but one that, in his Opinion, it were better to break, than obſerve: And then falls into the following Reflexion, how the *Danes* were reproach'd for Drunkenneſs, and what a Blot that Character was in their Eſcutcheons. *Act.* 1. *Sc.* 7. *p.* 365.

(1.) *This heavy-headed revel, eaſt and weſt* [;]
(2.) *Makes us traduc'd, and tax'd of other nations* [,]
(3.) *They* CLIP *us drunkards, and with ſwiniſh phraſe*
Soil our addition; and indeed it takes

From

From our atchievements, tho' perform'd at height,
The pith and marrow of our attribute.
(4.) *So* [ ] *oft it chances in particular men,*
(5.) *That for some vicious* MOLE *of nature in them,*
As in their birth (wherein they are not guilty,
(6.) *Since nature cannot chuse his origin* [ ])
By the o'ergrowth of some complexion,
Oft breaking down the pales and forts of reason;
Or, by some habit, that too much o'er-leavens
The forme of plausive manners; that these men
Carrying, I say, the stamp of one defect,
(7,8.) (*Being nature's livery, or fortune's* STAR [ ])
(9.) HIS *virtues else, be they as pure as grace,*
As infinite as man may undergo,
Shall in the general censure take corruption
(10.) *From that particular fault.* --- [*The Dram of* EASE
(11.) *Doth all the noble substance of* A DOUBT
To his own Scandal.]

I COME now to the Corrections, in which I'll endeavour to be as brief as the Proofs, in Support of them, will give me Leave. The first Three Lines are mighty easily rectified, being only accidentally, as I suppose, *wrong pointed*; and one Word as accidentally, for Want of due Care in the Revisal, *wrong spelt*: Which Mistakes, however, both alter and injure the Sense. They must be read, as some of the Editions rightly have them.

(1.) *This heavy-headed Revel, east and west,*
(2.) *Makes us traduc'd, and tax'd of other Nations;*
(3.) *They* CLEPE *us Drunkards,* -----

The Sense and Signification are very different betwixt the Words *Clip* and *Clepe*; and the latter is manifestly intended here, *viz.* They *call* us Drunkards. The same Error has slipt the Editor's Diligence in another of our Author's Plays, where this Word occurs again in the Sense of *calling*:

MAC-

MACBETH, pag. 552.

------- *Water-rugs, and demy-wolves are* CLIPT
All by the Name of Dogs.

Occaſional Correction.

In which Place it muſt be corrected,

------ *Water-rugs, and demy-wolves are* CLEP'T
All by &c.

And ſo **yclep'd**, and **yclep't**, are to be met with an hundred Times in *Chaucer*, *Spenſer*, and *Hudibras*. But, in another Place of our Poet, I obſerve, the *Editor* has taken Care to ſpell this Word as it ought to be.

WINTER'S TALE, *pag.* 556.

Three crabbed Months had ſowr'd themſelves to Death,
E're I could make thee open thy white Hand,
And CLEPE *thy ſelf my Love : Then didſt Thou utter,*
I'm yours for ever.

Now, to *Clip*, is illegally to *cut* or *maim* the *Coin*; and likewiſe to *gripe* or *embrace*: In Both which Senſes *SHAKESPEARE* has more than once uſed the Word. As, in the Senſe of *cutting the Coin*,

(1.) *KENT* in King *LEAR*, *pag.* 93.

To be acknowledg'd, Madam, is o'erpaid ;
All my Reports go with the modeſt Truth,
Nor more, nor clipt, *but ſo.*

(2.) So, King *HENRY* V. in the Play which bears his Name, *pag.* 459.

Indeed, the French *may lay twenty* French *Crowns to one they will beat us, for they bear them on their Shoulders : But it is no* Engliſh *Treaſon to cut* French *Crowns ; and to morrow the King himſelf will be a* Clipper.

So

So, in the other Senſe of *embracing*,

(1.) King *JOHN*, *pag.* 188.

---- O Nation, that Thou couldſt remove!
That Neptune's *Arms, who* clippeth *Thee about* &c.

(2.) *CORIOLANUS*, *pag.* 179.

------- Here I clip
The Anvil of my Sword, &c.

(3.) *ANTHONY* and *CLEOPATRA*, *pag.* 351.

Whate'er the Ocean pales, or Sky in-clips,
Is thine, if thou wilt ha't.

(4.) *CYMBELINE*, *pag.* 157.

------- His meaneſt Garment,
That ever hath but clipt *his Body*, &c.

(5.) And again, *pag.* 239.

Unknown to you, unſought, were clipt *about*
With this moſt tender Air.

(6.) And ſo *OTHELLO*, *pag.* 542.

Witneſs, you ever-burning Lights above!
You Elements, that clip *us round about!*

Occaſional Correction. There is one Place, indeed, in which Mr. *POPE*, and ſome of the former Editors, have writ this Word differently; but it ought to be corrected.

Second

Second Part of HENRY VI. *pag.* 169.

And now loud houling Wolves arouſe the Jades,
That drag the Tragic melancholy Night:
Who with their drowſy, ſlow, and flagging Wings
Cleap *dead Mens Graves;*

It ſhould be, clip *dead Mens Graves,* if I underſtand the Senſe of the Paſſage; i. e. *claſp, hover over, brood upon* &c. But to return to the Paſſage immediately under Correction.

Falſe Pointings, and Emendation.

(4.) *So* [ ] *oft it chances in particular Men,*
(5.) *That for ſome vicious* MOLE *of nature in them,*
As in their birth (wherein they are not guilty,
(6.) *Since nature cannot chuſe his origin* [ ])
By the o'ergrowth of ſome complexion,
Oft breaking down the pales and forts of reaſon;

What Relation is there betwixt a *vicious Mole* of Nature, and the Over-growth of a Complexion? Or how can a *Vicious Mole* be ſaid, or ſuppos'd, in any Degree to break down the Fences of *Reaſon,* or blemiſh the *Underſtanding?* A Mole is an exterior Defect, appearing upon the Surface of the Skin: and the Over-growth of a Complexion is, as I take it, an unequal Admixture of the Temperaments in the Frame and Compoſition of our Nature; thro' which we become faulty by the Defect of ſome good, or the Redundance of ſome ill, Quality. I am unwilling to be too poſitive in my Correction of this Place; but, I think from the Tenour of the Context, there is great Room to conjecture that our Author wrote;

So, oft it chances in particular Men,
That for ſome vicious MOULD *of Nature in them,* &c.

When Nature is unequally and viciouſly *moulded,* when any Complexion is too predominant, theſe Accidents may have an

Effect both on *Constitution*, and the *Intellectual Faculties* too; and then Reason, and the other Powers of the Mind, are impair'd and prejudic'd: And this I conceive to have been the Poet's Sentiment. To make Amends for my Doubt and Diffidence in this last Correction, I'll venture to be more positive in the Next I attempt.

> ------- *That these Men,*
> *Carrying, I say, the Stamp of one defect,*
> *(Being nature's livery, or fortune's* STAR [ ])

The Poet is insinuating, that Men carrying the Stamp but of one Defect, whether it be Nature's Livery, or Fortune's *Star*, (that is, whether it is owing to Nature, or Accident;) That shall in Character overpoise and blemish the whole Catalogue of their Virtues; and give them the Mark of vicious and corrupt Men. But is Fortune presum'd to give a *Star*, where she means a *Disgrace*? I should much rather suppose it an Ensign of her *Favour*, than design'd to set a Mark of *Infamy*. In short, the Cure of this Fault is so easy and obvious, that, I doubt not, but my Readers will acquiesce with me in thinking, that the Poet's Words were;

> *(Being Nature's Livery, or Fortune's* SCAR,)

And so the Sense of the whole Passage hangs together. I am very willing to believe that our Poet intends Nature's *Livery* as a Term of *Reproach*, and the Distinction of some *discrediting Quality*: And, in this Light, I find him using it in his Poem, call'd, *TARQUIN* and *LUCRECE*, *pag.* 41.

> *Oh! That is gone, for which I sought to live,*
> *And therefore now I need not fear to die;*
> *To clear this Spot by Death, at least I give*
> *A Badge of Fame to* Slander's LIVERY;
> *A dying Life to living Infamy.*

And

And the Word *Scar* is employ'd by our Poet, not only, in its natural Senſe, to ſignify a Wound in Body; but, metaphorically, a Blemiſh to Reputation. So, in his *ANTHONY* and *CLEOPATRA*, *pag.* 379.

> *The* SCARS *upon your Honour, therefore, he*
> *Does pity as conſtrained* BLEMISHES,
> *Not as deſerv'd.*

(9.) HIS *Virtues elſe, be They as pure as Grace,* Emendation.

The Poet ſpeaking all along before in the plural Number, as, *in particular Men, that theſe Men* &c. it is neceſſary, to preſerve the Concord, to read here;

THEIR *Virtues elſe*, &c.

Not but it is frequent with *SHAKESPEARE*, whether thro' Negligence, or Licentiouſneſs, to change his Numbers in this Sort.

I COME now to the concluding Sentence of this *degraded* Paſſage; Omiſſion *ſupplied, and* Emendation.

> (10.) [------ *The Dram of* EASE
> (11.) *Doth all the noble Subſtance of* A DOUBT
> *To his own Scandal.*]

Which, indeed, looks to be ſo deſperate, that, I ſuppoſe, Mr. POPE for that Reaſon only entirely left it out of his Quotation. In reality, I do not know a Paſſage, throughout all our Poet's Works, more intricate and deprav'd in the Text, of leſs Meaning to outward Appearance, or more likely to baffle the Attempts of Criticiſm in its Aid. It is certain, there is neither *Senſe*, *Grammar*, nor *Engliſh*, as it now ſtands: Yet with a ſlight Alteration I'll endeavour not only to give it all *three*, but a *Sentiment* too, that ſhall make the Poet's Thought cloſe nobly. What can a *Dram of* EASE mean? or what can it have to do with the Context, ſuppoſing it were the *allowed* Expreſſion here? Or, in a

 Word,

Word, what Agreement in Senſe is there betwixt a *Dram of Eaſe* and the *Subſtance* of a DOUBT? It is a deſperate Corruption; and the neareſt Way to hope for a Cure of it, is, to conſider narrowly what the Poet muſt be ſuppoſed to have intended here. The whole Tenour of the Sentences foregoing, is, That let Men have never ſo many, or ſo eminent, Virtues, if they have one Defect which accompanies them, that ſingle Blemiſh ſhall throw a Stain upon their whole Character; and not only ſo, (if I underſtand him right,) but ſhall deface the very Eſſence of all their Goodneſs, to its own Scandal; ſo that their Virtues themſelves will become their Reproach. This is not only a Continuation of his Sentiment; but carries it up with a fine and proper *Climax*. I think, therefore, it ought to be reſtor'd;

-------- *The Dram of* BASE
Doth all the noble Subſtance of WORTH OUT
To his own Scandal.

The Dram of *Baſe*, i. e. the leaſt Alloy of Baſeneſs or Vice. It is very frequent with our Poet to uſe the *Adjective* of *Quality* inſtead of the *Subſtantive* ſignifying the Thing. Beſides, I have obſerv'd that, elſewhere, ſpeaking of *Worth* he delights to conſider it as a Quality that adds *Weight* to a Perſon, and connects the Word with that Idea. So, particularly, in *All's Well that ends well.* Pag. 417.

Let every Word weigh *heavy of her* WORTH,
That he does weigh *too* light.

And I am the more inclin'd to flatter my ſelf that my Emendation may have retriev'd the Poet's very Words, becauſe I find him uſing ſomething like the ſame Thought and Metaphors in another of his Plays, and putting the ſame Terms of *Baſeneſs* and *Worth* in Oppoſition to One another.

CYM-

CYMBELINE, pag. 185.

> *From whose so many* Weights *of* BASENESS *cannot*
> *A* Dram *of* WORTH *be drawn.*

But I have intimated that it is frequent with our Poet to use the *Adjective* of *Quality*, instead of the *Substantive* signifying the Thing; and it may be expected of me to alledge a few Instances of this Practice in him.

(1.) MEASURE *for* MEASURE, *pag.* 358.

Proofs of Adjectives *instead of* Substantives.

> -------- *As for you,*
> *Say what you can, my* false *o'erweighs your* true.

i. e. My Falshood o'erweighs your Truth.

(2.) TWELFTH-NIGHT, *pag.* 488.

> *How easy is it for the proper* false
> *In Womens waxen Hearts to set their Forms!*

i. e. Falshood, or Disguise, in a proper outward Appearance.

(3.) King *LEAR, pag.* 71.

> *If Wolves had at thy Gate howl'd that stern time,*
> *Thou shouldst have said, Good Porter, turn the Key.*
> *All* cruels *else subscribe: But I shall see*
> *The winged Vengeance overtake such Children.*

i. e. All Things of Cruelty else.

(4.) And again, *pag.* 73.

> -------- *Full oft 'tis seen,*
> *Our* mean *secures us, and our meer Defects*
> *Prove our Commodities.* ----

i. e. Our Meanness, our low Fortune, middling State.

(5.) King

(5.) King *JOHN*, *pag.* 128.

> *This little Abstract doth contain That* large
> *Which dy'd in* Geff'ry.

i. e. That compleat Largeneſs, that full Size.

(6.) And *CORIOLANUS*, *pag.* 149.

> -------- *Th' Accuſation,*
> *Which they have often made againſt the Senate,*
> *All Cauſe unborn, could never be the* native
> *Of our ſo frank Donation.*

i. e. The natural Cauſe, the Nativity, Birth, Source.

BUT to proceed: As I have been oblig'd to branch out this *degraded* Speech into ſo many Parcells; and divide it, the better to give the Reaſons of the *Emendations*; it may not be improper to ſubjoine it once more entire, as corrected; and leave it to the Judgment of the Publick, whether, notwithſtanding the *Verboſeneſs* objected to it, it ought for the future to be *degraded*, or receiv'd into the Text of our Author.

> Haml. *This heavy-headed Revel, eaſt and weſt,*
> *Makes us traduc'd, and tax'd of other Nations;*
> *They* clepe *us Drunkards, and with ſwiniſh Phraſe*
> *Soil our Addition; and, indeed, it takes*
> *From our Atchievements, tho' perform'd at Height,*
> *The Pith and Marrow of our Attribute.*
> *So, oft it chances in particular Men,*
> *That for ſome vicious* Mould *of Nature in Them,*
> *As in their Birth, (wherein they are not guilty,*
> *Since Nature cannot chuſe his Origin;)*
> *By the O'ergrowth of ſome Complexion,*
> *Oft breaking down the Pales and Forts of Reaſon;*

Or

Or by ſome Habit, that too much o'er-leavens
The Forme of plauſive Manners: That theſe Men
Carrying, I ſay, the Stamp of one Defect,
(Being Nature's Livery, or Fortune's Scar,)
Their *Virtues elſe, be They as pure as Grace,*
As infinite as Man may undergo,
Shall, in the general Cenſure, take Corruption
From that particular Fault. The Dram of baſe
Doth all the noble Subſtance of Worth out,
To his own Scandal. ----

XXVIII.

WELL; Immediately after this Speech comes the *Ghoſt*; and *HAMLET*, in the Agonies of his Surpriſe and Concern, queſtioning, how it comes about, that his dead Father, whom he had ſeen quietly repoſited in his Sepulchre, ſhould be caſt up again, has theſe Words: *Falſe Pointing, and* Emendation.

HAMLET, Act 1. *Sc.* 7. *pag.* 366.

--------- *What may this mean?*
That thou dead coarſe again in compleat Steel
Reviſit'ſt thus the glimpſes of the moon,
(1,2,3.) *Making night hideous* [?] *and* WE *fools of nature* [,]
(4.) *So* HORRIDLY *to ſhake our diſpoſition*
(5.) *With thoughts beyond the reaches of our Souls* [.]
Say, why is this?

Beſides that this Paſſage is ſeveral times faulty in the *Pointing*, it is likewiſe faulty in *Language*. 'Tis true, WE *fools* --- is a Reading that has the Countenance of all the printed Copies; but That Authority muſt nor give a Sanction to Nonſenſe, and falſe Grammar, to the Injury of our Author, when a plain and unexceptionable Remedy is at hand. *Making Night hideous, and making*

making We *Fools of Nature* --- Every Body muſt immediately ſee is not *Engliſh*. I muſt not, however, diſſemble, that there are a few Paſſages more in our Poet, where I have obſerv'd the *Nominative* of *Pronouns* is uſed, tho' Grammar requires the *Accuſative*. As,

(1.) *CORIOLANUS, pag.* 202.

> -------- *And to poor* WE
> *Thine Enmity's moſt capital.*

But here it is a Fault as well as in *HAMLET*, and ought likewiſe to be correĉted, *And to poor* US. There is another of this Sort which I have obſerv'd too, in the Duke's Speech to *Angelo* in the ſecond Scene of MEASURE *for* MEASURE, *pag.* 322.

(2.)

> -------- *Thy ſelf and thy Belongings*
> *Are not thine own ſo proper, as to waſte*
> *Thy ſelf upon thy Virtues;* THEY *on Thee.*

It is requiſite, to make it true *Engliſh*, to read, THEM *on Thee. i. e.* As, either, to waſte thy ſelf on thy Virtues, or thy Virtues on thy ſelf. So again, in ANTHONY and CLEOPATRA, *pag.* 380.

(3.)

> ------- *Should I find them*
> *So ſawcy with the Hand of* SHE *here, (what's her Name,*
> *Since She was* Cleopatra?)

Grammar requires that it ſhould be, *So ſawcy with the Hand of* HER *here*. And ſo again in *MACBETH*, (where *Roſſe* is deſcribing the Miſeries of *Scotland* from the Cruelty of that Tyrant;) *pag.* 581.

(4.)

> ------- *The dead Man's Knell*
> *Is there ſcarce ask'd, for* WHO:

For ſo the ſecond *Folio* Edition, and ſome of the common Modern Editions read it; but Mr. *POPE*, in his Edition, has rightly cor-

corrected it *for* WHOM. It may be alledged from these Instances, and some few more that might be gather'd, that this was a Liberty which *SHAKESPEARE* purposely gave himself, and that therefore it is not an Error of the Copies. Be this, as it will; if *Grammar* and the *Idiom* of the Tongue be directly against it, we have sufficient Warrant to make him *now*, at least, speak true *English*.

BUT to proceed to my Remarks upon the next Line of this Passage,

> *So* horridly *to shake our Disposition* &c.

I suspect, in the Word *horridly*, a literal Deviation to have been made from the Poet by his Copyists: and I'll give my Reasons presently for this Suspicion. But, first, it will be proper to subjoin my Correction of the Passage, and the Pointing of it, which is manifestly faulty. For, why is there a Note of Interrogation at *hideous*, to divide the *Verb* from the Second *Accusative* Case which is govern'd by it, when the Question evidently goes on to the very Close of the Sentence? I think, it ought to be pointed, and restor'd thus;

> -------- *What may this mean ?*
> *That Thou dead Corse again in compleat Steel*
> *Revisit'st thus the Glimpses of the Moon,*
> *Making Night hideous, and* US *fools of Nature*
> *So* HORRIBLY *to shake our Disposition*
> *With Thoughts beyond the Reaches of our Souls?*
> *Say,* &c.

The Change of *horridly* into *horribly* is very trivial as to the Literal Part; and therefore, I hope, the Reason for the Change will be something more considerable. 'Tis true, *horrid* and *horrible* must be confess'd to bear in themselves the same Force and Signification: as *horridum* and *horribile* were wont to do among the *Latines*. But *horrid*, in the most common Acceptation and Use, seems to signify rather *hideous*, *uncouth*, *ugly*, *enormous*, than *terrible* or *frightful*: and it is generally so applied by our Author. I remember a Passage in his King *LEAR*, where it, par-

particularly, ſtands for *ugly.* It is in a Speech by the Duke of *Albany*, reproaching his Wife *Goneril* with her unnatural Behaviour.

LEAR, pag. 77.

------- *See thy ſelf, Devil;*
Proper Deformity ſeems not in the Fiend
So horrid *as in Woman.*

I cannot, however, deny, but that our Poet ſometimes employs the Word *horrid* in the Senſe of *frightful, terrible:* But every obſerving Reader of his Works muſt be aware that he does it ſparingly, and, ten times for every once, ſeems fond to uſe *horrible* and *terrible.* It is obvious, that he prefers both theſe Terms, as more ſonorous and emphatical than *horrid*; and the Proof that he does ſo, is, (which laid the Foundation of my Conjecture here,) that he almoſt conſtantly chuſes them, even where the *Numbers* of his Verſe naturally require *horrid.* I ſhall ſubjoin a few Inſtances of both for Confirmation; to which I could have amaſs'd twenty times as many; but theſe are enough, at leaſt, to excuſe me, tho' I ſhould be deceived in Judgment, from the Cenſure of being too *hypercritical* in my Obſervation.

Proofs of horrible *inſtead of* horrid.

(1.) *TEMPEST, pag.* 73.

Where but ev'n now with ſtrange and ſeveral Noiſes
Of roaring, ſhrieking, howling, jingling Chains,
And more Diverſity of Sounds, all horrible,
We were awak'd.

(2.) *LEAR, pag.* 41.

And with this horrible *Object, from low Farms,*
Poor pelting Villages, &c.

(3)

(3.) And again, *pag.* 55.

> *I tax not you, you Elements, with Unkindness;*
> *I never gave you Kingdom, call'd you Children,*
> *You owe me no Subscription. Then let fall*
> *Your* horrible *Pleasure;* -----

(4.) And again, *pag.* 83.

> Glouc. *Methinks, the Ground is even.*
> Edgar. ---------- Horrible *steep.*
> *Hark, do you hear the Sea?*

(5.) King *HENRY* VIII. *pag.* 457.

> ----- *With one Hand on his Dagger,*
> *Another spread on's Breast, mounting his Eyes,*
> *He did discharge a* horrible *Oath,* &c.

(6.) *TIMON, pag.* 61.

> --------- *For those Milk-paps,*
> *That thro' the Window-barn bore at Men's Eyes,*
> *Are not within the Leafe of Pity writ,*
> *Set 'em down* horrible *Traytors.* ---

(7.) *ANTHONY* and *CLEOPETRA, pag.* 342.

> *Hence,* horrible *Villain! or I'll spurn thine Eyes*
> *Like Balls before me!*

(8.) *MACBETH, pag.* 561.

> ------ *Hence,* horrible *Shadow!*
> *Unreal Mock'ry* [illegible]*nce!* ------

(9.) *Hamlet, pag.* 367.

What if it tempt you tow'rd the Flood, my Lord?
Or to the dreadful Summit of the Cliff,
That beetles o'er his Base into the Sea,
And there assume some other horrible *Form,* &c.

(10.) And *Othello, pag* 561.

Desd. *What is your Pleasure?*
Othell. ------- *Let me see your Eyes:*
Look in my Face.
Desd. --------- *What* horrible *Fancy's this?*

Proofs of terrible *instead of* horrid.

(1.) *Tempest, pag.* 15.

------- *This damn'd Witch* Sycorax,
For Mischiefs manifold, and Sorc'ries terrible
To enter human Hearing, &c.

(2.) And again, *pag.* 35.

Ev'n now we heard a hollow Burst of bellowing,
Like Bulls, or rather Lyons; did't not wake you?
It strook mine Ear most terribly.
Alon. --------- *I heard Nothing.*

(3.) *Macbeth, pag.* 535.

----- *I'm settled, and bend up*
Each corp'ral Agent to this terrible *Feat.*

(4.) And again, *pag.* 555.

But let both Worlds disjoint, and all Things suffer,
E'er we will eat our Meal in fear, and sleep
In the Affliction of these terrible *Dreams,* &c.

(5.) And ſo, *OTHELLO*, *pag.* 478.

What is the Reaſon of this terrible *Summons?*

XXIX. Act 1. Scene 8. Page 368.

Conjectural Emendation.

HAMLET being retir'd to a remote Ground with his Father's Apparition, the Ghoſt immediately diſcloſes himſelf, and the Circumſtances he was under in the *other State*, as far as he was licens'd, or it was proper for him, to declare.

-------- *I am thy father's ſpirit*;
Doom'd for a certain term to walk the night,
And for the day, confin'd to FAST *in fires;*
Till the foul crimes done in my days of nature
Are burnt *and* purg'd *away.*

Tho' all the Copies, old and modern, agree, in this Reading, I cannot help ſuſpecting (at leaſt, till I am better informed of the Force of it;) the Expreſſion, --- *to* faſt *in Fires.* If theſe are the Poet's Words, his Meaning in them muſt be, *to do* Penance *in fires*: as *Faſting* is often a Part of *Penance* injoin'd by the Church for our Sins. But could it be any great *Puniſhment* for a *Spirit*, a Being which requires no Suſtenance, to *faſt?* Or could *faſting* in Fires *burn* and *purge away* Crimes more effectually, than the not being in ſuch a State of *Abſtinence?* The Poet certainly, in my Opinion, intends to mix the old *Pagan* Syſtem here with the more *modern* Notion of a *local Purgatory*; and to intimate, that Souls are cleanſed and purified from their Mortal Stains by the Torment of Fire. The Variation will be but very ſmall, to ſuppoſe he might have wrote;

And, for the Day confin'd to ROAST *in fires*;

Now this takes in all the Ideas neceſſary to the Puniſhment, of being *burnt*, *ſcorched*, *pain'd*, *&c.* (and the Word, thus metaphorically

phorically uſed, conveys no meaner an Image than *carving*, *ſcalding*, *wringing*, and an hundred other *Technical* Terms do, frequent in the moſt elevated Poetry:) But that this was the very Caſe too of our Ghoſt, his own Words, in a Speech but juſt before, ſufficiently teſtify.

> --------- *My Hour is almoſt come,*
> *When I to ſulph'rous and* tormenting Flames
> *Muſt render up my ſelf.*

And our Poet, I remember, afterwards in this very Play, *pag.* 393. again uſes the Expreſſion; ſpeaking of *Pyrrhus* in the Heat of Rage, and running about the flaming Streets of *Troy*:

> ---------- ROASTED *in Wrath and Fire*, &c.

There is another fine Paſſage, that I at preſent remember, in which our Poet has touched this Subject of Puniſhments after Death, and there he does not ſay the leaſt Word of *faſting in fires*: But he makes a Suppoſition of *fiery Floods*, like the *Infernal Rivers*, fabled in the old *Heathen* Poets, and that the Spirits of the Deceaſed ſhould be doom'd to *bathe* in 'em.

MEASURE *for* MEASURE, *pag* 363.

> *Ay, but to die, and go we know not where:*
> *To lie in cold Obſtruction, and to rot;*
> *This ſenſible warm Motion to become*
> *A kneaded Clod; and the delighted Spirit*
> *To* BATHE *in* fiery Floods, *or to reſide*
> *In thrilling Regions of thick-ribbed Ice,*
> *To be impriſoned in the* Viewleſs Winds,
> *And blown with reſtleſs Violence round about*
> *The pendant World;* ------

Now, either to be *roaſted*, or *bath'd*, in Fire, takes in the Idea of being *burnt* and *puniſhed*; and comes up to the Term among the

the *LATINES*, *exurier igni*. Whoever will allow *SHAKESPEARE* to have imitated any Paſſages of the *Antients*, will, I believe, be of Opinion with me, that in theſe two Deſcriptions he had thoſe fine Verſes of *VIRGIL* in his Eye upon this Topick: There are ſuch Strokes of Similitude, as well in the Thought as the Diction, of both Poets.

VIRG. Æneid. VI. *v.* 736, &c.

> Non tamen omne Malum miſeris, nec funditùs omnes
> *Corporeæ excedunt Peſtes:* penitùſque neceſſe eſt
> Multa diù concreta modis inoleſcere miris.
> Ergò exercentur pœnis, *veterumque Malorum*
> *Supplicia expendunt: aliæ panduntur inanes*
> *Suſpenſæ ad Ventos*; aliis ſub gurgite vaſto
> *Infectum eluitur Scelus*, aut *exuritur igni.*

Which Paſſage is thus tranſlated by Mr. *DRYDEN.*

> *Nor Death it ſelf can wholly waſh their Stains;*
> *But long-contracted Filth ev'n in the Soul remains.*
> *The* Reliques of invet'rate Vice *they wear*;
> *And Spots of Sin obſcene in ev'ry Face appear.*
> *For this are various Penances injoin'd;*
> *And* Some are hung to bleach upon the Wind:
> *Some plung'd in Waters*, Others purg'd in Fires,
> 'Till all the Dregs are drain'd, *and all the Ruſt expires.*

XXX. Act 1. Scene 8. Page 369.

> *And each particular Hair to ſtand* ON *End*,
> *Like Quills upon the fretful Porcupine.*

Occaſional Emendation.

Thus Mr. *POPE* writes this Paſſage, as it ought to be; whereas all the Editions, both old and modern, that I have ſeen, concurr in reading --- *ſtand* an *end*, &c. And yet this Paſſage either ſeems

ſeems to have been rectified by Chance, or ſome others, where the ſame Phraſe recurs, have been reviſed with a ſtrange Careleſſneſs. For in the Second Part of *Henry* VI. *pag.* 164. we find him reading with the old Impreſſions,

Mine Eyes ſhould ſparkle like the beaten Flint,
Mine Hair be fixt AN *end, like One diſtraught.*

And ſo in *HAMLET*, *pag,* 424.

Your bedded *Hairs, like Life in Excrements,*
Start up, and ſtand AN *end.*

Occaſional Explanation. Whereas in both theſe Places we likewiſe ought to reſtore it, --- ON *end.* I cannot diſmiſs this laſt quoted Paſſage from *HAMLET*, without taking Notice, that I think the Expreſſion --- *like Life in Excrements,* as much wants an Explication, as any the moſt antiquated Word in our Poet wants a Gloſs. Mr. *HUGHS*, in his Impreſſion of *HAMLET*, has left it out; either becauſe he could make nothing of it, or thought it alluded to an Image too nauſeous. The Poet's Meaning is founded on a *Phyſical* Determination, that the *Hair* and *Nails* are *excrementitious* Parts of the Body, as indeed they are, without Life or Senſation: * And yet that Fear and ſurprize had ſuch an Effect upon *HAMLET*, that his Hairs, as if there were Life in thoſe Excrements, ſtarted up and ſtood on End: Or, as he expreſſes it in his *TEMPEST*, *pag.* 13.

With Hair upſtaring, then like Reeds, not Hair.

That our Poet was acquainted with this Notion in *Phyſics*, of the Hair being without Life, we need no ſtronger Warrant, than that frequently he mentions the *Hair*, as an *Excrement.* So,

---

* *This Doctrine, I ſuppoſe, is inculcated by the old Claſſical* Phyſicians; *a Point which I have not Leiſure here to look into: But* MACROBIUS, *I know, (the greater Part of whoſe Writings is from Collection;) in his* Saturnalia, (lib. 7. cap. 9.) *not only ſpeaks of thoſe Parts of the Humane Body, which have no Senſation; but likewiſe aſſigns the Reaſons, why they can have none.* Oſſa, Dentes, cum Unguibus & Capillis, nimiâ Siccitate ità denſata ſunt, ut penetrabilia nòn ſint effectui *Animæ* qui *Senſum* miniſtrat. &c.

Com.

Com. of ERRORS, *pag.* 432.

> *Why is Time ſuch a Niggard of Hair, being, as it is, ſo plentiful an* Excrement?

JEW *of VENICE, pag.* 49.

> *How many Cowards, whoſe Hearts are all as falſe*
> *As Stairs of Sand, wear yet upon their Chins*
> *The Beards of* Hercules, *and frowning* Mars;
> *Who, inward ſearch'd, have Livers white as Milk?*
> *And Theſe aſſume but Valour's* [a] Excrement
> *To render them redoubted.*

[a] *i. e.* a Beard.

And in *LOVE*'s *LABOUR LOST*, *pag.* 147.

> *For I muſt tell thee, It will pleaſe his Grace (by the World!) ſome time to lean upon my poor ſhoulder, and with his Royal Finger thus dally with my* Excrement, *with my Muſtachio.*

BUT beſides that he ſo often makes Uſe of this Term, to put the Matter out of all Diſpute, he has the very Thought, which he has here in *HAMLET*, again in his *MACBETH*, and expreſt in much plainer Words, *pag.* 592.

> *I have almoſt forgot the Taſte of Fears:*
> *The Time has been, my Senſes would have cool'd*
> *To hear a Night-ſhriek, and my Fell of Hair*
> *Would at a diſmal Treatiſe* rowze, *and* ſtir
> As Life were in't.

XXXI. Ibid.

The Ghoſt intimating how foully he had been murthered, conjures *HAMLET* by his filial Love to revenge his Death. The Prince ſtarting at this dreadful Information, and the Ghoſt proceeding to remark, that any Murther, tho' ever ſo favourable *Conjectural Emendation.*

I in

in its Circumſtances, is bad enough, but that the Murther of him was ſtrangely unnatural; *HAMLET*, impatient to be told the whole Story, ſays thus:

> *Haſte me to know, that I with wings as ſwift*
> *As meditation or the thoughts of love,*
> *May* SWEEP *to my Revenge.*

HAMLET makes uſe of the Metaphor here of a Bird uſing it's Wings ſwiftly, to expreſs his Speed in the purſuit of his Revenge. 'Tis true, to *ſweep* may carry the Senſe of *gliding ſmoothly*, and *ſwiftly* along; (generally, along the Surface of any thing;) but I don't remember the Word ever employ'd to ſignify the *Action* of a *Bird* in the Circumſtances of *purſuing* its *Prey*; that is, of moving its Wings *impetuouſly* for that Purpoſe. In Falconry, a Hawk is ſaid to *ſweep*, when ſhe wipes her Beak after ſhe has fed. But I obſerve that our Poet, for the moſt Part, uſes the Word in the plain and natural Senſe, of *clearing*, *bruſhing away*, or *trailing on the Earth*. So,

Second Part of *HENRY* VI. *pag.* 171.

> *Thy Lips, that kiſs'd the Queen, ſhall* ſweep *the Ground.*

HENRY VIII. *pag.* 541.

> *Pray, Sir, be patient. 'Tis as much impoſſible,*
> *(Unleſs we* ſwept *them from the Door with Cannons,)*
> *To ſcatter 'em, as 'tis to make them ſleep*
> *On May-day Morning,* &c.

ANTHONY and *CLEOPATRA*, *pag.* 373.

> -------- *Friends, be gone; you ſhall*
> *Have Letters from me to ſome Friends, that will*
> Sweep *your way for you.*

MACBETH

MACBETH, pag. 553.

> --------- *And tho' I could*
> *With bare-fac'd Power* ſweep *him from my Sight.*

He uſes it once, I think, to deſcribe the ſmooth March of a Body of Soldiers in gallant Array, and coming timely to the Succour of their Party

Third Part of *HENRY* VI. *pag.* 297.

> *And, lo! where* George *of* Clarence SWEEPS *along,*
> *Of Force enough to bid his Brother Battle.*

But in none of theſe Places, or elſewhere that I know, is it connected with the *Metaphor* of *Wings*, or introduced to denote the *ſwift* and *furious* Deſcent of any Fowl at its Prey, or Enemy. I had almoſt forgot to take Notice, that ſome of the Editors of this Play ſeem to have ſuſpected the *Propriety* of this Word here, by a Change which they have made of it: for both the *Quarto* Edition of 1703, and Mr. *HUGHS*'s, have ſubſtituted in its Place --- *May* fly *to my Revenge.* But to proceed to my own Conjecture: There is another Word, indeed, ſo very near it in Sound and Writing, and ſo peculiar to the Buſineſs of a Bird falling on its Prey, that, perhaps, the Poet might have wrote:

> *Haſte me to know, that I, with Wings as ſwift*
> *As Meditation or the Thoughts of Love,*
> *May* SWOOP *to my Revenge.*

I entirely ſubmit this Conjecture to Judgment; but I am ſure it is the very Phraſe of our Poet upon an Occaſion of the like kind. *MACBETH* having murthered the Wife and Children of *MACDUFF*, the latter, upon Notice of it, falls into theſe mixt Exclamations of Tenderneſs and Reſentment. *Pag.* 583.

He has no Children. --- All my pretty Ones?
Did you ſay, All? What, All? O Hell-kite! What?
What all my pretty Chickens, and their Dam,
At one fell SWOOP? ------

And to *ſwoop*, among Fowlers, is to fly down haſtily, and catch up with the Talons, as Birds of Prey do: An Action which, I humbly conceive, our Author intended to allude to, in the vehement Reſentment and Deſire of Revenge, with which he inflames his *HAMLET.*

XXXII. Ibid. Page 370.

*Various Reading, and E*mendations.

THE Ghoſt of *HAMLET*'s Father, having recounted to him the Proceſs of his Murther, proceeds to exaggerate the Inhumanity and Unnaturalneſs of the Fact, from the Circumſtances in which he was ſurprized.

Thus was I ſleeping, by a brother's hand,
Of life, of crown, of Queen at once diſpatcht;
Cut off ev'n in the bloſſoms of my ſin,
† UNHOUZZLED, † UNANOINTED, † *unanel'd;*
No reck'ning made, but ſent to my account
With all my imperfections on my head.

To which three Words Mr *POPE* has ſubjoined this Gloſs:

† unhouzzled, *without the Sacrament being taken.*
† unanointed, *without extream unction.*
† unanel'd, *no knell rung.*

I am very much afraid (and as apt to believe I ſhall prove it, to the Satisfaction of every Judge, before this Note is ended;) that this Paſſage is neither rightly read, nor, as it is read, rightly explained, throughout. In the firſt Place, inſtead of *unhouzzled* it ought to be reſtor'd --- *unhouſel'd*; from the old *Saxon* Word

Word for the Sacrament, *hufel*. So our *Etymologifts* and *Chaucer* write it; and *Spencer*, accordingly, calls the Sacramental Fire, *houfling* Fire. This, however, is but a trivial Slip, in comparifon with the next that offers it felf. I don't pretend to know what *Gloffaries* Mr. POPE may have confulted, and trufts to; but whofe foever they are, I am fure their Comment is very *fingular* upon the Word I am about to mention. I cannot find any Authority to countenance *unaneal'd* in fignifying, *no Knell rung*. This is, if I miftake not, what the *Greeks* were ufed to call an ἅπαξ λεγόμενον, *an* Interpretation *that never was ufed but once*. Nor, indeed, can I fee how this *participial Adjective* fhould be formed from the *Subftantive* Knell. It could not poffibly throw out the k, or receive in the a. We have an Inftance in our Poet himfelf, where the *participial Adjective* of the *Verb fimple* from this *Subftantive* retains the k; and fo Mr. POPE writes it there.

MACBETH, *pag*. 598.

> *Had I as many Sons as I have Hairs,*
> *I would not wifh them to a fairer Death;*
> *And fo his* Knell *is* knoll'd.

The *Compound Adjective*, therefore, from that Derivation muft have been written, *unknell'd*; (or, *unknoll'd*;) a Word which will by no Means fill up the Poet's Verfe, were there no ftronger Reafons to except againft it; as it unluckily happens, there are. Let us fee what Senfe the Word *unanel'd* then bears. SKINNER, in his *Lexicon* of *Old* and *Obfolete* ENGLISH Terms, tell us, that Anealed is *unctus*; a Præp. *Teut*: An, and Ole *Oleum*: fo that unanealed muft confequently fignify, *Not being anointed*, or, *not having the extream Unction*. But what muft we then do with the Word, immediately preceding it, *unanointed*? For, the Addition of it is fuch a manifeft and abfurd *Tautology*, as SHAKESPEARE could not be guilty of. We muft therefore have Recourfe to the Various Readings, and fee if any printed Copies will help us out. The Second Edition in *Folio*, the *Quarto* in 1637. the

HAM-

Hamlet revised by Mr. *Hughs*, and several other Impressions, all read, instead of *unanointed*,

------ DISAPPOINTED, *unanel'd;*

as I verily believe it ought to be read. Now, the Word **Appoint**, among other Significations, has that of *composing, reconciling:* and the Word *Disappointed* consequently means, *unreconcil'd* to Heaven, *unabsolv'd*, and no *Appointment* of *Penance* or *Atonement* made for Sin; a Work of the utmost Concern and Moment to a dying Person. And our Poet, I remember, in another of his Plays, as *Othello* is at the very Point of killing his Wife upon Suspicion of Adultery, makes him exhort her thus:

OTHELLO, pag. 587.

> *If you bethink yourself of any Crime*
> Unreconcil'd *as yet to Heav'n and Grace,*
> *Sollicit for it strait.* -----

But it happens very luckily too, in Support of the Old Reading which is necessary to be restor'd here, that the Poet has again, in another Play, made use of **Appointment** in this very Sense of *Reconciliation.* In MEASURE *for* MEASURE, *Claudio* is sentenced to die for having debauched a Maiden, and his Sister brings him Word, That his Execution is to be instant; therefore bids him prepare his *Self-examination*, and to make his Peace with Heaven with all Speed.

MEASURE *for* MEASURE, *pag.* 361.

> Isab. *Lord* Angelo, *having Affairs to Heav'n,*
> *Intends you for his swift Ambassador;*
> *Where you shall be an everlasting Leiger.*
> *Therefore your best* APPOINTMENT *make with Speed;*
> *To morrow you set out.*

So

So that, this Reading and this Senſe being admitted, the Tautology is taken away; and the Poet very finely makes his Ghoſt complain of theſe four dreadful Hardſhips, *viz.* That He had been diſpatch'd out of Life without receiving the (Hoste, or) *Sacrament*; without being *reconciled* to Heaven and *abſolved*; without the Benefit of *extream Unction*; or, without ſo much as a *Confeſſion* made of his Sins. The having no Knell rung, I think, is not a Point of equal Conſequence to any of theſe; eſpecially, if we conſider that the *Roman* Church admits the Efficacy of *Praying* for the *Dead.*

XXXIII. Act 1. Scene 9. Page 372.

HORATIO and *Marcellus* coming to *Hamlet*, after the Ghoſt is departed, and, queſtioning him with ſome Impatience, to know the Reaſon of the Spirit's walking; *Hamlet*, reſolv'd to keep the Contents a Secret, anſwers them in a wild, confuſed Manner; which not giving the deſired Satisfaction, *Horatio* replies to him. Emendation, *from Various Reading.*

Theſe are but wild and HURLING *Words, my Lord.*

The Editor, indeed, has the Countenance of ſeveral Editions for this Reading: Tho' here again, as it happen'd in a former Inſtance, ſome of the Editions ſeem to have ſuſpected the Word, and therefore have printed this Paſſage thus;

Theſe are but wild and windy *Words, my Lord,*

But in what Senſe is *hurling* to be taken here? It is always uſed to ſignify, *throwing*, *caſting*, *darting out*, and, as we are told, in the Old ENGLISH, *making a Noiſe:* None of which are within the Poet's Meaning, who intends, *wild* and *giddy*. It muſt, therefore, certainly be reſtor'd, as my *Quarto* Edition of 1637, tho' corrupt in the Spelling, meant to exhibit it.

Theſe are but wild and WHIRLING *Words, my Lord.*

The Acceptation of this Word is ſo univerſally known, as well as ſo apt and peculiar to our Author's Meaning, that, I believe, few

few will doubt that it was his own Expreſſion in this Place: And I have nothing more to do (in Support of this Conjecture, if it needs any;) than to produce a few Inſtances from him, to ſhew that he underſtood and uſed *hurl*, and *whirl*, in the reſpective and diſtinct Senſes which I have above mentioned to belong to them.

(1.) King *RICHARD* II. *pag.* 96.

And interchangeably hurl *down my Gage*
Upon this over-weening Traytor's foot, &c.

(2.) Firſt Part of *HENRY* VI. *pag.* 21.

Then broke I from the Officers that led me,
And with my Nails digg'd Stones out of the Ground,
To hurl *at the Beholders of my Shame.*

(3.) *JULIUS CÆSAR*, *pag.* 293.

--------- *Come*, Anthony;
Defiance, Traytors, hurl *we in your Teeth.*

(4.) *ANTHONY* and *CLEOPATRA*, *pag.* 313.

What our Contempts do often hurl *from us,*
We wiſh it ours again.

(5.) And *OTHELLO*, *pag.* 587.

-------- *When we ſhall meet at Compt*,
This Look of thine will hurl *my Soul from Heav'n,*
And Fiends will ſnatch at it.

In all which Paſſages *hurl* ſignifies to *throw*, or *caſt*, and nothing elſe.

(1.) LOVE'S LABOUR *loſt*, *pag.* 144.

And Juſticealw ays whirls *in equal Meaſure.*

(2.) King

(2.) King *JOHN*, *pag.* 154.

> *I am with Both, each Army hath a Hand,*
> *And in their Rage, I having Hold of Both,*
> *They* whirl *asunder, and dismember me.*

(3.) And again, *pag.* 175.

> *My Lord, they say, Five Moons were seen to Night;*
> *Four fixed, and the Fifth did* whirl *about*
> *The other Four,* &c.

(4.) *First Part of HENRY* VI. *pag.* 24.

> *My Thoughts are* whirled *like a Potter's Wheel.*

(5.) *TITUS ANDRONICUS*, *pag.* 486.

> *To calm this Tempest* whirling *in the Court.*

(6.) And again, *pag.* 502.

> *And then I'll come and be thy Waggoner,*
> *And* whirl *along with thee about the Globes:*

(7.) And *TROILUS and CRESSIDA*, *pag.* 58.

> *I'm giddy; Expectation* whirls *me round.*

In all which Passages *whirl* signifies *agitating, turning round*, in a vehement and giddy Manner.

XXXIV. Ibid. Page 374.

WE come now to a Speech towards the Conclusion of this Act, which labours under so many Faults of Pointing, as well as some of Language, that the Sense is very much perplex'd, and the Text false both in Meaning and Grammar. I must transcribe the Whole first, as it stands; and then give it entire with its Corrections. *False Pointings, and* Emendation.

K *But*

-------- But come,
Here as before, never [ ] *so help you Mercy* [,]
[( ] *How strange or odd soe'er I bear my self,*
[ ] *As I perchance hereafter shall think meet*
To put an antick Disposition on [ ])
That you [ ] *at such Time seeing me, never shall*
[ ] *With Arms encumber'd thus, or this head-shake* [;]
Or by pronouncing of some doubtful Phrase [;]
As [ ] *well, --- we know, -- or, we could, and if we would ---*
Or, if we list to speak, -- or, there be and if there might ---
Or such ambiguous giving out [ ] TO NOTE,
That you know ought of me; this do ye swear [.]
So grace and mercy at your most need help you.

Whoever will take this Speech asunder, and examine the Structure and Connection of it, will easily find that something is wanting to support the *Sense* and *Grammar* of the Whole. *HAMLET* is conjuring them to a Repetition of their Oath of Secrecy, as to what they knew concerning the Walking of his Father's Spirit. Let's dismount it from the Verse, and see what we can make of the Passage, as the Sense plainly will lead us. *Here, as before,* says he, *you shall swear* (*so Mercy help you!*) *that, however oddly I shall think fit to carry myself, you seeing me so transform'd,* never shall --- (*by Motions, Shruggs, or any ambiguous* Giving out to note,) --- *that you know any Thing of me.* This is the whole Scope, in Miniature, of this Passage; and now for the *Syntax* of it. *Never shall* --- do what? The *Verb* is manifestly wanting, and the Sense consequently defective. Then, why, *ambiguous Giving out to note?* Does not, *ambiguous Giving out*, comprehend all the Poet intends here, without Words in the Tail to clog the Clearness of his Meaning? In short, it is necessary, to make the whole intelligible, to point and correct it thus:

But

-------- But come ;
Here as before, Never, --- So help you Mercy!
How ſtrange or odd ſoe'er I bear myſelf,
(As I, perchance, hereafter ſhall think fit
To put an antick Diſpoſition on :)
That you, at ſuch time ſeeing me, never ſhall
(With Arms encumber'd thus, or this Head-ſhake,
Or by pronouncing of ſome doubtful Phraſe,
As, well, --- we know --- or, we could, and if we would ---
Or, if we liſt to ſpeak, --- or, there be, and if there might ---
Or ſuch ambiguous Giving out;) DENOTE
That you know aught of me. This do you ſwear;
So Grace and Mercy at your moſt Need help you!

This ſmall Change of two Letters not only gives us a *Verb* that makes the whole Tenour of the Speech clear and intelligible; but a *Verb* too, that carries the very Force and Senſe which we before wanted in this Place. To *denote*, as very raw *Grammarians* know, implies, to *ſignify*, to *ſhew by Marks:* And thus it is uſual with our Poet to employ this very Word. So in OTHELLO, *pag.* 540.

Othell. *O monſtrous! monſtrous!*
Jago. *-------- This was but his Dream.*
Othell. *But it* DENOTED *a fore-gone Concluſion.*

And ſo *HAMLET*, in a Speech to his Mother, upon the Nature of his Grief for his Father's Death, *pag.* 354.

'Tis not alone my inky Cloak, good Mother,
Nor cuſtomary Suits of ſolemn Black,
Nor windy Suſpiration of forc'd Breath,
No, nor the fruitful River in the Eye,
Nor the dejected 'Haviour of the Viſage,
Together with all Forms, Moods, Shews, of Grief,
That can DENOTE *me truly.*

I HAVE, at length, got through the firſt Act of this Tragedy; and hope, as well for the Eaſe of my Readers as my ſelf, that, in the remaining Parts, Faults will neither riſe ſo numerous, nor require ſo much Prolixity in the grubbing up. The Proofs of ſeveral Kinds, which I have already given to maintain any Correction, muſt naturally ſave ſome Trouble in what is to follow: And I am ſufficiently aware what Room my APPENDIX will demand; in which I have engaged to ſhew, that the ſame Sorts of Errors are ſcattered through the other Plays; and that *SHAKESPEARE* is to be reſtor'd to his genuine Reading, with the ſame Method and Eaſe of Cure.

XXXV. Act. 2. Scene 1. Page 376.

Falſe Pointing, and Conjectural Emendation.

POLONIUS, about to diſpatch his Servant *Reynoldo* for *France* with Commands to his Son *Laertes*, bids him, before he makes his Viſit, firſt enquire into his Son's Character; and the better to ſift into it, commiſſions him to lay ſeveral Levities to his Charge; (ſuch as are uſual with Youth, but none ſo rank in Quality, as might diſcredit him;) as Gaming, Drinking, Fencing, Swearing, Quarrelling, Drabbing. *Reynoldo* objecting, that, to accuſe him of *Drabbing*, might diſhonour him, *Polonius* replies;

> *Faith* [ ] *no* [,] *as you may ſeaſon it in the charge*;
> *You muſt not put* ANOTHER *Scandal on him*,
> *That he is open to incontinency*,
> *That's not my Meaning*; - - - -

The old Gentleman, 'tis plain, is of Opinion, that to charge his Son with *wenching* would not *diſhonour* him, conſequently would be no *Scandal* to him: For every Scandal, in ſuch Degree as it affects any Man, proportionably diſhonours him. Why then ſhould he caution *Reynoldo* from putting ANOTHER *Scandal* on him? Methinks, there is ſome Reaſon to ſuſpect this Word of not being altogether ſo proper here, if no Scandal at all had been yet offer'd. There can be no *Second* Scandal ſuppoſed

ſuppoſed, without a *Firſt* implied. The Poet's Meaning is, as I conceive it, ſimply this: To ſay, that he wenches, without Aggravation in the Circumſtances, lays but a venial Liberty of Youth at his Door; but to ſay, That he is open and addicted to Incontinency, amounts to an Habit of Licence, and throws an actual Scandal. A very ſlight Change will reconcile the Paſſage to this Senſe; and therefore, if I am right in the Author's Meaning, we may ſuppoſe he wrote;

> *No, faith; as you may ſeas'n it in the Charge;*
> *You muſt not put* AN UTTER *Scandal on him,*
> *That he is open to Incontinency,*
> *That's not my Meaning;* but breath his Faults ſo quaintly,
> That they may ſeem the Taints of Liberty;

i. e. So far from their being an abſolute, entire, and utter Scandal to him, that they may be none at all, but appear at worſt the Liberties of Youth.

XXXVI. Ibid.

Emendation, from Various Reading.

> - - - - - - - - *Marry, Sir, here's my Drift;*
> *And I believe it is a Fetch of* WIT.

THERE is a various Reading upon this Paſſage, which deſerved the Notice of the Editor; becauſe, if I am not much deceived, it ſeems to have the genuine Stamp of our Author upon it. The ſecond Edition in *Folio*, and ſome other of the Impreſſions, read;

> *And, I believe, it is a Fetch of* WARRANT.

Which I take to be the very Words and Meaning of the Poet for this Reaſon, becauſe he makes *Polonius* ſpeak dubiouſly of his Intention. No body is ſo doubtful of his own Judgment and Talents, but that he knows abſolutely whether his Drifts and Purpoſes are deſigned with *Wit*, or no, tho' he cannot be ſo certain

certain, as to their being *juſtifiable.* A Man may much eaſier be miſtaken, as to the *Legality,* than as to the *Sagacity,* of any Fact; becauſe ſomething more than private Opinion, or naked Belief, is wanting to determine poſitively whether a Thing be *warrantable.* Beſides, I obſerve, that it is very familiar with *SHAKESPEARE* to uſe the Words *Warrant* and *Warranty* to ſignify a Juſtification. So,

(1.) *OTHELLO, pag.* 484.

> *I therefore apprehend, and do attach Thee,*
> *For an Abuſer of the World, a Practiſer*
> *Of Arts inhibited, and out of* Warrant,

(2.) *TITUS ANDRONICUS, pag.* 509.

> *A Reaſon mighty, ſtrong, and effectual,*
> *A Pattern, Precedent, and lively* Warrant,
> *For me, moſt wretched, to perform the Like.*

(3.) King *JOHN, pag.* 176.

> *It is the Curſe of Kings to be attended*
> *By Slaves, that take their Humours for a* Warrant,
> *To break into the bloody Houſe of Life.*

(4.) And again, *pag.* 189.

> *Look, where the holy Legate comes apace,*
> *To give us* Warrant *from the Hand of Heav'n.*

(5.) JEW *of VENICE, pag.* 9.

> *And from your Love I have a* Warranty
> *T' unburthen all my Plots and Purpoſes,* &c.

(6.) And *OTHELLO, pag.* 580.

> -------- *never lov'd* Caſſio,
> *But with ſuch general* Warranty *of Heav'n*
> *As I might love.*

Not

Not, *Warrantry*; as it is in this laſt Place erroneouſly printed in Mr. POPE's Edition. *Occaſional Correction.*

XXXVII. Ibid.

Correction, from Various Reading.

You laying theſe ſlight SALLIES *on my Son,*
As 'twere a thing a little ſoil'd *i' th' working,*

'Tis true, *Sallies* and *Flights* of Youth are very frequent Phraſes; but what Agreement is there betwixt the Metaphors of *Sallies*, and a Thing *ſoil'd?* Correct, as all the Editions, that I have ever ſeen, have it;

You laying theſe ſlight SULLIES *on my Son,*

Perhaps, this *Subſtantive* may be of his own coining, from the *Verb* to *ſully:* But that, as I have already amply prov'd, is a Liberty which he eternally aſſumes through his whole Works.

XXXVIII. Act 2. Scene 4. Page 381.

CORNELIUS and *Voltimand*, being returned from their Embaſſy to *Norway*, bring Word, that That Monarch had ſuppreſs'd his Nephew *Fortinbras*'s Expedition; which he at firſt ſuppoſed deſigned againſt *Poland*, but found, upon Enquiry, to be levell'd at *Denmark:* That he had put *Fortinbras* under Arreſt, who had obey'd it; and, upon a Check receiv'd, had made Proteſtation before his Uncle never more to make any hoſtile Attempts againſt the *Daniſh* State. *Conjecture, from Various Reading.*

Whereon old Norway, *overcome with Joy,*
Gives him THREE *thouſand Crowns in annual Fee;*
And his Commiſſion to employ thoſe Soldiers,
So levied as before, againſt the Polack.

So,

So, indeed, the Generality of the Editions read; but my two *Quarto's*, of 1637 and 1703, both have it;

> *Whereon old* Norway, *overcome with Joy,*
> *Gives him* THREESCORE *thousand Crowns in annual Fee*, &c.

This Addition of a Syllable gives a little Roughness to the Beginning of the Verse; but one Syllable in the first *Foot* of it must be *resolv'd* in the Pronunciation; which is very usual, as I have observ'd, with our Poet. 'Tis true, this Alteration is of no Moment to the Sense of the Passage; but, methinks, *Threescore thousand* Crowns are a much more suitable Donative from a King to his own Nephew, and the General of an Army, than so poor a Pittance as *Three thousand* Crowns, a Pension scarce large enough for a dependant Courtier.

XXXIX. Ibid. Page 382.

Correction, from Various Reading.

> *That He is mad 'tis true; 'tis true, 'tis pity;*
> *And pity,* it is true: -----

Thus, indeed, several of the Editions read this Place; but they don't seem to enter entirely into the Poet's Humour. *Polonius*, (an officious, impertinent, old Courtier,) priding himself in the Discovery which he supposes he has made of the Cause of *HAMLET*'s Madness, is so full of the Merit of it, that he can't content himself to deliver it in a plain and easy Manner; but falls into an affected jingling Sort of Oratory, as he fancies; and ringing the Chimes, backwards and forwards, upon the same Words. No Body can read this Speech without observing, that these Figures and Flowers of Rhetorick are not only sprinkled, but poured out, through the whole. They are Strokes of low Humour, thrown in purposely, *ad captandum populum*; or, to use the Poet's own Phrase, *to set on some Quantity of barren Spectators to laugh at.* I think, therefore, it should be wrote, as as three of my Editions have it; and as I know it is conſtantly pronounc'd on the Stage:

> *That he is mad*, 'tis *true*; 'tis *true*, 'tis *Pity*;
> *And Pity* 'tis, 'tis *true*.

XL. Ibid.

> *For this effect defective* [,] *comes by cauſe* [,]

Falſe Pointing.

Either the *Comma* after *defective* muſt be taken out, or another added before it; otherwiſe, the *Subſtantive* is disjoined from its *Verb*. Reſtore it,

> *For this Effect, defective, comes by Cauſe;*

XLI. Ibid. Page 384.

> *Into the Madneſs wherein now he raves,*
> *And all we wail for.*

Correction from Various Reading.

King. Do you think [ ] this?
Queen. --------- *It may be very likely.*

POLONIUS having explain'd to them the Nature of HAMLET's Lunacy, and from what Cauſe he imagines it to have ſprung; the King asks the Queen, if ſhe is of Opinion that it had ſuch a Riſe; which, ſhe confeſſes, ſeems very probable to her that it might. Reſtore, therefore, as all my Editions have it.

King. D' you think 'tis This?
Queen. -------- *It may* &c.

XLII. Ibid.

> *Take this from this, if this be otherwiſe* [,]

Falſe Pointing.

POLONIUS thinks himſelf ſo certain of being right in his Diſcovery, that he is willing the King ſhould take his Head from his

his Shoulders, if he is out in his Politicks. It must be pointed;

Take This from This, --- if This be otherwise;

XLIII. Ibid.

Various Reading

--------- *If he love her not,*
And be not from his reason fall'n thereon,
Let me be no assistant for a state,
AND *keep a farm and carters.*

Instead of the *Copulative* AND, which does not make the Sense so clear, my two *Quarto Editions* read it, I think, better, with a *Conjunction disjunctive.*

-------- *If he love her not,*
And be not from his Reason fall'n thereon,
Let me be no Assistant for a State,
BUT *keep a Farm and Carters.*

XLIV. Act 2. Scene 6. Page 391.

Conjectural Emendation.

These are now the FASHION, *and so berattle the common* STAGES *(so they call them,) that many wearing rapiers are afraid of goose-quills, and dare scarce come thither.*

I'll give the Reading first as I think it ought to be restor'd, and then assign the Reasons.

These now are the FACTION, *and so berattle the common* STAGERS *(so they call them,) that Many wearing Rapiers are afraid of Goose-quills, and dare scarce come thither.*

The Poet, as it were, here steps out of *Denmark* into *England*, and makes *Rosencraus*, in talking of Theatres, allude to the Plays per-

performed at home by the Children of the *King's Chappel*; who were in great Eſtimation at that Time of day, and out-rival'd the Gentlemen of the *Profeſſion*. The Variation *of Faſhion* into *Faction* we owe to Mr. *HUGHS*; I think it much the more forcible and expreſſive Term: implying, that thoſe Children were not only in Faſhion and Eſteem; but were a Prevailing Faction againſt the other Playhouſes, or had a Faction made by the Town in their Favour. As to the other Alteration of *common Stages* into *common Stagers*, which is a Conjecture of my own, my Reaſon for it is this: The Poet certainly cannot intend by his *Many wearing Rapiers*, that Gentlemen-Spectators were afraid to go to the common Theatres, for Fear of the Reſentment of theſe Children, who ſo berattled the common Stages. What greater Affront could *SHAKESPEARE* put upon his Audience, than to ſuppoſe any of them were of ſuch tame and cowardly Spirits? No, if I underſtand him, he ſeems to me to hint, that this young Fry were ſo pert upon the profeſt *Actors*, that even they, tho' they wore Swords, were afraid of going near them, leaſt they ſhould be *banter'd*, or *inſulted*, paſt Sufferance. What farther induces me to think, it ſhould be *common Stagers*, rather than *common Stages*, is, that, in the Speech immediately following, *HAMLET*, ſpeaking of theſe Children, retorts upon them, --- *If they ſhould grow themſelves to* common PLAYERS --- and does not ſay, *If they ſhould come themſelves to the* common PLAY-HOUSES, or *Stages*.

XLV. Ibid.

What, are they Children? who maintains them? how are they eſcoted? will they purſue the quality no longer than they can ſing? *will they not ſay afterwards, if they ſhould grow themſelves to common players* [?] [ ] *as it is moſt like, if their Means are no better:* [ ] *their writers do them wrong to make them exclaim againſt their own Succeſſion* [.] *Falſe Pointing.*

 The

The Pointing of the latter Part of this Speech is ſo very faulty, that the Senſe of it is but barely intelligible. Reſtore it, as Mr. *HUGHS*'s Edition partly leads the way;

> *Will they not ſay afterwards, if they ſhould grow themſelves to common Players, (as it is moſt like, if their Means are not better;) their Writers do them wrong to make them exclaim againſt their own Succeſſion?*

I cannot help obſerving, that the Beginning of this Speech contains one of thoſe Paſſages in which the Poet may be ſaid to overſhoot himſelf; and be guilty of an Abſurdity, by making his *Actor* ſay what he cannot be ſuppoſed to know *in Character:* Which is confounding the *Perſon* of the *Drama* with a *Poeta loquitur. HAMLET*, replying to *Roſencraus* concerning theſe young Players, aſks, --- *What, are they Children? who maintains them? how are they eſcoted?* Theſe Queſtions argue him a Stranger to them, and their Quality: Yet, without any Information, he immediately after cries, *Will they purſue the Quality no longer than they can ſing?* --- which is intimating tacitly, as I take it, that, he knew them to be the *Singing-Boys* of the *King's Chappel*: a Knowledge, no ways to be accounted for, as I can imagine, unleſs the Poet had given his *HAMLET* a Portion of Sir *John Falſtaffe's* INSTINCT. I muſt own, *SHAKESPEARE* is not without ſome more Samples of theſe Self-Contradictions; and one Great one, that has been generally imputed to him, will fall under Conſideration in the next Act. But of That in its own Place.

XLVI. Ibid.

Conjecture.

> *Faith, there has been much to do on both ſides; and the Nation holds it no ſin, to* tarre *them* [ ] *to controverſie.*

I think it will be more numerous to the Ear, and, perhaps, requiſite in point of Language, to read;

> ----- *And the Nation holds it no Sin to* tarre *them* on *to Controverſie.*

To

To *tarre on* is an *old* ENGLISH Word, ſignifying, to *provoke, urge on, ſet on,* as we do Dogs to fighting. And ſo, I obſerve, *SHAKESPEARE* in other Paſſages writes it.

King *JOHN, pag.* 169.

> *And like a Dog, that is compell'd to fight,*
> *Snatch at his Maſter that doth* tarre *him* on.

And, ſo again, in *TROILUS* and *CRESSIDA, pag.* 32.

> *Two Curs ſhall tame each other; Pride alone*
> *Muſt* tarre *the Maſtives* on, *as 'twere their Bone.*

XLVII. Act 2. Scene 7. Page 391.

I will propheſie, he comes to tell me of the Players [.] *Mark it* [,] *you ſay right, Sir;* *Falſe Pointing.*

This ought to be pointed as in Mr. *HUGHS*'s Impreſſion.

I will propheſie, he comes to tell me of the Players; Mark it: --- You ſay right, Sir;

XLVIII. Ibid. Page 392.

I remember one ſaid, there was No ſalts in the lines, to make the matter ſavoury; nor no matter in the phraſe, that might indite the author of AFFECTION; *but call'd it, an honeſt method.* *Various Reading, and Omiſſion ſupply'd.*

I muſt own, I can have no tolerable Comprehenſion of what is meant here by the Word *Affection: HAMLET* is ſpeaking of ſome Play, to the Stroling Players, which he liked very well, but which did not ſo currently go down with the Multitude. One, it ſeems, who had a Mind to make a Criticiſm upon it, hints, That there was no *Matter* in its *Phraſe* that could indite the Author of *Affection.* Now, what can *Affection,* as a Quality with regard to a Play, ſignify, but *Paſſion?* Yet ſurely the Author

Author could not intend to mean that it wanted That. *HAMLET* ſpeaks to the Maſter-Player to give him a Taſte of his Quality in a *paſſionate* Speech; directs him to a Tragedy, which he ſays, in his Judgment was an *excellent Play, well digeſted in the Scenes, and ſet down with as much Modeſty as Cunning:* And then points out a Speech in it, which he chiefly loved, and which contained the Account of *Priam*'s ſlaughter, and the Diſtreſs of *Hecuba* at the Sight of that terrible Action. The Subject alone, never ſo inartificially told, certainly could not be altogether diveſted of *Paſſion.* Beſides, Could not the Phraſe of a Play carry *Paſſion* with it, and yet the Poet uſe an *honeſt Method?* The ſecond *Folio* Edition (which, in the Generality, is eſteemed as the beſt Impreſſion of *SHAKESPEARE*;) has a different Reading, which, at leaſt, deſerved a ſlight Notice from the Editor: And which, I believe, is more likely to expreſs our Author's Meaning. We, there, find it written thus;

> *I remember, one ſaid, there was no Sallets* (which Mr. POPE very juſtly reſtores to, *Salts*) *in the Lines to make the Matter ſavoury; nor no Matter in the Phraſe, that might indite the Author of* AFFECTATION; *but call'd it an honeſt Method.*

i. e. if I underſtand it at all, That as there was no *Poinancy* of *Wit* or *Virulence* of *Satire*, on the one hand; ſo there was Nothing to condemn it of *Affectation*, on the other. And if it wanted *Affectation*, the Poet might more properly be ſaid to uſe an *honeſt Method:* For *Affectation*, is either the *Maſquerade* of Nature in an Habit of *Ridicule*; or the *Abuſe* of it, by a *deſign'd Diſguiſe* of a worſe Sort. Three of my Editions (the oldeſt of which is the *Quarto* in 1637;) exhibit this Paſſage with an Addition in its Cloſe; which tho' I can't warrant to be the Author's own genuine Words, yet make the Sentence end more roundly, and therefore might have been *degraded*, at leaſt, to the Bottom of Mr. POPE's Page, and been noted as an Interpolation of the Stage, as, perhaps, indeed they may be. The Words however are theſe.

---- *But*

----- *But called it an honest Method, as wholesome as sweet; and, by very much, more handsome than fine.*

XLIX. Ibid. Page 393.

False Printing.

And thus o'er-cised *with coagulate gore,*

It must be restored with the second *Folio* Edition, and some of the more modern Ones,

And thus o'er-sized *with coagulate Gore,*

For the Glue, or Composition used by Plaisterers, Painters, *&c.* is called *Size,* and derived from the *Sisa* of the *Italians.*

L. Ibid.

Conjecture.

--------- *unequal* MATCH'D,
Pyrrhus *at* Priam *drives, in rage strikes wide;*
But with the whif and wind of his fell Sword
Th' unnerved father falls [.] THEN SENSELESS [ ] Ilium,
Seeming to feel this blow, with flaming top
Stoops to his base, &c.

In the first Place, *unequal matched* by the Position must be a Nominative, and consequently relate to *Pyrrhus.* Now if *Pyrrhus* was *unequal matched,* in the Sense and general Acceptation we must understand that he was *over-match'd,* and *had the worst of it:* Not that he was an *Over-match* for *Priam,* which was the Truth of the Fact. I believe therefore it should be, as the second *folio* Edition has it, (and the Impression, said to be revised by Mr. ROWE, whether by Chance or Design;) with an Alteration in the Pointing ;

------- *Unequal* MATCH !

For

For the Subſtantive thus, with a Note of Admiration after it, relates indifferently to *Pyrrhus* and *Priam*, and ſignifies that each was unequal to the other, the firſt in *Strength*, the latter in *Weakneſs*. But to go lower into the Paſſage, (tho' all the Editions agree in the Reading,) I can hardly be perſwaded it is printed as the Poet intended it; or that he would have induſtriouſly choſen to prefix an *Epithet* to *Ilium*, which makes a Paradox in the Context. If *Ilium* was *then* ſenſeleſs, why ſhould it ſeem to *feel* the Blow? Or, if *Ilium* was ſenſeleſs, why ſhould it *then* ſeem to *feel* it? For one of the two Ways it muſt be taken. I know very well it may be reſolved thus; that *Ilium, quoàd* the Bricks and ſtones, was abſolutely *ſenſeleſs*; yet the Buildings, falling into the Fire juſt at the Inſtant when *Priam* fell to the Ground, ſeemed, as it were, to be ſenſible of that Blow. I confeſs, this may be a poetical Inference; but a little hard-ſtrained, and in no wiſe neceſſary. Perhaps, with a ſmall Variation in the Text and Pointing, the Paſſage may lie more eaſy and natural thus.

> ------- *Unequal* Match!
> Pyrrhus *at* Priam *drives; in Rage ſtrikes wide;*
> *But with the Whif and Wind of his fell Sword*
> *Th'unnerved Father falls* DOWN SENSELESS. --- Ilium,
> *Seeming to feel this Blow, with flaming Top*
> *Stoops to his Baſe*, &c.

I propoſe this laſt Alteration but as a Conjecture, and without laying any Streſs upon it: and the rather too, becauſe, perhaps, the whole Paſſage concerning *Priam* and *Hecuba* may not be of our Poet's writing, but a Quotation from ſome Play of a Contemporary, which he had a mind to put in the Mouth of a ſtroling Player. I ſhould, indeed, ſuſpect it to be our Poet's from one Reaſon only; and that is, from its Subject. I think the Obſervation has never yet been made, and therefore I ſhall give it here; That there is ſcarce a Play throughout all his Works, in which it was poſſible to introduce the Mention of them,

them, where he has not by *Simile*, *Allusion*, or otherwise, hinted at the *Trojan* Affairs; so fond was he of that Story.

LI. Ibid.

Emendation.

But as we often see against some storm,
A silence in the heav'n, the RACK *stand still,*
The bold wind speechless, and the orb below
As hush as death;

Tho' all the Editions, that have fallen in my Way, write this Passage as the Editor does; I know no Sense, in which the Word *Rack* is ever used, that will serve the Purpose here. It must certainly be corrected,

A Silence in the Heav'n, the WRACK *stand still,*

Occasional Emendation.

i. e. the Tempest; the Hurry, Confusion, and Outrage of the Elements: And so, in this admirable Passage of the *TEMPEST*, *p.* 60.

--------- *Those our Actors,*
As I foretold you, were all Spirits, and
Are melted into Air, into thin Air;
And, like the baseless Fabrick of their Vision,
The Cloud-capt Tow'rs, the gorgeous Palaces,
The solemn Temples, the great Globe it self,
Yea, all which it inherit, shall dissolve,
And, like this insubstantial Pageant faded,
Leave not a RACK *behind!*

It must be corrected;

Leave not a WRACK *behind!*

i. e. if I conceive the Poet's Meaning rightly, not a *Fragment*, or *minutest Particle*, to shew that a *Wrack* has been.

LII. Ibid. Page 395.

Various Reading.

Look IF *he has not turn'd his Colour, and has Tears in's Eyes. Pr'ythee no more.*

All the Editions, that I have ever met with, read;

Look, WHERE *he has not turn'd his Colour, and has Tears in's Eyes. Pr'ythee, no more.*

i. e. Look, whether *he has not,* &c. 'Tis true, as Mr. *Pope* writes it, the ſame Senſe is convey'd; but the other is the Poet's Word: And it is frequent with him, tho' the *Editor* did not remember it here, to uſe it in that Signification. So in the Second Part of *Henry* VI. *pag.* 162.

And therefore do they cry, tho' you forbid,
That they will guard you where *You will, or no.*

And again, *pag.* 168.

Died he not in his Bed? where ſhould he die?
Can I make Men live where *they will, or no?*

As, in theſe Inſtances, (and, perhaps, where ever elſe it occurs in our Author;) the Strictneſs of the *Numbers* requires a *ſingle Syllable* in the Place where this Word ſtands, it may be, it is uſed by Contraction only, for *whether.*

LIII. Ibid. Page 395.

False Printing.

After your death, you were better have a bad epitaph, then *their ill report while you liv'd.*

This is only a ſlight literal Fault of the Preſs, and the Reviſer. Correct it, as it ought to be,

After

After your Death you were better have a bad Epitaph, than *their ill Report while you* live.

THE next, with which my Remarks on this Act conclude, is a *Slip* of ſuch a kind, that I don't know to whoſe Account, properly, to place it. There are many Paſſages of ſuch intolerable Careleſſneſs interſpers'd thro' all the ſix Volumes, that, were not a few of Mr. POPE's *Notes* ſcatter'd here and there too, I ſhould be induced to believe that the Words in the Title Page of the *Firſt* Volume,--- COLLATED, *and* CORRECTED *by the former* EDITIONS, *By Mr.* POPE,---- were plac'd there by the *Bookſeller* to enhaunce the *Credit* of his *Edition*; but that he had play'd falſe with his *Editor*, and never ſent him the Sheets to reviſe. And, ſurely, this muſt have been the Caſe ſometimes: For no Body ſhall perſwade me that Mr. POPE could be awake, and with his Eyes open, and reviſing a Book which was to be publiſh'd under his Name, yet let an Error, like the following, eſcape his Obſervation and Correction.

LIV. Act 2. Scene 8. Page 397.

For murther, tho' it have no Tongue, will ſpeak *Correction.*
With moſt miraculous Organ. I'll OBSERVE HIS LOOKS,
Play ſomething like the murther of my father
Before mine uncle. I'll obſerve his Looks,
I'll tent him to the quick; if he but blench,
I know my courſe.

This is palpable Nonſenſe, from an Error in the *Compoſitor* to the *Preſs*; occaſion'd by his throwing his Eye two Lines lower than he ſhould have done, and ſo printing the ſame *Hemiſtich* twice over. This Error could not be repeated by an *Editor* in *reviſing*, his Eye and Attention going together in that Task: This, therefore, muſt be one of thoſe Sheets, which, as I before hinted, were never ſent to Mr. POPE for his *Reviſal*. Reſtore it, as the Meaning of the Place requires, and as all the former Editions have it;

For Murther, tho' it have no Tongue, will ſpeak
With moſt miraculous Organ. I'll HAVE THESE PLAYERS
Play ſomething like the Murther of my Father
Before mine Uncle. I'll obſerve his Looks;
I'll tent him to the Quick; if he look pale,
I know my Courſe.

But becauſe it may ſeem a little too hard, upon a ſingle Inſtance of this kind, to ſuſpect that the Sheets might not be *all* reviſed by the Editor, as I juſt now hinted; I'll ſubjoin another *flagrant* Teſtimony of the ſame Sort of Negligence: And I ſhall do it the more willingly, becauſe I would embrace an Opportunity of clearing *Brutus* from the Imputation of a Murther, which *SHAKESPEARE* is made to throw upon him, tho' he never had it in his Head to think him guilty of it.

WILLIAM de la Poole, the wicked Duke of *Suffolk*, being baniſhed out of *England* by King *Henry* the Sixth, as he is making off in Diſguiſe, is upon the Coaſt of *Kent* taken by Pirates: And behaving himſelf to them in a Manner they did not care to brook, was ordered to the long Boat's Side, there to have his Head ſtrook off. As he is dragging away, he comforts himſelf that his Death will be memorable, from the Circumſtance of his being murther'd by ſuch mean and vile Fellows; as it had happen'd to many *Great Men* before him.

Second Part of *HENRY* VI. *pag.* 173.

Omiſſion. *ſupplied.*

That this my death may never be forgot.
Great men oft die by vile Bezonians.
A Roman *ſworder and* Bandetto *ſlave*
Murther'd ſweet Tully. Brutus' *baſtard hand*
Pompey *the Great; and* Suffolk *dies by pirates.*

Tully

Tully indeed was kill'd by *Herennius* a Centurion, whom the Poet here calls, by way of Ignominy, a *Roman* Sworder; and by *Popilius* a Tribune, who is likewiſe here call'd a *Bandetto* Slave, probably, becauſe he had formerly murthered his Father, and was defended, upon his Tryal for that Fact, by *Tully*. But would not any Body now, taking Mr. POPE's for a *correct* and *infallible* Edition, begin to wonder how *SHAKESPEARE* could be ſo preciſe in *Roman* Hiſtory as to the Death of *Cicero*; and ſo ignorant, as to lay the Murther of *Pompey* upon *Brutus*? If we were to take this Fact for granted, we ſhould find our Poet guilty of a ſtrange Self-Contradiction, or *Pompey* the Father of a very degenerate Son. For *Sextus Pompeius*, in another of our Author's Plays, gives *Brutus* ſuch a Character and Commendations, as no Man certainly would beſtow on his Father's Murtherer. See

ANTHONY and *CLEOPATRA*, *pag*. 345.

------------ I do not know,
Wherefore my Father ſhould Revengers *want,*
Having a Son *and Friends; ſince* Julius Cæſar,
(*Who at* Philippi *the* GOOD Brutus *ghoſted,*)
There ſaw you lab'ring for him. What was it
That mov'd pale Caſſius *to conſpire? And what*
Made thee ALL-HONOUR'D, HONEST Roman Brutus,
With the arm'd reſt, Courtiers of beauteous Freedom,
To drench the Capitol, but that they would
Have but one man, a man? *And that is it*
Hath made me rig my Navy: At whoſe Burthen
The anger'd Ocean foams, with which I meant
To ſcourge th' Ingratitude *that deſpiteful* Rome
Caſt on my noble *Father.*

The Sentiments of filial Piety, and Reſolutions of avenging his Father's Murther, are too ſtrongly expreſs'd, to ſuppoſe he would in the ſame Breath beſtow an Encomium on the Man who kill'd him

Occaſional Correction.

him. But when I firſt quoted this Paſſage, I little ſuſpected it would have furniſhed freſh Work for Correction. What! were the Conſpirators preſumed to have kill'd CÆSAR, *becauſe they would have* but one *Man*, a Man? What Mock-reaſoning is this? If they would have but *one man, a man,* (*i. e.* a Man κατ᾽ ἐξοχήν· a Man eminent above, and over-topping, all others;) it was the Height of *Cæſar*'s Ambition to be ſuch a One, and therefore they ſhould rather have let him live. If I underſtand the Meaning of the Poet, he would infer, that the noble Conſpirators ſtabb'd *Cæſar*, becauſe they would have, or ſuffer, any one Man to be *but a Man*; *i. e.* they would have no one aim at arbitrary Power, and a Degree of Preheminence above the reſt. Reſtore the Place therefore with the ſecond *Folio* Edition;

> -------------- *but that they would*
> Have One Man, but a Man?

But to return again to the Queſtion of *Pompey* being kill'd by *Brutus*. I have before hinted, that our Poet never deſign'd a Charge of this ſort againſt poor *Brutus*; and in ſhort, SHAKESPEARE will preſently ſtand acquitted of this Blunder; and the Fault appear to have ariſen from a Negligence of *Reviſal*, or rather from the Want of *reviſing at all*. But that this Suſpicion of mine may not appear a meer *gratis dictum*, I'll now give the Reaſon that induced me to it; and from which, I think, the Source of the Error may be fairly accounted for. The Caſe is, a Material Line is left out, in this Paſſage, by Mr. POPE's Impreſſion; which very Line is left out of another Edition, in *Duodecimo*, likewiſe publiſh'd by Mr. *Tonſon* about ten Years ago; ſo that it ſeems moſt probable, that the Preſs was ſet to Work and corrected by this *Duodecimo* Edition; without any *Collation* with the old Editions mentioned in Mr. POPE's Table of Editions at the End of his *Sixth Volume*. This Deduction, I am ſure, is fair and natural: for the ſecond *folio* Edition (one of the Editions there mentioned,) exhibits the Paſſage entire, and as the Poet wrote it: and even the fourth Edition in *folio* (which, indeed, is but a faulty one;) printed no longer ago than the

the Year 1685, likewiſe has it as it ſhould be. Reſtore it therefore with them, and we come back both to the Truth of the Hiſtory, and the Poet's Text into the Bargain.

That This my Death may never be forgot.
Great Men oft die by vile Bezonians.
A Roman *Sworder, and* Bandetto *Slave*
Murther'd ſweet Tully. Brutus' *baſtard Hand*
STAB'D Julius Cæſar. SAVAGE ISLANDERS
Pompey *the Great: And* Suffolk *dies by Pirates.*

I cannot help, tho' this Paſſage has already taken up ſome Length, throwing in an Explication upon it, which will be new to *ſome* Readers, at leaſt, of *SHAKESPEARE*: and, conſequently, I ſhall not loſe all my Labour in it. I had once a Suſpicion that the Poet intended to make *Suffolk* reproach *Brutus* with Cowardice, for diſhonourably ſtabing *Cæſar*; and that the Text, to ſupport this Meaning, ſhould have been alter'd to *Occaſional Explication.*

--------- Brutus' DASTARD *Hand*
Stab'd Julius Cæſar:

A Miſtake of the like kind has happen'd upon the very ſame Words in another of our Author's Plays. In King *Richard* II. *Bolingbroke* being required to throw down the Duke of *Norfolk*'s Gage, and withdraw his own Challenge, refuſes at firſt upon a point of Honour, and throws out this contemptuous Reflexion againſt the Duke.

Shall I ſeem creſt-fall'n in my Father's Sight?
Or with pale beggar-fear impeach my Height,
Before this out-dared DASTARD? ---

Where ſome of the Editions erroneouſly expreſs it,

Before this out-dared BASTARD? ---

But

But I have ſince found Reaſons to retract this Opinion, and to be convinced that the Poet, in calling *Brutus* BASTARD, deſigned a much deeper Contumely than That of *Cowardice*; *viz.* the blackeſt *Ingratitude* and moſt deteſtable *Parricide* SHAKESPEARE has elſewhere taken Notice of *Cæſar's* exceſſive Love to *Brutus*, and of the Ingratitude of the latter for being concern'd in his Murther.

JULIUS CÆSAR, pag. 271.

Thro' This, the well-beloved *BRUTUS ſtabb'd,*
And, as he pluck'd his curſed Steel away,
Mark how the Blood of Cæſar *follow'd it!*
As ruſhing out of Doors to be reſolv'd,
If Brutus *ſo unkindly knock'd, or no:*
For BRUTUS, as you know, was Cæſar's ANGEL.
Judge, oh, you Gods, how dearly *CÆSAR lov'd him!*
This, This, was the unkindeſt Cut of all;
For when the noble Cæſar *ſaw* Him *ſtab,*
INGRATITUDE, *more ſtrong than Traytors Arms,*
Quite vanquiſh'd him; ----

But this amounts to no more than a poſitive Accuſation againſt *Brutus* of Ingratitude, becauſe *Cæſar* lov'd him to that Degree. We know Nothing from hence of the Spring of *Cæſar's* Affection, or why *Brutus*, even for aſſiſting in his Murther, ſhould be ſtigmatiz'd with *Baſtardy*. As this Piece of ſecret Hiſtory is no where elſe ſo much as hinted at, that I know of, or can recollect, throughout all our Author's Works, I ſhall give it from PLUTARCH in the Life of MARCUS BRUTUS. *Cæſar*, before the great Battle of *Pharſalia*, had order'd his Commanders to ſpare *Brutus*, and bring him ſafe to him, if he would willingly ſurrender himſelf: But if he made any Reſiſtance, to ſuffer him to eſcape, rather than to kill him. "And this he "is believed to have done (ſays the HISTORIAN,) out of a "Tenderneſs to *Servilia*, the Mother of *Brutus*: For *Cæſar* had

" had it ſeems, in his Youth, been very intimate with her, " and ſhe paſſionately in Love with him. And conſidering " that *Brutus* was born about that Time, in which their Loves " were at the higheſt, *Cæſar* had ſome Reaſon to believe that he " was begot by him. " --- This *SHAKESPEARE* knew, and therefore reviles *Brutus* with being the Baſtard Iſſue of the Man whom he ſo ungratefully kill'd.

LV. Act 3. Scene 1. Page 399.

Various Reading.

Good Gentlemen, give him a further edge,
And drive his purpoſe INTO *theſe delights.*

But Two Speeches above, *Roſencraus* had informed the Queen, that there did ſeem a kind of Joy in *Hamlet* to hear of the Actors Coming, and that they had already Orders to play before him: What Occaſion, therefore, was there to drive his Purpoſe *into* theſe Delights? He already ſeem'd to give *into* them; and the King deſires *Roſencraus* and *Guildenſtern* to promote and further that Bent and Diſpoſition which *Hamlet* ſhew'd to that Sort of Pleaſures. I think, therefore, the ſecond *Folio* Edition expreſſes this Paſſage more rightly;

Good Gentlemen, give him a further Edge,
And drive his Purpoſe ON TO *theſe Delights.*

And ſo the Poet expreſſes himſelf before in the ſecond *Act* of this Play, where the King entreats *Roſencraus* and *Guildenſtern*, as old School-fellows of *Hamlet*, to ſtay a while at Court in order to divert him. See *pag.* 379.

----------- *I entreat you Both,*
That being of ſo young Days brought up with him,
And ſince ſo neighbour'd to his Youth and Humour,
That You vouchſafe your Reſt here in our Court
Some little Time, ſo by your Companies
To draw him ON TO *Pleaſures,* -----

LVI. Act 3. Scene 2. Page 400.

Text Vindicated.

To be, or not to be? --- That is the question, ---
Whether 'tis nobler in the mind, to suffer
The slings and arrows of outrageous fortune;
Or to take arms against a SEA *of troubles,*
And by opposing end them? ---

A late *Eminent* AUTHOR, I think, took the beginning of this noble Speech to Task, for employing too great a Diversity of *Metaphors*, that have no Agreement with one another, nor any Propriety and Connexion in the Ideas. *To take Arms against a Sea,* literally speaking, would be as unfeasible a Project, as the Attempt (mentioned in a Speech of the Lord *Haversham,* in a late Reign;) *to stop the Tide at* Gravesend *with a Man's Thumb.* Mr. POPE subjoins a Note, that instead of a *Sea* of Troubles, it might have been --- *perhaps,* siege; *which continues the Metaphor of* slings, arrows, taking Arms; *and represents the being encompassed on all Sides with Troubles.* The EDITOR is not the *first* who has had the same Suspicion: And I may say, because I am able to prove it by Witnesses, it was a *Guess* of mine, before he had enter'd upon publishing *SHAKESPEARE.* But, perhaps, the Correction may be, at best, *but* a *Guess*; considering the great Liberties that this Poet is observed to take, elsewhere, in his *Diction,* and *Connexion* of *Metaphors*: And considering too, that a *Sea* (amongst the antient Writers, sacred and prophane, in the *Oriental,* as well as the *Greek* and *Latin,* Tongues;) is used to signify not only the great, collected, Body of Waters which make the Ocean, but likewise a vast Quantity, or Multitude, of any thing else. * The Prophet *Jeremiah,* particularly, in one Passage, calls a prodigious *Army* coming up

* *Vid.* Schindleri *Lexic. Pentaglottum*; Kircheri *Concordantias Veteris Testamenti*; Becmannum *de Origine Linguæ Latinæ*; Martinii *Lexicon Philologicum,* &c.

up againſt a City, a *Sea.* Chap. 51. 42. *The Sea is come up upon* Babylon ; *ſhe is covered with the Multitude of the Waves thereof.* So here, I conceive, *to take Arms againſt a* Sea *of Troubles*, is, *figuratively*, to bear up againſt the Troubles of human Life, which flow in upon us, and encompaſs us round, like a Sea.

BUT there is another Paſſage in this Soliloquy of *HAMLET*, which, I hinted, in my Remarks upon the laſt Act, would demand ſome Conſideration in its proper Place ; and, therefore, it naturally falls in here.

Self-Contradiction *in the Poet examin'd.*

But that the Dread of Something after Death
(*That* undiſcover'd Country, *from whoſe Bourn*
No Traveller *returns* ;) *puzzles the Will* ;
And makes us rather bear thoſe Ills we have,
Than fly to Others that we know not of.

The *Criticks* have, without the leaſt Scruple, accuſed the Poet of *Forgetfulneſs* and *Self-Contradiction* from this Paſſage ; ſeeing that in this very Play he introduces a Character from the other World, the *Ghoſt* of *HAMLET*'s Father. I would not be ſo hardy to aſſert peremptorily, that *SHAKESPEARE* was aware of this *ſeeming Abſurdity*, and deſpiſed it ; any more than I would pretend to juſtify him againſt this Charge to all his Objectors. If he foreſaw any thing of it, perhaps, he ſhelter'd himſelf from their Criticiſms under ſome Reſerve like this. 'Tis certain, to introduce a *Ghoſt*, a Being from the other World, and to ſay that *no Traveller* returns from thoſe Confines, is, literally taken, as abſolute a Contradiction as can be ſuppoſed, *& facto & terminis.* But we are to take Notice, that *SHAKESPEARE* brings his Ghoſt only from a *middle State*, or *local Purgatory* ; a *Priſon-houſe*, as he makes his Spirit call it, where he was doom'd, for a Term only, to expiate his Sins of Nature. By the *undiſcovered Country*, here mentioned, he may, perhaps, mean that *laſt* and *eternal* Reſidence of Souls in a State of *full* Bliſs or Miſery : which Spirits in a *Middle* State (either under *Purgation*, or in the *Priſons of Hope*, as, I think, one of the APOSTLES calls them ;) could not be acquainted with, or explain. So that, if any Latitude of Senſe may be allow'd to the Poet's Words, tho' he admits the *Poſſibility* of a Spirit *returning* from the Dead, he yet holds that the *State* of the *Dead* cannot be *communicated*, and, with that Allowance, it remains ſtill an *undiſcover'd Country.* We are to obſerve too, that even his Ghoſt who comes, as I hinted above, from *Purgatory*, (or, whatever elſe has been underſtood under that Denomination;) comes under Reſtrictions: And tho' he confeſſes himſelf ſubject to a Viciſſitude of Torments, yet he ſays at the ſame time, that *he is forbid to tell the Secrets of his Priſon-houſe.* If theſe Qualifications will not intitle the Poet to ſay, that *no Traveller* returns from the Verge of the other World, *i. e.* to *diſcloſe* any of its *Myſteries*, without a Contradiction to the Liberty he has taken of bringing *Apparitions* upon the Stage; it is all the *Salvo* I can put in for him, and I muſt give him up to the Mercy of the Cavillers. The Antients had the ſame Notions of our abſtruſe and twilight Knowledge of an *After-Being.* *VALERIUS FLACCUS*, I remember, (if I may be indulged in a ſhort Digreſſion,) ſpeaking of the lower Regions, and State of the Spirits there, has an Expreſſion which, in one Senſe, comes cloſe to our AUTHOR's *undiſcovered Country*; *viz.* --- *Superis* incognita Tellus. And it is obſervable that VIRGIL, before he enters upon a Deſcription of Hell, and of the *Elyſian* Fields, implores the Permiſſion of the Infernal Deities, and profeſſes, even then, to diſcover no more than *Hear-Say* concerning their Myſterious Dominions. VIRG. *Æneid.* VI.

Dii, quibus imperium eſt Animarum, Umbræque ſilentes,
Et Chaos, & Phlegethon, loca nocte tacentia latè,
Sit mihi fas *audita* loqui, ſit *numine veſtro*
Pandere res altâ terrâ et caligine merſas.

The Note of *Donatus* upon this Paſſage is very remarkable to our Poet's Subject: But That the Curious may refer to at their Leiſure.

I SHALL conclude all I have to remark on this fine *Soliloquy*, when I have ſubjoin'd an Explication to *one* Word; in which, perhaps, I may

I may take the Poet in a Meaning different from what the Generality of his Readers underſtand him. But if my *Singularity* in this Point be juſtify'd by a Reaſon, I hope it will ſecure me from the Cenſure of being *idly ſingular.* He is ſaying, That were it not for the Dread of an unknown State after this, who would bear the Plagues and Calamities here, when he could himſelf put an End to them, and his own Life too? His Words are theſe;

For who would bear the Whips, and Scorns of Time,

Occaſional Gloſs.

- -

When as himſelf might his Quietus *make*
With a bare BODKIN?

I know that the Poet is generally interpreted to mean in this Place, When we might give ourſelves a Releaſe by *any*, the *leaſt*, Weapon of Offence that can be. 'Tis true, This exaggerates the Thought in that particular; but I can ſcarce ſuppoſe that he intended to deſcend to a Thought, that a Man might diſpatch himſelf with a *Bodkin*, or little Implement with which Women ſeparate, and twiſt over their Hair. I rather believe, the Poet deſigned the Word here to ſignify, according to the old Uſage of it, a *Dagger*. Tho' the *Gloſſaries* give us no ſuch Interpretation, the uſe of an Old and Learned Poet, who may weigh againſt their Comments, I am ſure will ſupport me in it. *CHAUCER*, in his *Monke's* Tale, recounting the Murther of *Julius Cæſar*, has this Stanza.

This Julius *unto the Capitol went,*
Upon a day, as he was wont to gone,
And in the Capitol anon him hent
This falſe Brutus, *and his other fone,*
And ſticked him with BODKINS *anone*
With many a Wound, and thus they let him lie:
But never grutch'd he at no ſtroke but One,
Or elſe at two, but if his ſtory lie.

'Tis

'Tis plain, that the Poet here means *Daggers* by this Word : And no one ever yet thought that *Brutus* and *Caſſius*, or any other of the Conſpirators, ſtabb'd *Cæſar* with their *Ladies* Bodkins.

LVII. Act 3. Scene 6. Page 407.

Falſe Pointing.

King. *I have nothing with this anſwer,* Hamlet, *theſe words are not mine.*

Haml. *No, nor mine* [*n*] *ow, my Lord* [.] *You play'd once i'th' University, you ſay?*

HAMLET gives the King an abrupt, gruff, Anſwer; and immediately applies himſelf and his Diſcourſe to *Polonius.* Correct it therefore, as the ſecond and fourth *Folio* Editions have it.

King. *I have Nothing with this Anſwer,* Hamlet; *theſe Words are not mine.*

Haml. *No, nor mine. --- Now, my Lord, --- You play'd once i'th' Univerſity, you ſay?*

LVIII. Ibid. Page 408.

Omiſſion *ſupply'd.*

Haml. *Lady, ſhall I lie in your Lap?*

Ophel. *No, my Lord.*

[ ]

Haml. *Do you think I meant Country matters!*

Certainly, *HAMLET*'s Anſwer is more natural, and leſs abrupt, if we reſtore this Paſſage from the ſecond *folio* Edition thus:

Haml. *Lady, ſhall I lie in your Lap?*

Ophel. *No, my Lord.*

Haml. I mean, my Head upon your Lap?

Ophel. Ay, my Lord.

Haml. *Do you think I meant Country Matters?*

But

But, indeed, if ever the Poet deserved Whipping for low and indecent Ribaldry, it was for this Passage; ill-tim'd in all its Circumstances, and unbefitting the Dignity of his Characters, as well as of his Audience.

LIX. Act 3. Scene 7. Page 408.

Enter a King and Queen very lovingly; the Queen embracing him, and he her. [ ] *He takes her up, and declines his Head upon her Lap.* Omission *supply'd.*

Mr. *POPE* here makes the King, as we say upon a different Occasion, *take her up, before she's down.* It must be restor'd as the second *folio* Edition, and several others, rightly have it.

Enter a King and Queen, very lovingly; the Queen embracing him, and he her. She kneels, and makes Shew of Protestation unto him: *He takes her up, and declines his Head upon her Lap.*

LX. Ibid. Page 410.

And women's fear and love hold quantity, Emendation.
'Tis either none, or in extremity;
Now what my love is, proof hath made you know,
And as my love is FIX'D, *my fear is so.*

So several of the Editions exhibit this Passage; but, I think, the Sense of the Context shews it to be wrong. My *Quarto* Edition of 1637 has it;

And as my Love is CIZ'D, *my Fear is so.*

And the Second *folio* Edition reads,

And as my Love is SIZ, *my Fear is so.*

Now,

Now, from theſe two miſtaken Readings, and as the Queen evidently is talking here of the *Quantity* of her Love and Fear, their *Proportion*, not their *Continuance* or *Duration*, I am perſwaded, the whole Paſſage ought to be reſtor'd thus;

And Women's Fear and Love hold Quantity,
'Tis either None, or in Extremity;
Now what *my Love is, Proof hath made you know,*
And as my Love is SIZ'D, *my Fear is ſo:*

i. e. As you know by Proof the *Quantity* of my Love; ſo my Fear for you is of the ſame *Size* as my Love is.

LXI. Ibid. Page 412.

Falſe Printing.

King. *What do you call the Play?*
Haml. *The* Mouſe-trap. *Marry, how?* TOPICALLY.
This play is the image of a murther done in Vienna;
Gonzago *is the duke's Name, his* WIFE Baptiſta;
&c

Correct it, as it ought to be.

King. *What do you call the Play?*
Haml. *The* Mouſe-trap. *Marry how?* TROPICALLY.
This Play is the Image of a Murther done in Vienna;
Gonzago *is the Duke's Name, his* WIFE's Baptiſta;
&c.

Well; immediately upon this enters *Lucianus*; and *HAMLET*, continuing his Relation, tells his Uncle;

LXII. Ibid.

This is one Lucianus, *nephew to the* KING. Emendation.

All the Editions whatever, 'tis true, concur in this Reading; and therefore we are to preſume the Blunder was original, either in the Poet's Inadvertence, or the Miſtake of the firſt Tranſcript. *Nephew to* what *King?* The Story of the introduc'd Play is the Murther of *Gonzago*, Duke of *Vienna*: As is plain from the preceding Part of this very Speech. It therefore ought to be corrected, in Spight of all the printed Copies;

This is one Lucianus, *Nephew to the* DUKE.

So, wherever the *Player-King* and *Queen* are mentioned, it ought to be DUKE and DUTCHESS. The Source of theſe Miſtakes is eaſily to be accounted for, from the Stage's *Dreſſing* of the Characters. *Regal* Coronets, perhaps, being by the Poet at firſt ordered for the *Duke* and *Dutcheſs*, the ſucceeding Players, who did not ſo ſtrictly obſerve the *Quality* of the Characters and *Circumſtances* of the Story, miſtook them for a *King* and *Queen*; and ſo the Error was deduced down from thence to the preſent Times.

LXIII. Ibid.

Ophel. *You are keen, my Lord, you are keen.* Emendation.
Haml. *It would coſt you a groaning, to take off my edge.*
Ophel. *Still* WORSE *and worſe.*
Haml. *So you* muſt take *your Husbands.*

Surely, this is the moſt uncomfortable Leſſon that ever was preached to the poor Ladies: And I can't help wiſhing, for our own ſakes too, it mayn't be true. 'Tis too foul a Blot upon our Reputations, that every Husband that a Woman takes muſt be *worſe* than her *former*. The Poet, I am pretty ſure, intended no ſuch Scandal upon the Sex. The Second and Fourth *folio* Editions, and the *Quarto* of 1637, read the latter Part of this Dialogue thus.

Ophel. *Still* better *and worſe.*

Haml. *So you* miſtake *Husbands.*

Miſtake, in the *Laſt* Line, runs thro' all the printed Copies, that I have ever ſeen, from the ſecond *folio* Edition downwards. Mr. POPE, who very juſtly reſtores the true Reading there, takes no manner of Notice of the Various Reading in the *laſt* Line but *One*: Tho', if I underſtand the Poet's Conceit at all, the whole Smartneſs of the *Repartee* depends upon it. I think, therefore, the entire Paſſage ought to ſtand thus.

Ophel. *You are keen, my Lord, you are keen.*

Haml. *It would coſt You a Groaning to take off mine Edge.*

Ophel. *Still* BETTER *and* WORSE.

Haml. *So you* muſt take *your Husbands.*

In ſhort, *HAMLET* has been all along talking to the young Lady in *double Entendre's*, or, rather, in a Strain of *Freedom* which ſcarce admits of that nice Diſtinction. She tells him once before, that *he's naught*, and *ſhe'll mark the Play.* He ſtill keeps up his Vein of *Drollery*, and throws in ſuch *plain Hints*, that ſhe is forced to parry them by an indirect Anſwer; and remarks, as I conceive, that his Wit is *ſmarter*, tho' his Meaning is more *blunt*. This, I think, is the Senſe of her --- *Still* better *and* worſe, --- and then there is ſome Reaſon and Acuteneſs in *HAMLET*'s Anſwer, *So you* muſt take *your Husbands.* For he certainly alludes to the Words in the Church-Service of *Matrimony*, where the Husband and Wife promiſe alternately to take each other *for* BETTER, *for* WORSE; *for* richer, *for* poorer, *&c.*

LXIV.

LXIV. Ibid. Page 413.

Ophel. *The King riſes,* Omiſſion *ſupply'd*

[ ]

Queen. *How fares my Lord?*

Polon. *Give o'er the play.*

King. *Give me ſome light, away.*

As *Hamlet* had thrown ſome appoſite Lines into the Play, in Order to ſift the King's Conſcience as to the Fact of his Father's Murther, and was reſolved to watch his Looks and Behaviour narrowly during the Repreſentation; when the Scene comes to touch the Poyſoning in the Garden, and the King, ſtruck with the Image of his own Deed, can ſet it out no longer, methinks, it is very improbable that *Hamlet*, upon this pleaſing Stroke of Conviction, ſhould not expreſs his Satisfaction in one half-line at leaſt, upon the Play having a proper Effect, and his being convinced of his Uncle's Guilt. The Paſſage ought certainly to be ſupplied from the Second *Folio* Edition, and Three more Impreſſions now before me.

Ophel. *The King riſes.*

Haml. What, frighted with falſe Fire?

Queen. *How fares my Lord?*

Polon. *Give o'er the Play.*

King. *Give me ſome Light, away.*

LXV. Act 3. Scene 8. Page 413.

Would not this, Sir, and a foreſt of feathers, if the reſt of my fortunes turn Turk *with me, with two provincial roſes on my* RAY'D *Shoes, get me a fellowſhip in a cry of players, Sir?* *Conjectural* Emendation.

Hamlet, applauding himſelf upon the Diſcovery his additional Lines in the Play have made of his Uncle's Villany, asks *Horatio*, whether he does not think, that his Skill, and a few Theatrical Equipments join'd with it, would not, upon a Shift, help him into a Share among the Players by their own Voices. But, what are we to underſtand by *ray'd* Shoes? Mr. POPE tells us, at the Bottom of his Page, that in ſome Books he had found it *rac'd*; in others, *rack'd*. 'Tis true; and no leſs than three Editions that I know of, (*viz.* the *Quarto*'s of 1637 and 1703, and Mr. *Hughs*'s Impreſſion,) have it, *raz'd*: And all the four Readings, I believe, are equally miſtaken; tho' the laſt mentioned, perhaps, will bring us neareſt to the *true* one. 'Tis plain to me, *Hamlet*, from the Diſcovery that his Lines in the Play have extorted, is complimenting himſelf on his Taſte and Judgment in the Powers of Tragedy; and ſeems to think that he wants Nothing but a Stock of *Plumes*, and *Buskins*, to ſet him up for one of the Profeſſion. If this be the true Senſe of the Paſſage, as I believe verily it is, I am apt to think the Poet wrote it thus.

> *Would not This, Sir, and a Foreſt of Feathers, if the reſt of my Fortunes turn* Turk *with Me, with two provincial Roſes on my* RAIS'D *Shoes, get me a Fellowſhip in a Cry of Players, Sir?*

By *rais'd* Shoes, as I take it, he means the Tragedy-Buskin, (or *Cothurnus*, as it was call'd by the *Romans*;) which was as much higher in the Heel than other common Shoes, as the *Chioppines*, worn by the *Venetians*, are, mention'd by our Poet in the foregoing *Act* of this Play. It was the known Cuſtom of the Tragedians of Old, that they might the nearer reſemble the Heroes they perſonated, to make themſelves as tall in Stature, and, by an artificial Help to Sound, to ſpeak as big, as they poſſibly could. But of this I ſhall have Occaſion to ſpeak more at large in the *Diſſertation* to be prefix'd to my *Tranſlation* of ÆSCHYLUS's *Tragedies.* HORACE, in his ſhort Hiſtory of the Progreſs of the Stage, takes Notice of theſe two Things, as peculiar Supplements to Tragedy; --- *magnumque loqui, nitique Cothurno*: And SHAKESPEARE himſelf, in his *Troilus* and *Creſſida*, ſeems to rally the Actors both on Account of ſtretching their Voices and Perſons, (*pag.* 24.)

And

And like a ſtrutting *Player, whoſe Conceit*
Lies in his Ham-ſtring, *and doth think it rich*
To hear the wooden Dialogue, and Sound,
'Twixt his STRETCH'D FOOTING *and the Scaffoldage;*

LXVI. Ibid.

For thou doſt know, oh Damon *dear,*
This realm diſmantled was
Of Jove *himſelf, and now reigns here*
A very very PEACOCK.

Conjectural Emendations.

The Generality of Editions have another Reading, (which is, indeed, a corrupt one as printed,) but Mr. *POPE* has eſpouſed This, and ſubjoined a Note for his Reaſon; that it *alludes to a Fable of the Birds chuſing a King, inſtead of the* Eagle, *a* Peacock. I ſuppoſe, the EDITOR muſt mean the Fable of *Barlandus*, in which it is ſaid, the Birds, being weary of their State of Anarchy, moved for the ſetting up of a King. The *Peacock*, on Account of his gay Feathers, put in for the Office; and the Choice upon the Poll falling to him, a *Pye* ſtood up with this Speech in his Mouth; *May it pelaſe your Majeſty*, ſays he, *we ſhould be glad to know, in Caſe the* Eagle *ſhould fall upon us in your Reign, as he has formerly done, how will you be able to defend us?* But, with Submiſſion, in this Paſſage of *SHAKESPEARE*, there is not the leaſt Mention made of the *Eagle*, unleſs, by an uncommon Figure, *Jove* himſelf ſtands in the Place of his *Bird*. Then, we do not find that *Hamlet* intends to ſpeak of his Uncle, as of a Perſon unable to defend the Realm; nor, indeed, do we find that the Realm had been yet attack'd, or wanted a Defender. In ſhort, I think, *Hamlet* is here ſetting his Father's and Uncle's Characters againſt each other; and means to ſay, that by his Father's Death, the State was ſtript of a Godlike Monarch, in Excellence rivalling *Jove*: And that now, in his ſtead, reign'd the moſt deſpicable *Animal* that could be. I ſay, that *Hamlet* intends a Compariſon betwixt his Father and his Uncle; or, at leaſt, to ſpeak greatly to the Diſadvantage, and in Contempt of the latter. But the

Peacock,

Peacock, ſurely, is too fine a Bird to be thus degraded; tho' the *Eagle* has the Preference in Strength, Spirit, and Fierceneſs. Beſides, what Features of Reſemblance are there betwixt a *tame Peacock*, and a King, who had *Courage* enough to uſurp a Crown, to make away with his own Brother to make way for himſelf, and to juſtle his Brother's Son, *Hamlet*, out of the Election, tho' he was a Favourite of the People?

First Conjecture. Were it neceſſary to ſuppoſe, that the Poet meant, *Hamlet* ſhould revile his Uncle here for a *tame*, cowiſh Spirit, and as one inheriting none of the *maſculine* Qualities of his Predeceſſor; the Change of a ſingle Letter will give us this Senſe, and a Word too that has the Warrant of our Poet, in another Place, to bear that Signification. I would then read,

------------- *and now reigns here*
A very, very, MEACOCK.

Now a * **Meacock** or **Mewcock**, beſides its proper Signification of a *cravenly* Bird, is taken *metaphorically* to mean a *daſtardly, effeminate* Fellow: And in that Acceptation we find it uſed in the TAMING *of the* SHREW, *pag.* 312.

Oh, you are Novices; 'tis a World to ſee,
How tame (when Men and Women are alone,)
A MEACOCK *Wretch can make the curſteſt Shrew.*

But not to fix ourſelves down abſolutely to this Reading, let's firſt have Recourſe to the various Reading in ſome of the Copies, and ſee what Help we can derive from thence. The Second and Fourth Editions in *Folio*, the *Quarto* of 1637. and, if it be worth mentioning, the *Duodecimo* Impreſſion, publiſh'd by Mr. *Tonſon* in 1714, all have it;

---------- *and now reigns here*
Various Reading. *A very, very,* PAJOCK.

I muſt

* Skinner's *Lexicon Etymolog. in* Meacock.

I muſt own, I know no ſuch Term; but there is one ſo very near it in Sound, and one which ſuits the Author's Meaning in Senſe ſo aptly, that it is not improbable but he might write originally;

Second Conjecture.

------- *and now reigns here*
A very, very, PADDOCK.

Here you have the old Word itſelf which *Minſhew* derives from padde, *Bufo*, a Toad. * Our Author was very well acquainted with the Word, and has uſed it more than once, or twice. In the Firſt Witch-Scene of his *Macbeth*, we have theſe Words.

1ſt Witch. -------- *I come,* Grimalkin;
2d Witch. PADDOCK *calls.*

Where the *Haggs* ſpeak of the *Screaming* of the *Cat*, and the *Croaking* of the *Toad*, which they are ſuppoſed to hear from the Organs of their *Familiars*. But what makes it the more probable that this Term ſhould be uſed here, *Hamlet*, again, afterwards, ſpeaking of his Uncle to the Queen his Mother, among other contemptuous Additions, gives him this very Appellation of *Paddock*.

--------- *'Twere good, you let him know;*
For who, that's but a Queen, fair, ſober, wiſe,
Would from a PADDOCK, *from a Bat, a Gib,*
Such dear Concernings hide?

Third Conjecture.

But, again: If we will, with Mr. POPE, ſuppoſe, that the Poet alludes to the *Eagle*, and ſome *inferior* Bird in *Quality* that has got the Start of him; another ſmall Variation from the Text will bring us to all we want for this Purpoſe. Why, then, might not the Poet make his *Hamlet* ſay,

-------- *and now reigns here*
A very, very PUTTOCK.

i. e.

---

* Idem, *in* Paddock.

i. e. a ravenous *Kite*, a mere Bird of Prey; a Devourer of the State and People; without any of the Excellencies and *defensive* Virtues of the Royal *Eagle*, his Father? Here again we have a Word, which the Poet was as well acquainted with, as with the *two* already quoted.

Second Part of King *HENRY* VI. *pag.* 160.

> *Who finds the Partridge in the* PUTTOCK's *Nest,*
> *But may imagine how the Bird was dead,*
> *Although the* Kite *soar with unbloodied Beak?*

But what might go a good Way towards supporting a Conjecture that this was our Author's Word here, is, that there is a particular Passage in another of his Plays, where the *Eagle* and *Puttock* are placed comparatively, and in a Light of Opposition to one another.

CYMBELINE. pag. 128.

> Cymb. *Thou might'st have had the sole Son of my Queen.*
> Imog. *O blest, that I might not!* --- *I chose an* EAGLE,
> *And did avoid a* PUTTOCK. ---

I shall leave these Conjectural Readings entirely to the Arbitration of better Judgments: But, I think, I may with Modesty affirm every one of them to be more just, and better grounded, than that espoused by the Editor; and that therefore the *Peacock* may e'en be content to wait for another *Election.*

LXVII. Ibid. Page 415.

Various Reading, and Pointing.

> *Oh wonderful son, that can so astonish a Mother* [.] *But is there no sequel at the heels of this* Mother-Admiration?

Correct, as some of the better Books exhibit it;

> *O wonderful Son, that can so astonish a Mother!* --- *But is there no Sequel at the Heels of this* Mother's-Admiration?

LXVIII.

LXVIII. Ibid. Page 416.

Haml. *Methinks it is like an* † Ouzle. *Various Reading.*

Pol. *It is* black *like an* Ouzle.

† An *Ouzle*, or *Black-Bird*, it has been printed by Miſtake a *Weeſel*, which is not black.

I have nothing to object againſt this Alteration made by Mr. POPE; or, why an *Ouzle* may not be as proper as a *Weeſel*: But I am afraid his Reaſoning, that *it has been printed by* Miſtake *a* Weeſel, *becauſe a* Weeſel *is not* black, --- will not be altogether ſo inconteſtible; when we come to ſee that the Second Edition in *Folio*, and ſeveral other of the Copies have a *various Reading*, in which there is not the leaſt Intimation of *Blackneſs*. There, you read it,

Haml. *Methinks, it is like a Weeſel.*

Polon. *It is* BACK'D *like a Weeſel.*

LXIX. Ibid.

Haml. *Then will I come to my Mother by and by; they fool me to the top of my bent. I will come by and by. Leave me, friends.* I will ſay ſo. By and by is eaſily ſaid. *Falſe Printing.*

We have already, in the Courſe of theſe Remarks, convers'd with a Place or two, which have given Reaſon to preſume, that, if corrected at all, they could be corrected only by the Servants at the Preſs. Here again is a Paſſage ſo confuſed, and ſo indiſcriminately printed, that it furniſhes a ſtrong Suſpicion of never having been *reviſed* by the *Editor*. Could ſo nice a Judge as Mr. POPE paſs over ſuch abſurd Stuff as is jumbled here together, and not obſerve a Fault that is ſo plain and palpable? Correct it with all the Editions that I have ever ſeen, except the *Quarto's* of 1637, and 1703. in which the Text is likewiſe ſhuffled and faulty;

Haml. *Then will I come to my Mother by and by. --- They fool me to the Top of my Bent. --- I will come by and by.*
Polon. *I will say so.* *Exit* Polon.
Haml. *By and by is easily said. Leave me, Friends.*
Exeunt Rosen. *and* Guilden.

LXX. Ibid. Page 417.

Omission *supply'd.*

I will speak daggers to her, but use none.
My Tongue and soul in this be hypocrites!
[ ] Exit.

The Editor might have taken Notice that a *Couplet* follows here, in several of the printed Copies, which he mistrusted not to be *SHAKESPEARE*'s. I will not warrant the Lines to be his, but they are obsolete enough in the Phrase to be so; neither are they so bad, as to be positively disputed. He has many *Couplets* full as bald and poor in the *Diction*; and These have an Authority as old as the second *Folio* Edition, and have found a place in most of the more modern Copies too. The Verses are these.

I will speak Daggers to her, but use none.
My Tongue and Soul in This be Hypocrites!
How in my Words soever She be † shent,
To give them Seals never my Soul consent. Exit.

† put to Confusion, roughly treated.

LXXI. Act 3. Scene 9. Page 417.

False Printing.

I like him not, nor stands it safe with us
To let his Madness rage. -----

Restore, with all the Editions.

To let his Madness range. -----

LXXII.

LXXII. Ibid.

Correction, *from Various Reading.*

Most holy and religious fear it is,
To keep those many bodies safe, that live
And feed upon your majesty.

The last Line here is *lame*, and shorter by a *Foot* than it should be, without any Necessity. The second *Folio* Edition is likewise faulty, for there the last Line but One is defective, and the Verses are plac'd thus.

To keep those many Bodies safe,
That live and feed upon your Majesty.

A different Disposition of the Verses, and of so long a Date, gives a Proof of a Fault, and a sort of Inlet to the Cure. The *Quarto* Edition of 1637, is the only One that I have observ'd, which makes the Verses compleat; and adds a fine and forcible *Emphasis* to the Sentence, by the Repetition of one Word; a Figure (as I have before observ'd in the Remark, N°. XI.) very familiar with *SHAKESPEARE.* Restore them thus:

Most holy and religious Fear it is,
To keep those many, many, *Bodies safe,*
That live and feed upon your Majesty.

LXXIII. Ibid. Page 418.

Conjecture.

Oh my offence is rank, it smells to heav'n,
It hath the primal eldest curse upon it,
[ ] *A Brother's murther. Pray, I cannot,* &c.

Here again the last Verse halts in the *Measure*, and, if I don't mistake, the *Sense* is a little *lame* too. Was a *Brother's Murther* the *eldest Curse?* Surely, it was rather the *Crime*, that was the *Cause* of this *eldest Curse.* We have no Assistance, however,

 either

either to the Senſe or Numbers, from any of the Copies. All the Editions concur in the Deficiency of a *Foot*; but if we can both cure the Meaſure, and help the Meaning, without a Diſgrace or Prejudice to the Author, I think, the Authority of the printed Copies is not ſufficient to forbid a Conjecture. Perhaps, the Poet wrote;

> *It has the primal eldeſt Curſe upon't,*
> THAT OF *a Brother's Murther. Pray, I cannot,* &c.

LXXIV. Act 3. Scene 10. Page 420.

Emendation.

> *Up, ſword, and know thou a more horrid* TIME;
> *When he is drunk, aſleep, or in his Rage,* &c.

This, as I take it, is a *ſophiſticated* Reading, eſpouſed by Mr. POPE from the more modern Editions. The ſecond *Folio* Edition and the *Quarto* of 1637, both read;

> *Up, Sword, and know Thou a more horrid* HENT;

The *Editor* has taken Notice, at the Bottom of his Page, of this Word, as a *various Reading*; but, as I humbly preſume, without gueſſing at the Reaſon of it. 'Tis true, there is no ſuch Subſtantive, I believe, as *Hent*; and yet the true Word of the Poet, I am ſatisfied, lies hid under it, by a ſlight literal Corruption. Reſtore it therefore;

> *Up, Sword, and know Thou a more horrid* BENT;

i. e. *Drift, Scope, Inclination, Purpoſe,* &c. and there is ſcarce any Word more frequent than This with our Poet, where he has Occaſion to expreſs himſelf in thoſe Senſes.

(1.) *MUCH ADO ABOUT NOTHING. pag.* 510.

> *They have the Truth of This from* Hero, *they ſeem to pity the Lady: it ſeems, her Affections have the full* BENT.

(2.)

(2.) *WINTER's TALE. pag.* 559.

> *To your own* BENTS *dispose you; you'll be found,*
> *Be you beneath the Sky.*

(3.) *JULIUS CÆSAR, pag.* 243.

> --------- *Leave me to work;*
> *For I can give his Humour the true* BENT
> *And I will bring him to the* Capitol.

(4.) *TROILUS and CRESSIDA, pag.* 28.

> *I bring a Trumpet to awake his Ear,*
> *To set his Sense on that attentive* BENT,
> *And then to speak.*

(5.) *CYMBELINE. pag.* 123.

> --------- *But not a Courtier,*
> (*Altho' they wear their Faces to the* BENT
> *Of the King's Looks;*) *but hath a Heart that is not*
> *Glad at the Thing they scoul at.*

(6.) *ROMEO and JULIET, pag.* 274.

> *If that thy* BENT *of Love be honourable,*
> *Thy Purpose, Marriage;*

(7.) So twice before in *HAMLET*; as, *pag.* 380.

> ------- *But we Both obey,*
> *And here give up ourselves in the full* BENT,
> *To lay our Service freely at your Feet.*

(8.) And again, *pag.* 416.

> *They fool me to the Top of my* BENT.

I am

I am ſurpriz'd the Editor could remember this Word from None of theſe Inſtances, and a Number more that lie interſpers'd in our Poet; eſpecially as it is a Word of his *own* too in his Preface to the Edition, *pag.* 4. *He hits upon that particular Point, on which the* BENT *of each Argument turns, or the Force of each Motive depends.* I did not think, when I began this Work, to *collate* the more recent *Folio* Editions, eſpecially the *fourth*, publiſh'd in 1685, for I had it not then by Me; but upon throwing my Eye over it lately, I find it is there printed, as I have here corrected it —— *a more horrid* BENT. I thought my ſelf obliged to make this *Confeſſion*, that I might not be accus'd of *Plagiariſm*, for an *Emendation* which I had made, before ever I ſaw a ſingle Page of That Book.

LXXV. Ibid. Page 421.

Various Reading.

Queen. *Have you forgot me?*
Haml. - - - - - *No, by the Rood, not ſo;*
You are the Queen, your husband's brother's wife,
A N D *(would it were not ſo) you are my mother.*

If I underſtand at all what *Hamlet* ſhould be preſum'd to ſay here, I think, the *Editor* has adopted a Reading directly oppoſite to the Sentiment the Poet would expreſs. Surely, *Hamlet* does not ſo much wiſh that the Queen was not his Mother, as that She was not his Uncle's Wife. He loves and honours her as his Mother; and therefore, out of thoſe Regards, wiſhes She had not that Diſgrace upon her Character, of having married his Uncle, whom he knew to be his Father's Murtherer. The Paſſage, certainly, ought to be diſtinguiſhed as the ſecond *Folio* Edition, and ſeveral other of the better Copies, lead the way.

Queen. *Have you forgot me?*
Haml. - - - - - - *No, by the Rood, not ſo;*
You are the Queen, your Husband's Brother's Wife,
BUT, *'would you were not ſo! ---- You are my Mother.*

LXXVI. Ibid. Page 422.

Omission supply'd.

---------- *Ha! have you eyes?*
You cannot call it love; for at your age,
The hey-day of the blood is tame, it's humble,
And waits upon the judgment; and what judgment
Would step from this to this? [
] *what devil was't*
That thus hath cozen'd you at hoodman blind?

There is an Addition, in several of the Copies, which, tho' it has not the Sanction of any older Edition, that I know of, than the *Quarto* of 1637. yet has so much of the Style, Diction, and Cast of Thought peculiar to our Poet, that, I think, we may warrant it to be his, and not an Interpolation of the Players without that Authority. Perhaps, it was not written when he first finish'd the Play; or it was left out in the shortning the Play for the *Representation*, and so lost its Place in the *first* Editions, which were printed from the Players Copies. The Verses are these;

----------- *Ha! have you Eyes?*
You cannot call it Love; for at your Age
The Hey-day of the Blood is tame, it's humble,
And waits upon the Judgment; and what Judgment
Would step from This --- to This ---? Sense sure you have,
Else could you not have Motion; but That Sense
Is apoplex'd: for Madness would not err;
Nor Sense to Ecstasie was ne'er so thrall'd,
But it reserv'd some Quantity of Choice
To serve in such a Difference. *What Devil was't*, &c.

The same Book exhibits another small Addition, which is so much inferior to the former, that I dare not so boldly vouch for it's being genuine.

---- *What*

---------- What Devil was't,
That thus hath cozen'd you at hoodman blind?
Eyes without Feeling, Feeling without Sight,
Ears without Hands or Eyes, Smelling ſans all,
Or but a ſickly Part of one true Senſe,
Could not ſo mope.

LXXVII. Ibid. Page 423.

Various Reading reſtored, and explained.

----------- Nay, but to live
In the rank ſweat of an INCESTUOUS *bed,*
Stew'd in corruption, honying and making love
Over the naſty ſty:

Here again, as I conceive, we have a *ſophiſticated* Reading palmed upon us, probably, from the Players firſt, who did not underſtand the Poet's *Epithet,* and therefore conſcientiouſly ſubſtituted a *new* one. If we go back, however, to the ſecond *folio* Edition (which is one of thoſe collated by the *Editor*) we have there a *various Reading*, of which he is not pleaſed to take the leaſt Notice, tho', as I verily believe, it reſtores us the Poet's own Word.

--------- Nay, but to live
In the rank Sweat of an ENSEAMED *Bed,*
Stew'd in Corruption, honying and making Love
Over the naſty Sty.

i. e. groſs, fulſome, ſwiniſh Bed. For, not to dwell too long upon an *unſavoury* Image, the Sweat of any *other* Bed of Pleaſure will be as *rank* as that of an *inceſtuous* Bed. But beſides, when we come to the *Etymology*, and *abſtracted* Meaning of *enſeam'd*, we ſhall have a Conſonancy in the *Metaphors*, and a Reaſon for the Poet's calling the Bed a naſty *Sty*. In ſhort, the Gloſſaries tell

us,

us, that Seam † is properly the *Fat*, or *Grease*, of a *Hog*: And tho' I do not remember the *compound Adjective* from it used in any other Place of the Poet than this before us; yet he has elsewhere employ'd the Substantive; and making *Ulysses* speak contemptuously of *Achilles*, who had sequester'd himself from the *Græcian* Captains and the War, he compares him tacitly to a Hog in his Sty, feeding on his own Pride, and Self-sufficiency.

TROILUS and *CRESSIDA pag.* 49.

> ---------- *Shall the proud Lord,*
> *That* basts *his Arrogance with his own* SEAM,
> *And never suffers Matters of the World*
> *Enter his Thoughts, save such as do revolve*
> *And ruminate himself; Shall He be worshipp'd*
> *Of That we hold an Idol more than* Him?
> --------------------------
> *That were t'* enlard *his Pride, already* fat, &c.

LXXVIII. Ibid. Page 426.

False Pointing.

> *No, in despight of sense and secrecy,*
> *Unpeg the basket on the house's top,*
> *Let the birds fly, and like the famous ape* [ ]
> *To try conclusions* [;] *in the basket creep,*
> *And break your own neck down.* ------

The Ape crept into the Basket, to try Conclusions; that is the Meaning of the Poet: But by the *Semicolon*, wrong-placed, the Sense is interrupted, and the *Substantive* divided from its *Verb*. It ought to be pointed, as some of the Editions rightly have it;

† Seam *is derived from a Contraction of* Sebum, *or* Sevum, *among the* Latins; *which Words* ISIDORE *brings* à Sue, quasi Suebum, vel Suevum; quià Animal hoc pingue. *So* Arvina *is a Ram's Fat, from the old Word* Arvix (*i. e.* Aries) *a Ram.* Vid. VOSSII Etymolog. Latinum.

-------- and like the famous Ape,
To try Conclusions, in the Basket creep,
And break your own Neck down. ---

I have at last, I think, got thro' all the Errors of this long *Act*, save a slight one, in which SHAKESPEARE is no ways concern'd, committed by Mr. POPE, in a *Note* of his own, upon the last Speech of it. *The* ten *following Verses*, says he, *are added out of the old Edition.* It must for the future be printed, *The* Nine *following Verses*, &c. for no more than *that* Number are restored either from the *old* Edition, or those *modern* ones which have inserted them.

LXXIX. Act 4. Scene 1. Page 428.

Various Reading.

We would not understand what was most fit,
But like the owner of a foul disease,
To keep it from divulging, LETS *it feed*
Ev'n on the pith of life.

The *Syntax* of this Passage is evidently bad, for WE is the *Nominative* to both *Verbs*, and therefore they both must be *Plural.* Three of my Impressions, *viz.* the *Quarto*'s of 1637, and 1703, and that by Mr. *Hughs*, have it as it ought to be.

We would not understand what was most fit;
But like the Owner of a foul Disease,
To keep it from divulging, LET *it feed*
Ev'n on the Pith of Life.

LXXX.

LXXX. Ibid. Page 429.

Omiſſion *ſupply'd, and* Text *conjecturally* reſtored.

Come, Gertrude, *we'll call up our wiſeſt Friends,*
And let them know both what we mean to do,
And what's untimely done: [
] *O come away,*
My ſoul is full of diſcord and diſmay.

The *Quarto* Edition of 1637 has an Addition in this Place, which has been admitted into moſt of the *modern* Editions; tho' it has not the Authority of any earlier Date in *Print,* as I know of, than that *Quarto*; and yet ſeems to bear the very Stamp of *SHAKESPEARE* upon it. The Coin, indeed, has been clipt from our firſt receiving it; but it is not ſo diminiſhed, but that, with a ſmall Aſſiſtance, we may hope to make it paſs current. The Reading, as it has hitherto come to us, is thus;

Come, Gertrude, *we'll call up our wiſeſt Friends,*
And let them know both what we mean to do,
And What's untimely done.
Whoſe Whiſper o'er the World's Diameter,
As level as the Cannon to his Blank,
Tranſports his poyſon'd Shot, may miſs our Name,
And hit the woundleſs Air: *O, come away;*
My Soul is full of Diſcord and Diſmay.

'Tis plain here the *Senſe* is defective, as well as the *Verſe* imperfect, which introduces it: and from the Additional Lines beginning with the *Relative* WHOSE, without any preceding *Nominative* of which it is govern'd, it is as plain that the latter Part of the foregoing *Hemiſtich* fell out in the *printing,* or was ſo blind in the *Copy* as not to be gueſs'd at, and therefore neceſſarily came to be omitted. I wonder, Mr. *HUGHS,* who inſerted this Paſſage in his Impreſſion, and could not but ſee that ſomething was wanting, did not at the ſame time endeavour to ſupply it. We have not, indeed, ſo much as the Footſteps, or Traces, of a corrupted Reading here to lead us to an Emendation; nor any Means left of reſtoring what is loſt but Conjecture. I ſhall therefore offer only what the Senſe of the Context naturally ſeems to require. I am far from affirming that I ſhall give the Poet's very Words, but 'tis probable that they were, at leaſt, very near what follows in Subſtance.

Come, Gertrude, *we'll call up our wiſeſt Friends,*
And let them know both what we mean to do,
And what's untimely done. Happily, * Slander,
Whoſe Whiſper o'er the World's Diameter,
As level as the Cannon to his Blank,
Tranſports his poyſon'd Shot, may miſs our Name,
And hit the woundleſs Air. O, come away;
My Soul is full of Diſcord and Diſmay.

* *Or* Rumour.

'Tis evident, This reſtores us the Sentiment ſeemingly requiſite, and there is the more Room to ſuppoſe it the very Sentiment of our *SHAKESPEARE*. The Poet, I remember, has the ſame Thought about the diffuſive Powers of *Slander* in another of his Plays; tho' he has expreſs'd it with ſome Difference, as well as with greater Diverſity of *Metaphor* and *Alluſion.*

CYMBELINE, pag. 176.

---------*No, 'tis* SLANDER,
Whoſe Edge is ſharper than the Sword, whoſe Tongue
Out-venoms all the Worms of Nile, *whoſe Breath*
Rides on the poſting Winds, and doth belye
All Corners of the World.

LXXXI.

LXXXI. Act 4. Scene 3. Page 432.

False Pointing; and Various Reading restored.

> - - - - - - - - *Thou may'st not coldly set*
> *Our sovereign Process, which imports at full* [ ]
> *By letters* CONGRUING *to that effect,*
> *The present death of* Hamlet.

Methinks, there is an unnecessary Tautology in this Term *Congruing*, which is avoided by the Various Reading that possesses many of the Editions, and is taken Notice of by the *Editor* at the Bottom of his Page. If the *Letters*, importing the Tenour of the Process, were to *that* Effect, they were certainly *congruing*; but of no great Use, when the sovereign Process imported the *same* Thing. Now a Process might import a Command, and Letters *conjuring* a Compliance with it be sent, and be of great Efficacy, where the Execution of the Command was to be doubted of, or might admit of a Demur. I cannot therefore but think the other Reading the truest; and the Passage ought to be pointed thus;

> - - - - - - - - - *Thou may'st not coldly set*
> *Our Sovereign Process, which imports at full,*
> *By Letters* CONJURING *to that Effect,*
> *The present Death of* Hamlet; - - - -

Hamlet, who put a Change upon his Uncle's Commission, and reversed the Substance of it, 'tis likely, kept to the Model of it in That which He drew up: And, where he recounts the Contents of it to *Horatio*, we find him beginning his Command by forcible Conjurations implying the Necessity of it. See *pag.* 460.

Haml. - - - - - - - - *Wilt Thou know*
Th' Effect of What I wrote?
Hor. - - - - - - - - - *Ay, my good Lord.*
Haml. *An earnest* CONJURATION *from the King,*
As England *was his faithful Tributary,*
As Peace should still &c.

Perhaps, the *Editor* might dislike the word *conjuring* here, because the Cadence of the Verse requires that the Accent should lie upon the *Antepenultima*; and the Sense, that it should lie upon the *Penultima.* To explain this Difference; when we intend by *conjure,* to signify a *solemn Adjuration* only, we lay the Accent upon the *last* Syllable; where we mean by it a *magical Invocation* or *Effect,* the Accent falls upon the *first.* But our Poet uses the Word in both these Senses promiscuously, without regard to this Difference in the Pronunciation; and, I believe, generally, if not always, will be found to lay the Stress upon the *first* Syllable. So, again, in

HAML. *pag.* 457.

- - - - - - *What is He, whose Griefs*
Bear such an Emphasis? whose Phrase of Sorrow
Conjures *the wand'ring Stars, and makes them stand*
Like wonder-wounded Hearers?

So, in *MACBETH, pag.* 568.

I conjure *You by That which you profess,*
Howe'er you come to know it, answer Me.

So, in *ROMEO and JULIET, pag.* 268.

I conjure *Thee by* Rosaline'*s bright Eyes,*
By her high Forehead, &c.

And,

And, again, in the next Page;

> --------- *my Invocation is*
> *Honeſt and fair, and in his Miſtreſs' Name*
> *I* conjure *only but to raiſe up Him.*

Indeed, but three Lines before the laſt quoted Inſtance, he ſeems to lay the Accent upon the *laſt* Syllable of this Word by the Neceſſity of the Numbers; tho' the Senſe and Acceptation, which it carries, require it to be pronounced with the Accent on the *firſt.*

> --------- *letting it there ſtand,*
> *Till She had laid it, and* conjur'd *it down.*

But, perhaps, either the *Copyiſts*, or the *Preſs*, by Miſtake, made a ſmall Variation from the Author here; and this wrong Cadence is eaſily cur'd by only taking out the firſt *it*, which is of no Uſe there; and extending the Second Verb to three Syllables, by pronouncing it, without the *Apoſtrophe*, at length; than which Nothing is more frequent throughout our Author's Works: As, *Occaſional* Conjecture.

> *Till She had laid, and* conjured *it down.*

LXXXII. Act 4. Scene 7. Page 440.

Falſe Pointing; and Correction *from Various Reading.*

> *It ſhall as level to your judgment pierce,*
> *As day does to your eye.* [*A Noiſe within.*
> *Enter* Ophelia *fantaſtically dreſt*, &c.
> Laert. Let her come in. *How now? what noiſe is that?*
> *O heat* [ ] *dry up my brains* [,] *tears* [ ] *ſeven times ſalt* [ ]
> *Burn* ON *the ſenſe and vertue of mine eye.*

Had I never ſeen any other Edition of *SHAKESPEARE* than Mr. POPE's, I could not but have ſuſpected Something wrong here, tho' I ſhould not, perhaps, have known ſo eaſily how to to rectify it. Just before the Entrance of *Ophelia*, a Noise is heard behind the Scenes, *viz.* of Some, that would have the Young Lady admitted; and of Others, that would keep her out. *Laertes*'s Friends, as we may observe at the Beginning of the preceding Scene, where he rushes in by force upon the King, are set to guard the Door; and they might be sollicitous that *Laertes* should see his Sister in her Madness, to heighten his Resentments for the Death of his Father. But it is certainly very absurd that *Laertes* should know who it is *without*, upon the Noise made; that *Ophelia* should come in; and then that he should desire, that She may come in; and then after all, that he should enquire into the Meaning of the Noise. I think, the second *Folio* Edition sets the whole Passage right; and it seems to Me that it ought to be corrected as *that* Copy, and several Others, which come after, exhibit it with more Propriety thus;

It shall as level to your Judgment pierce,
As Day does to your Eye.
[A Noise within, *Let her come in.*

Laert. *How now? What Noise is that?---*

Enter *Ophelia* fantastically drest, &c.

O Heat, dry up my Brains; Tears, sev'n times salt,
Burn OUT *the Sense and Virtue of mine Eye.*

'Tis natural for *Laertes*, who was in a riotous Proceeding against the King, to be alarm'd at the Tumult *without*, least his Party could not maintain the Door: And as soon as he sees the Occasion of the Noise, in the Admission of his distracted Sister, his deep Concern makes him wish at once that he were depriv'd both of Sense and Sight. But why, *burn* ON *the Sense?* This Reading, in Mr. POPE's Impression, is, as I apprehend, a literal Mistake of the Press instead of *burn* OUT; and it is a Mistake so easy to happen, that I think in another Place the same Error has passed thro' all the Editions of *SHAKESPEARE*; and, as I suppose, was not so much as suspected

ſuſpected by our *Editor*, becauſe he has given us the Paſſage as he found it.

In the *WINTER*'s *TALE*, *Florizel*, Prince of *Bohemia*, in a paſtoral Habit, addreſſes *Perdita*, an Outcaſt Princeſs of *Sicily*, but ſuppoſed of mean Extraction; who was taken up an Infant, in a Deſart of *Bohemia*, by a Shepherd, and educated as his Daughter. As the Prince is courting, careſſing, and whiſpering her at a Sheep-ſheering Feaſt, *Polixenes* his Father, and an old Courtier attending him, come to the rural Entertainment. They fix their Eyes on the young amorous Couple, and obſerving Something in the Virgin above her outward Seeming and Rank, fall to making theſe Obſervations on them.

Occaſional Emendation.

Polix. *This is the* pettieſt *low-born Laſs that ever*
Ran on the Green-ſord; Nothing She does, or ſeems,
But ſmacks of Something greater than herſelf,
Too noble for this Place.
Camil. --------- *He tells her Something,*
That makes her Blood look ON 'T.

Winter'*s* Tale. *Act* 4. *Sc.* 5. *p.*613.

In the firſt Verſe a literal Error is committed at Preſs, for the other Editions all read, as it ought to be;

This is the prettieſt *low-born Laſs* ------

But what Senſe is there in *Camillo*'s Speech, that *the Prince tells her Something which makes her Blood look* on't? This to me ſeems obſcure even to the Degree of being unintelligible. The *SPECTATOR*, if I remember right, tells us ſomewhere a Story of a Climate ſo cold at one Seaſon, that it congealed Words even in the Pronunciation; and ſo ſoon as a Thaw came, they were diſtinctly repeated and heard: But, I muſt own, I never heard of any Words ſo *condens'd* as to be *viſible* to the *Eye*, much leſs to the *Blood*. If I underſtand any thing of the Poet's Meaning here, he certainly wrote;

> -------- *He tells her Something,*
> *That makes her Blood look* OUT.

i. e. *that calls the Blood up into her Cheeks, and makes her blush.* *PERDITA*, but a little before, in the self-same Page, uses a like Expression to describe the Prince's Sincerity, which appear'd in the honest Blood rising on his Face.

> *Your Praises are too large; but that your Youth*
> *And the true* Blood, *which* peeps forth *fairly* through *it,*
> *Do plainly give you out an unstain'd Shepherd,* &c.

LXXXIII. Act 4. Scene 9. Page 444.

Various Reading restored.

> *I lov'd your father, and we love* YOUR *self;*
> *And that I hope will teach you to imagine,* ---

My *Quarto* Editions of 1637 and 1703, have a different Reading of this Passage, which is espoused too by Mr. *HUGHS*, and which I take to comprehend the genuine Meaning of our Poet.

> *I lov'd your Father, and* We *love* OUR *self;*
> *And That, I hope, will* &c.

I'll now give the Reasons for my being on this Side of the Question. *Laertes* is complaining, that (because the King durst not pursue *Hamlet* to Death for killing *Polonius*, but had only sent him out of the way;) he has lost a Father, and the Opportunity of being reveng'd on his Murtherer. The King bids *Laertes* not break his Sleep about the Want of his Revenge; *for,* says He, *I lov'd your Father, and I love my self; and both These are my Motives to That End.* But how did the King's Love of *himself* contribute to his *Desire* of *Revenge* on *Hamlet?* for thereon lies the Stress of the Alteration. Now there are two Speeches of the King in this very *Scene*, that perswade me to espouse this

this Reading, and believe it preferable to That of the Editor: For the King ſays expreſsly, that *Hamlet* had ſought *his* Life too; and that He was not ſo unapprehenſive of Danger, as to be negligent in defending himſelf from it.

Page 443.

> *Sith you have heard, and with a knowing Ear,*
> *That* He, *which hath your noble Father ſlain,*
> Purſued my Life.

And *pag.* 444.

> -------- *You muſt not think*
> *That We are made of Stuff ſo flat and dull,*
> *That* We can let our Beard be ſhook with Danger,
> And think it Paſtime.

LXXXIV. Ibid. Page 444.

> *And that I hope will teach you to imagine* ----- Omiſſion *ſupply'd.*
> Enter Meſſenger.
> [ ]
> Meſſ. *Theſe to your Majeſty, this to the Queen.*
> King. *From* Hamlet? *who brought them?*

The King, as the Text here ſtands, had no other way of knowing that his Letter was from *Hamlet*, than by knowing his Character upon the Superſcription. And he had very little Reaſon to credit the Similitude of the Hand, or to expect a Salutation from *Hamlet*; whom, he knew well, he had diſpatch'd away for *England*, with an abſolute Order for his Execution as ſoon as ever He ſhould ſet Footing there. The ſecond *Folio* Edition, I think, ſets right this Paſſage, by a ſmall Addition, which, tho' it ſhould have no earlier Authority from the Preſs, we have no Reaſon but to think came from the Poet's own Hand.

And That, I hope, will teach you to imagine -------

Enter Meſſenger.

How now? what News?

Meſſ. Letters, my Lord, from *Hamlet.*

Theſe to your Majeſty: This to the Queen.

King. *From* Hamlet? *Who brought them?*

Now here the King asks the Queſtion, as he naturally might, with a Surprize, and a reaſonable Diſtruſt, Circumſtances conſidered, that he could have any Letter from *Hamlet:* And, perhaps, the Pointing would be juſter, if the firſt *Interrogation* was turn'd into a Note of *Admiration.*

King. *From* Hamlet! ---- *Who brought them?*

LXXXV. Ibid. Page 445.

Falſe Printing.

----------- I will work him
To an Exploit now ripe in my deviſe,
Under the which he ſhall not chuſe but fall:

It muſt be reſtor'd, as all the Editions have it;

------------- I will work him
To an Exploit now ripe in my Device,
Under &c.

To *deviſe*, the *Verb*, is written with an *ſ*; but the *Subſtantive* from it always with a *c*.

LXXXVI.

LXXXVI.

Various Reading.

> ----------- *He made Confeſſion of You,*
> *And gave you ſuch a maſterly report*
> *For art and exerciſe in your defence;*
> *And for your rapier moſt* eſpecial,
> *That he cry'd out 'twould be a* FIGHT *indeed,*
> *If one could match you.*

All the Editions, that I have ſeen, except the *Duodecimo* publiſhed by Mr. *Tonſon* in 1714, with a ſmall Variation in the Pointing, read this Paſſage thus;

> ----------- *He made Confeſſion of You,*
> *And gave You ſuch a maſterly Report*
> *For Art and Exerciſe in your Defence,*
> *And for your Rapier moſt* eſpecially,
> *That he cry'd out, 'Twould be a* SIGHT *indeed,*
> *If One could match You.*

LXXXVII. Ibid.

Omiſſion ſupply'd.

The *Quarto* Edition of 1637, has an Addition immediately following the laſt quoted Paſſage, which has been inſerted in the *Quarto* of 1730, and Mr. *HUGHS*'s Impreſſion; and which, if an Interpolation by the Players, has ſuch a Reſemblance of *SHAKESPEARE*, and exaggerates the Deſcription of *Laertes*'s Excellence at the Sword ſo aptly, that I think it may be given to our Author without any Injury.

That

> *That he cry'd out, 'Twould be a Sight indeed,*
> *If One could match You.* The * SCRIMERS of their Nation,
> He ſwore, had neither Motion, Guard, nor Eye,
> If You oppos'd them. *Sir, this Report of his,* &c.

The two latter Editions, which, as I ſaid, have inſerted this Addition, inſtead of *Scrimers* ſubſtitute *Fencers*. Perhaps, they might underſtand the *firſt* Term, (but thought it too obſolete to be retained;) for the Alteration is juſt and pertinent to the Senſe. *SHAKESPEARE*, I am well ſatisfied, knew the Propriety of the old Word, and its Derivation. I think, his Acquaintance with the *Italian* Tongue neither has been, nor can be, diſputed; as he has founded ſo many of his *Plots* on *Italian* Novels, and ſo often ſcatters Remnants of *that* Tongue thro' his Plays.

LXXXVIII. Ibid. Page 447.

Falſe Printing.

> *And then this* ſhould *is like a* Spend-thrift'*s ſigh*
> *That hurts by eaſing;*

I look upon this to be a ſlight Error of the *Preſs* and *Reviſal:* For how does a *Spendthrift's* Sigh hurt more than any *other* Body's? All the Editions that I have ſeen, which inſert this Paſſage, concur in reading it, as undoubtedly it ought to be;

> *And then this* ſhould *is like a* ſpend-thrift *Sigh,*
> *That hurts by eaſing.*

* **Scrimer** *is properly a* Gladiator, Fencer, *or One that ſtands on his* Guard. SKINNER'*s* Etymolog. (*in the Word,* **Skirmiſh**;) *gives us a Number of Derivations of it, but All cent'ring in the ſame Point. Among the reſt, he tells Us, that the* Ars Gladiatoria, *or Science of Defence, was call'd by the* DUTCH, **Scherm**; *by the* ITALIANS, Scherma *and* Scrima; *and by the* FRENCH, Eſcrime: *As the* ANGLO-SAXONS *of Old uſed to call a Fencer or Swordſman,* Scrimbre; *which (the* b *being left out, and a ſmall* Metatheſis *made in the Letters of the* laſt *Syllable;) is the very Word uſed by our Author.*

LXXXIX.

LXXXIX. Ibid.

Conjectural Emendation.

-------- He being remiss,
Most generous and free from all contriving,
Will not peruse the foils; so that with ease,
Or with a little shuffling, you may chuse
A sword UNBATED, *and in a pass of practice*
Requite him for your father.

We meet this Word again, afterwards, in *pag.* 468.

The treach'rous Instrument is in thy hand,
UNBATED *and envenom'd.*

The Generality of the Editions consent in reading, as the Derivation of the Word seems to require, UNBAITED. But still, I must confess, I want to be taught how *unbaited* comes to signify *baited?* Un is a *negative Particle* (equivalent to the ἀνεῦ of the *Greeks*;) which is prefixed to Thousands of *English* Words, and always deprives them of their native Sense, making them signify the direct contrary. And whenever it is so prefixed, I don't know an Instance either in our Poet, in *SPENCER*, or in *CHAUCER*, that the *compound* Word signifies what the *simple* Word did before it was annexed. If I am not mistaken in this Observation, or it has not its particular Exceptions to which I am a Stranger, perhaps, we may with a very slight Change set our two Passages right. Why might not the Poet write,

A Sword IMBAITED,-----

And so in the other Passage,

IMBAITED *and envenom'd*,----

To *imbait*, is exactly what the *Latines* express by their *inescare*, or *escâ illinere*; and we have a Multitude of Words, in our own Idiom,

Idiom, compounded in the ſelf ſame Manner; as, *imbargo, imbark, imbaſe, imbattle, imbelliſh, imbezzle, imbibe, imbody, imbolden, imboſs, imbowel, imbroil, imbrue, imbue, imburſe, immerge, immit, immolate, immure, impact, impair, impale:* Cum multis aliis, *&c.*

Occaſional Conjecture. I can remember but a ſingle Paſſage, in all the Works of *SHAKESPEARE*, where a Word, with the Particle *un* prefixed to it, ſhould ſeem to ſignify the ſame Thing as the *ſimple* Word would do; and even there I violently ſuſpect the preſent Reading. It is in his King *JOHN*, *pag.* 151. where Lady *CONSTANCE* adviſes the *Dauphin* of *France* not to ſacrifice his Oath and Conſcience to the Temptations of a young fair Bride. Her Words are theſe;

> Lewis, *ſtand faſt; the Devil tempts thee here*
> *In Likeneſs of a new* UNTRIMMED *Bride.*

I cannot conceive what the Poet is ſuppoſed to mean here by *untrimm'd*, unleſs its oppoſite, as I take it, in Senſe, *trim*; i. e. neat, ſpruce, fine. But I cannot admit it, without ſome Proof for Conviction, to carry that Signification. Again, there is no Room ſurely to imagine that the Poet intends to compare the Lady *BLANCH*, as *unmarried*, to a Veſſel wanting either the Proportion of her Ballaſt or Rigging, or not being *compleat in her Trim*, as the Sea-phraſe is; and therefore calls her *untrimmed.* This would be a remote *Alluſion* with a Vengeance; and, eſpecially, when it is put in the Mouth of a Woman too.

As I profeſs my ſelf to have ſuſpected the Paſſage, ſo I endeavour'd as far as an unſupported Conjecture, or two, would go, to reconcile it to an intelligible Meaning. I ſay, a Conjecture or two, for which I have no Warrant or Aſſiſtance from the Copies; and therefore I ſhall urge them barely as ſuch, and leave them to be embraced, or renounced, at Pleaſure. If it did not depart too widely from the preſent Text, to make ſuch a Correction reaſonable, it is not impoſſible but the Poet might have wrote;

Firſt Conjecture.

> -------- *the Devil tempts thee here*
> *In Likeneſs of a new* UNTAMED *Bride.*

i. e.

i. e. a *Virgin-Bride*; a Bride yet *unbedded.* I cannot, indeed, recollect any Instance, in which the Poet has ever taken the Liberty of using this *Epithet* in that *metaphorical* Sense: But it is a Sense, in which I am sure he may be born out, and justified, by the Usage of other Languages. An *untamed Bride* exactly amounts to what the *Latines* call'd *Virgo indomita*; which I believe they borrow'd from the παρθένος ἀδάματος of the *Greeks*; that is, a Bride *untasted, unenjoy'd.* And it will be no new Doctrine, to say, that Temptation and Desire are generally heighten'd in Men by that Circumstance.

But I observe that *trim* is used as an *Epithet* by our Author, to signify not only *neat, spruce,* &c. but *substantively* too, for a peculiar Quaintness and Elegance of Habit.

So in the *First* Part of *HENRY* IV. *pag.* 200.

> *When I was dry with Rage, and extream Toil,*
> *Breathless and faint, leaning upon my Sword,*
> *Came there a certain Lord, neat,* TRIMLY *dress'd*;
> *Fresh as a Bridegroom,* &c.

So in *CYMBELINE. pag.* 181.

> ------------- *and forget*
> *Your laboursome and dainty* TRIMS, *with which*
> *You made great* Juno *angry.*

And he employs it besides to signify personal Beauty, and the Hue and Brightness of Colours. So in his *Poem* of *VENUS* and *ADONIS*, *pag.* 41.

> *The Flow'rs are sweet, their Colours fresh and* TRIM,
> *But true sweet Beauty liv'd, and dy'd, in Him.*

It is not improbable therefore, that the Passage before us ought to be restor'd thus; *Second* Conjecture.

> Lewis, *stand fast; the Devil tempts thee here*
> *In Likeness of a new* BETRIMMED *Bride.*

i. e. adorn'd, and *deck'd with Charms.* It is familiar with our Poet to use the word *betrim* in these Senses; and it is certainly of *Saxon* Derivation; among whom *getrymmed* signified *neat, fine, finished*, &c. The Transmutation of *g* into *b* was customary in Words of *Saxon* Original; as *gewarian*, to *beware*; *geleafan*, to *believe*, &c. Of which Changes, thro' all the Letters of the Alphabet, *SKINNER* has discours'd at large in his *Prolegomena Etymologica.*

Third Conjecture. But if *betrimmed* may seem to any to depart too far from the Traces of the Text, as it now stands, I'll propose another Correction, that requires but a very minute Change, and comes up to the Sense of the former; As,

> Lewis, *stand fast; the Devil tempts thee here*
> *In Likeness of a new* AND TRIMMED *Bride.*

i. e. of a *new Bride*, and one, as I said before, *deck'd* with all the Charms of personal Beauty.

I have hinted above, that I remember'd but a single Passage in our Author, where a Word, with the Particle *un* prefixed to it, should seem to signify the same Thing as the *simple* Word would do: But I find since, there are some other Instances of this kind; One, at least, in which *Shakespeare* is countenanc'd by the Usage of other Writers: Some, in which his present Reading is certainly to be disputed, and therefore ought to be corrected. See King *HENRY* VIII. *pag.* 487.

> ------- *for where I'm robb'd and bound,*
> *There must I be* unloos'd, *&c.*

'Tis evident here, that *unloos'd* signifies *loos'd*; and so we find it used by other Writers. To go no farther for Authorities than the Translation of our New Testament, there is a Passage where, in three of the *Evangelists*, the Word *unloos'd* is made to mean *loosed*; --- *Whose Shoe-latchet I am not worthy to* unloose, *&c.* This Term therefore, without any more ado, must be admitted

equivocal

equivocal in its Signification. But let us try our Author upon another doubtful Paſſage, and then I have done with this Remark. I obſerve he uſes the Term, to *bonnet*, in the Senſe of ---- to *pull off the Cap to.*

CORIOLANUS, pag. 130.

> *He hath deſerv'd worthily of his Country*; *and his Aſcent is not by ſuch eaſy Degrees as Thoſe who have been ſupple and courteous to the People*, bonnetted *without any further Deed to heave them at all into their Eſtimation and Report.*

i. e. that have won the People's Hearts, only by Submiſſion, and pulling off the Hat to them. Now as *bonnetted* here manifeſtly ſignifies *pulling off* the Hat; ſo, on the other hand, if you can believe our Author's Text, *unbonnetted* is in another place employ'd to mean *having the Hat on.*

OTHELLO, pag. 482.

> --------- *I fetch Life and Being*
> *From Men of royal Siege*; *and my Demerits*
> *May ſpeak,* unbonnetted, *to as proud a fortune,*
> *As This that I have reach'd.*

Will any Body pretend that the Idiom of our Tongue can admit *unbonnetted* here to intend, *with the Hat on*, as the Senſe of the Place neceſſarily requires? I cannot help ſaying with *HORACE*,

> --------- Credat *Judæus* apella,
> Non ego. ---------

Occaſional Emendation.

In ſhort, I dare affirm, the Preſs, or the Tranſcribers, have palm'd a Reading upon the Author contrary to his Intention. I am of Opinion, that, to *bonnet*, is equivocal, and ſignifies, as the Context may require, either to *pull off*, or *put on*, the Hat; but that, to *unbonnet*, is always to *pull it off*. I make no Scruple, therefore, but that the Author wrote thus;

- - - - - - - - - I fetch Life and Being
From Men of royal Siege; and my Demerits
May speak, and bonnetted, *to as proud a Fortune,*
As This that I have reach'd.

i. e. may speak with the Hat on, without shewing any Degrees of Deference, or Inequality to: Which small Alteration restores us the plain Sense of the Poet.

XC. Act 5. Scene 1. Page 450.

Correction, *from Various Reading.*

For here lies the point; if I drown my self wittingly, it argues an act; and an act hath three *branches. It is* AN ACT TO DO *and* TO PERFORM, argal, *&c.*

Very notably made out! If an Act has *Three* Branches, as the honest Clown here defines it to have, it would puzzle a good Arithmetician to find them out from this Reading. 'Tis true, the *Folio* Editions exhibit it thus; and so, indeed, does the *Duodecimo* Edition publish'd by Mr. *Tonson* in 1714. But, surely, to *do*, and to *perform*, can be but two Branches; and if we admit This for the true Reading, then we ought to correct the Passage: - - - *And an Act hath* Two *Branches; it is an Act to* do, *and to* perform. But the *Quarto* Edition of 1637, I believe, will instruct Us to read the Place exactly as the Poet intended it.

For here lies the Point; if I drown my self wittingly, it argues an Act; and an Act hath three *Branches; it is, - - - to* ACT, - - - *to* DO, - - - *and to* PERFORM, - - - *argal,* &c.

XCI. Act 5. Scene 2. Page 456.

False Printing.

- - - - - - - - - What is that they follow,
And with such maimed RIGHTS?

The Church-Ceremonies, that are ordered either in Marriages or Funerals, are always written *Rites,* (from *Ritus,* in the *Latine;*) and not *Rights.* Correct therefore,

- - - - *What*

. - - - - - - - - *What is That they follow,*
And with ſuch maimed RITES?

The ſame literal Miſtake, I find, is made in the *TEMPEST*, *pag.* 55.

If Thou doſt break her Virgin Knot, before
All ſanctimonious Ceremonies may
With full and holy RIGHT *be miniſter'd*, &c.

Occaſional Correction.

Where, likewiſe it muſt be reſtor'd, RITE. And ſo Mr. *Pope* at other times takes care to ſpell this Word; as thrice in this very Play of *Hamlet.*

Page 442.

No noble RITE, *nor formal Oſtentation,*

And, *pag.* 457.

Yet here She is allowed her Virgin RITES,

And again, *pag.* 471.

- - - - - - - - - - *And for his Paſſage,*
The Soldier's Muſick, and the RITES *of War,*
Speak loudly for him. - - - - -

And ſo in *ROMEO and JULIET*, *pag.* 274.

If that thy Bent of Love be honourable,
Thy Purpoſe Marriage, ſend me Word to morrow,
By One that I'll procure to come to Thee,
Where, and what time, thou wilt perform the RITE.

And in many other Places.

XCII.

XCII. Act 5. Scene 3. Page 461.

Various Reading.

Horat. --------- *How was this seal'd?*
Haml. *Why ev'n in that was Heaven* ORDINATE.

So the *Folio* Editions write this Passage with the *Editor*; and so I find, Mr. TONSON's *Duodecimo*, so often mention'd, likewise exhibits it. But why a *Passive* Participle here, when the Sense, I think, plainly requires an *Active? Ordinate*, must signify order'd, directed, agreed to; not ordering, directing, concurring with, as the Poet's Meaning seems to demand. My *Quarto* Editions, which are follow'd by Mr. HUGHS in his Impression, read, as I verily believe the Passage ought to be restor'd.

Horat. --------- *How was This seal'd?*
Haml. *Why ev'n in That was Heaven* ORDINANT.

XCIII. Ibid.

Omission *supply'd.*

Horat. *So* Guildensterne *and* Rosencraus *go to't.*
Haml. [ ]
They are not near my Conscience; their Defeat
Doth by their own insinuation grow.

The second *Folio* Edition begins *Hamlet*'s Speech with a Verse, which we have no Reason to believe is not SHAKESPEARE's; and which, I think, is very essential to explain the two Verses that follow it. I don't know whether Mr. POPE suspected, or overlook'd it; but, I am sure, it may be restor'd without any Detriment.

Horat. *So* Guildenstern *and* Rosencraus *go to't.*
Haml. Why, Man, they did make Love to this Employment:
They are not near my Conscience; their Defeat
Doth by their own Insinuation grow.

XCIV

XCIV. Act 5. Scene 4. Page 464.

Haml. *It is but Foolery; but it is ſuch a kind of* Game-giving *as would perhaps trouble a Woman.*

Hor. *If your mind diſlike any thing, obey it. I will foreſtal their repair hither, and ſay you are not fit.*

Various Reading reſtored, and explained.

I do not know whether the *Editor* deſigned this Reading, which, I find, poſſeſſes ſome of the Editions beſides; or whether it be a literal Error of the Preſs only. I muſt own, I am at a Loſs to underſtand the Meaning of *Game-giving*. The *Quarto* Edition of 1703, and Mr. *Hughs* agree in reading, *But it is ſuch a kind of* boding, *&c.* 'Tis certain, they expreſs the Author's Senſe exactly in this Word; but they have put a Change upon him, for Want of underſtanding his Original. The ſecond *Folio* Edition reads the Paſſage, as it ought to be reſtor'd;

It is but Foolery; but it is ſuch a kind of gain-giving, *as would, perhaps, trouble a Woman.*

To *Gain-give*, is to *diſtruſt*, or, as we more vulgarly expreſs it, to *miſgive*. It is of *Saxon* Derivation, among whom *gean* ſignified *againſt*; and ſo we at this day uſe *gain-ſay*, to imply *contradict*, ſay *againſt*.

XCV. Act 5. Scene 5. Page 466.

And in the Cup an ONYX *ſhall he throw,*
Richer than that which four ſucceſſive kings
In Denmark'*s crown have wore.*

Various Reading reſtor'd, and aſſerted.

So again, *pag.* 468.

Drink off this potion: is the ONYX *here?*

I find

I find, this Reading possesses several of the Editions, and even That of the accurate Mr. *HUGHS*. I don't know upon what Authority it first obtain'd; but it seems evident to Me, whoever introduced it, did not mind to expound the Author by himself; which is the surest Means of coming at the Truth of his Text. The second *Folio* Edition, has it in both places.

And in the Cup an UNION *shall he throw,*
Richer than That, &c.

And so in the second Passage;

Drink off this Potion; Is thy UNION *here?*

Mr. *Pope*, indeed, takes Notice of this as a Various Reading, but in Both places substitutes *Onyx*. I am clearly for the *Union* being restor'd; and shall submit my Reasons for it to Judgment. An *Onyx*, as we may find from PLINY and the other *Naturalists*, was a small Stone-Gemm; and was likewise a coarser Species of *lucid* Stone, of which they made both Columns and Pavements for Ornament. An *Union* is a fine Sort of *Pearles*, so call'd, either because they are found *single*, or because they resemble an *Onion* in Shape, &c. But the Etymology of the Name is of no Consequence here. I'll transcribe the King's whole Speech, by which it will appear for what, and upon what Terms, he promises to throw a Jewel into the Cup; and after that Another short Speech, from which I believe it will be apparent, that *Union* ought to be restor'd instead of *Onyx*.

Set me the Stoops of Wine upon that Table:
If Hamlet *give the* first *or* second Hit,
Or quit in Answer of the third Exchange,
Let all the Battlements their Ord'nance fire:
The King shall drink to Hamlet's *better Breath;*
And in the Cup an Onyx *shall he throw,*

Richer

Richer than That which four successive Kings
In Denmark's *Crown have worn.*

Well; *Hamlet* and *Laertes* immediately fall to play with the Foils; *Hamlet* gives *Laertes* the *first Hit*; and the King thereupon, in Performance of his Promise, says;

Stay, give me Drink: Hamlet, *this* PEARL, *is thine*;
Here's to thy Health; *give him the Cup.*

Now if an *Union* be a Species of *Pearl*, as it certainly is; and if an *Onyx* be a transparent Gemm, quite differing in its Nature from *Pearls*; the King saying that *Hamlet* has earn'd the Pearl, I think, amounts to a Demonstration, that it was an *Union-pearl* he meant to throw into the Cup; and that therefore, as I said before, *Union* ought to be restor'd into the Poet's Text; and *Onyx* casheer'd as a spurious Reading. Besides, if I am not mistaken, neither the *Onyx*, nor *Sardonyx*, are Jewels, which ever found Place in an Imperial Crown.

XCVI. Act 5. Scene 6. Page 470.

Various Reading.

---------- *Oh proud death!*
What feast is tow'rd in thine ETERNAL *Cell*,
That thou so many princes at a shot
So bloodily ha'st strook?

I can see no great Propriety here in this Epithet of *eternal*; nor does it communicate any Image suitable to the Circumstance of the Havock, that *Fortinbras* looks on, and would represent in a Light of Horror. He, upon the Sight of so many dead Bodies, exclaims against Death, as an execrable, riotous Destroyer; and as preparing to make a savage and hellish Feast. The *Quarto* Edition of 1637 seems to give us an Epithet more forcible, and peculiar to this Scene of Action.

------- O proud Death!
What Feast is tow'rd in thine INFERNAL *Cell,*
That Thou so many Princes at a Shot
So bloodily ha'st strook?

XCVII. Ibid. Page 471.

Correction, *from Various Reading.*

Fortinb. *--------- Let four captains*
Bear Hamlet *like a soldier* OFF *the stage;*

As Errors made their Appearance very early in this Play, so they keep their Ground to the very Close of it. Why *bear* Hamlet OFF *the Stage?* I meet with this Reading no where but in the fourth *Folio* Edition; and in the *Duodecimo* publish'd by Mr. *Tonson*, which does not much out-do the Other in Correctness. Surely, *Fortinbras* cannot be supposed to consider either himself, or *Hamlet*, here, as *Actors* before an *Audience*; and upon the *Stage* of a Theatre. The Poet must very strangely forget himself, to be guilty of such an Absurdity: But I dare say, he may be clear'd from a Suspicion of it. In short, the Case is This: *Hamlet*, upon the Point of Death, conjures *Horatio*, who was desirous to have poison'd himself, to relinquish those Thoughts, and to live, and by a true Representation of Occurrences, rescue *his* Character and Memory from Scandal.

Page 469.

Oh, good Horatio, *what a wounded Name,*
Things standing thus unknown, shall live behind Me!
If Thou did'st ever hold me in thy Heart,
Absent thee from Felicity awhile,
And in this harsh World draw thy Breath in Pain,
To tell my Tale.

Horatio,

Horatio, in Obedience to this Command, desires *Fortinbras* will order, that the dead Bodies may be placed on a *publick Stage*, or Scaffold, and he will speak to the Business of their disastrous Deaths.

Page 470.

> ----------- *Give Order that these Bodies*
> *High* ON A STAGE *be placed to the View,*
> *And let Me speak to th' yet unknowing World*
> *How these Things came about.*

Nay, and he desires that This may be done with al possible Dispatch, lest, thro' a Delay, any farther accidental Mischief might intervene.

Page 471.

> *But let this same be presently perform'd,*
> *Ev'n while* * *Mens Minds are wild, least more Mischance*
> *On Plots and Errors happen.*

Fortinbras likes the Proposal, expresses himself in Haste to hear what *Horatio* has to say; and is for convening the Noblest Persons of the State to the Audience of it. There is no doubt, therefore, but we ought to restore this Passage, as all the better Editions have it;

* *It is in Mr.* Pope's *Edition, by a Fault of the Press,* men minds.

Fortinb. - - - - - *Let four Captains*
Bear Hamlet *like a Soldier* TO *the Stage*;

that is, to the *Stage*, or *Scaffold*, from whence *Horatio* desired to explain the casual and plotted Calamities, that had befall'n them in the Persons of their Princes.

THE

THE

APPENDIX.

HE Examination of this ſingle Play has drove out into ſuch a Length, that I am almoſt afraid to think of an *Appendix* to it. But I have tied my ſelf down by expreſs Engagement, at my ſetting out; and I am ſatisfied, unleſs an Author acquits himſelf very badly, the Publick never care to bate him his Promiſes. I undertook, I think, boldly to prove, That, whatever Errors occurr'd in HAMLET, Errors of the ſame Sorts ſhould be found in the other Plays, throughout all the Volumes. 'Tis evident, the *Faults* of that Play have branched out into many *Claſſes:* And I have an ample Stock of Matter before Me, to make good my Aſſertion upon every individual *Species.* As this is but a *Specimen*, I ſhall be excuſed from pointing out thoſe innumerable *literal* Faults of the Preſs, which every Reader can correct, that does but throw his Eye over the Paſſages. As to the Faults of *Pointing* too, I ſhall confine my ſelf to remark on Such only, in which the Senſe is palpably injured; in which the *Editor* has followed the old printed Copies, and in which he has either not ſeem'd to ſuſpect a Fault, or not underſtood how to rectify it.

The Deſign of this Work was an honeſt Endeavour to reſtore SHAKESPEARE from the Corruptions, that have taken Place in all his Editions: And, to this End, I gave it as my Opinion, that an *Editor* of Him, ought to be a *Critick* upon him too. The Want of *Originals* reduces us to a Neceſſity of *gueſſing*, in order to amend him; but theſe Gueſſes change into Something of a more *ſubſtantial* Nature, when they are tolerably ſupported by *Reaſon* or *Authorities.* There is certainly a Degree of Merit in a good Conjecture; tho' it be not ſo thoroughly ſatisfactory and convincing, as the Party, who advances it, flatters himſelf it muſt be. This calls to my Mind a Sentiment in an old *Latin* Verſe, though I do not remember at preſent to what Author we owe it;

Benè qui *conjiciet*, *Vatem* hunc perhibebo *optimum.*

I am far from entertaining ſo vain an Hope, that every Conjecture, which I have ventur'd to make, ſhall be followed with the Concurrence and Applauſe of the Readers: But I may dare to aſſert, Some of them are ſo well-grounded and certain, that They renew in Mé a Wiſh, that Mr. POPE had propoſed to himſelf to enter upon this Province. This would naturally have led him to weigh every Line of his Author with that Care and Judgment, that, I believe, *Then* he would have *retracted* ſome few of thoſe Conjectures which he has made; and in which he ſeems to have err'd, either from Want of duly conſidering the Poet, or of a competent Knowledge of the Stage. The Cauſe of SHAKESPEARE is here engaged, and the Reſtitution of Him concern'd; and therefore I muſt beg Mr. POPE's Pardon for contradicting Some of his Conjectures, in which he has miſtaken the Meaning of

our

(our Author.) No other Cause, but This, should provoke me to run so bold a Risque; and if I have the ill Fortune to deceive my self in the Attempt, I shall willingly submit to own my self, (as HAMLET says to LAERTES,) *his Foil in my Ignorance*.

The exceptionable Conjectures of the *Editor*, I think, may be ranged under these Heads; as, where he has *substituted* a *fresh Reading*, and there was no Occasion to depart from the Poet's Text; where he has *maim'd* the Author by an unadvis'd *Degradation*; where he has made a *bad* Choice in a *Various Reading*, and degraded the better Word; and where he, by *mistaking* the *Gloss* of any Word, has given a wrong Turn to the Poet's Sense and Meaning.

Of the first Species of These I shall produce but a single Instance, because my Defence of the Poet will take up some Room: But, I am in hopes, the Novelty of the Subject, and the Variety of the Matter, will make it not appear too tedious. The Passage, upon which I make my Observation, is This:

New Reading disputed, *and Text* defended. * Vid. infrà.

I. TROILUS *and* CRESSIDA, *p.* 42.

> Paris *and* Troilus, *you have Both said well:*
> * And *on the Cause and Question now in hand*
> *Have gloss'd but superficially; not much*
> *Unlike Young Men, whom* GRAVER SAGES *think*
> *Unfit to hear moral* Philosophy.

† *Page* 22.

The EDITOR, I remember, in his Preface, † speaking of the Method taken in his Edition, tells us that *the Various Readings are fairly put in the Margin, so that every one may compare them; and those he has preferr'd into the Text are* CONSTANTLY ex fide Codicum, *upon Authority*. I heartily beg the Pardon of this Gentleman, if, thro' Ignorance, I shall assert a Falshood here, in being bold to say, that This may be call'd an Exception to his Rule; that *Graver Sages* is preferr'd into the Text without *any* Authority, and that all the printed Copies read the Passage thus;

> -------------- *not much*
> *Unlike Young Men, whom* ARISTOTLE thought
> *Unfit to hear moral Philosophy.*

Anachronism *consider'd.*

'Tis certain, indeed, that *Aristotle* was at least 800 Years subsequent in Time to *Hector*; and therefore the Poet makes a remarkable Innovation upon Chronology. But Mr. POPE will have this to be One of those *palpable Blunders*, which the Illiteracy of the first Publishers of his Works has father'd upon the Poet's Memory, and is of Opinion that it could not be of our Author's penning; *it not being at all credible, that these could be the Errors of any Man who had the least Tincture of a School, or the least Conversation with such as had.** 'Tis for this Reason, and to shelter our Author from such an Absurdity, that the *Editor* has expung'd the Name of ARISTOTLE, and substituted in its place *graver Sages*. But, with Submission, even herein he has made at best but half a Cure. If the Poet must be fetter'd down strictly to the Chronology of Things, it is every whit as absurd for *Hector*, to talk of PHILOSOPHY, as for him to talk of *Aristotle*. We have sufficient Proofs, † that *Pythagoras* was the first who invented the Word *Philosophy*, and call'd himself *Philosopher:* And he was near 600 Years after the Date of *Hector*, even from his beginning to flourish. 'Tis true, the Thing, which we now understand by Philosophy, was *then* known; but it was only *till then* call'd *Knowledge* and *Wisdom*. But to dismiss this Point; I believe this Anachronism of our Poet, (and, perhaps, all the Others that he is guilty of,) was the Effect of Poetick Licence in him, rather than Ignorance.

* *Pref. Page* 14.

† Diogenes Laertius, *and* Cicero, *from* Heraclides Ponticus; Iamblichus, *in the Life of* Pythagoras, *&c.*

Anachronisms *familiar with* Shakespeare.

It has been very familiar with the Poets, of the *Stage* especially, upon a Supposition that their Audience were not so exactly inform'd in Chronology, to anticipate the Mention of Persons and Things, before either the *first* were born, or the *latter* thought of. SHAKESPEARE again, in the same Play * compares the Nerves of AJAX with those of *bull-bearing* MILO of *Crotona*, who was not in Being till 600 Years after that *Greek*; and was a Disciple of *Pythagoras* †. Again, *Pandarus*, at the Conclusion of the Play, ‡ talks of a *Winchester-Goose:* Indeed, it is in an Address to the Audience; and then there may be an Allowance, and greater Latitude for going out of Character. Again, in § CORIOLANUS, *Menenius* talks of *Galen*, who was not born till the second Century of the Christian Æra: And

* Troilus, *Page* 51.

† Strabo, Aulus Gellius, *&c.*

‡ *Page* 120.

§ *Page* 123.

And the very Hero of that Play talks of the Grievance that he must stoop to, in begging Voices of *Dick* and *Hob**: Names which I dare say the *Editor* does not imagine, that SHAKESPEARE believ'd were ever heard of by that *Roman*. From his many Plays founded on our *English* Annals, and the many Points of History accurately transmitted down in them, I suppose it must be confess'd that he was intimately versed in that Part of Reading: Yet, in his King LEAR, he has ventur'd to make † *Edgar* talk of the *Curfew*, a Thing not known in *Britain*, till the *Norman* Invasion: In his King JOHN he above fifty times mentions *Cannons*, tho' *Gunpowder* was not invented till above a Century and an half after the Death of that Monarch; and what is yet more singular, (as he could not be a Stranger to the Date of a remarkable Man, who liv'd so near his own Time;) twice in the Story of *Henry* VI. he makes Mention of *Machiavel* as a subtle Politician: Tho', 'tis very well known, He was chief Counsellor to the wicked *Cæsar Borgia*, and a Favourite to the Popes *Leo* X. and *Clement* VII. the latter of whom did not come to the Papal Chair till the 15th Year of K. *Henry* VIII.

* *Page* 139.

† *Page* 62.

All these Transgressions in Time therefore, as I said before, are Liberties taken knowingly by the Poet; and not Absurdities flowing from his Ignorance. There is one Passage, I remember, in our Author, in which, if I am not mistaken, he may be presum'd to sneer at his own Licentiousness in these Points. It is in his LEAR: The King's Fool pronounces a sort of Dogrel Prophecy; and as soon as he has finish'd it, cries, ‡ *This Prophecy* Merlin *shall make; for I do live* before his time.

‡ *Page* 58.

Nor have these Liberties been taken alone by SHAKESPEARE among our own Poets: In the *Humorous Lieutenant* of BEAUMONT and FLETCHER, all the Characters of which Play are the immediate Successors of *Alexander* the Great: *Demetrius*, Prince of *Macedon*, comes out of his Chamber with a *Pistol* in his Hand, above 1500 Years before *Fire-Arms* were ever thought of. So, in the *Oedipus* of DRYDEN and LEE, there is a Mention of the *Machines* in the *Theatre* at *Athens*; tho' neither *Plays*, nor *Theatres*, were so much as known to the World till above 500 Years after that Prince's Days. And yet I dare say, neither *Beaumont* and *Fletcher* ever supposed, or thought to make their Audiences believe, that Pistols were used in *Demetrius*'s Time; nor were *Dryden* and *Lee* so ignorant in Dramatical Chronology, as to suppose *Tragedy* of as early a Date as *Oedipus*.

But that the Poets of our own Nation may be justified in these Liberties by Examples of the Antients, I'll throw in a few Instances of the like sort from their Predecessors in the Art at *Greece*. The Great SOPHOCLES, in his *Electra*, supposes that *Orestes* was thrown from his Chariot, and kill'd, at the *Pythian* Games; which Games, as the Scholiast tells us, were not instituted till 600 Years afterwards by *Triptolemus*. And frequent Instances occur in *Athenæus*, that shew, beyond Exception, how free the Comick Poets made with Chronology. ALEXIS, in his Comedy call'd *Hesione*, introduces *Hercules* drinking out of a *Thericlean* Cup: Now this was a Species of Cups, invented by *Thericles* a *Corinthian* Potter, who was Contemporary with *Aristophanes*, above 800 Years after the Period of *Hercules*. ANAXANDRIDES, in his *Protesilaus*, a Hero that was kill'd by *Hector*, brings in *Hercules* again, and talks of *Iphicrates* the *Athenian* General, and *Cotys* the *Thracian* King, both living in the Poet's own Days. And DIPHILUS, in his *Sappho*, makes *Archilochus*, and *Hipponax*, both address that poetical Lady, tho' the *first* was dead a Century before *She* was born; and tho' *She* was dead and rotten before the *latter* was born.

If these Instances of Transgression in Time may go any Way towards acquitting our Poet for the like Inconsistencies, I'll at any Time engage to strengthen them with ten Times the Number, fetch'd from the Writings of the best Poets, ancient and modern, foreign and domestick.

II. I come now to consider a *Degraded* Passage, by which I think we may safely affirm the Poet's Sense to be maim'd. It may be very justly said of SHAKESPEARE's *Style*, as He himself says of the Web of human Life, *it is of a mingled Yarn, good and ill together*. And therefore it must be own'd, Mr. POPE has very often with great Judgment thrown out of the Text such low Trash, as is unworthy of the Poet's Character, and must disgust a Reader who is desirous to be pleased. But if unhappily some of his mean Conceits are so intermingled either with the Business, or the Sense of the Context, that they cannot be rejected without leaving an Imperfection, there we must dispense with them; and content ourselves to be sorry for the *Levity* of the Author's *Pen*, or the *Vice* of the Times that forc'd him to bring in such *bald Witticisms*. Let us now examine the *Editor*'s Rule in making these *Degradations*. *Some suspected Passages*, says He, ‡ *which are excessively bad*, (*and which seem* Interpolations, *by being* so inserted *that one can intirely* omit *them without any* Chasm *or* Deficience *in the Context*,) *are* degraded *to the Bottom of the Page*; *with an* Asterisk *referring* to

Degraded Passage restor'd.

‡ *Pref. Page* 22.

to the Places of their Insertion. I am afraid, all the *degraded* Passages are not thrown out with that due Care, but that there is left an actual Deficience in the Context for want of their Insertion. As for Example;

In TROILUS and CRESSIDA, Page 87. *Antenor* the *Trojan*, a Prisoner to the *Greeks*, being agreed to be exchang'd for *Cressida* the Daughter of *Calchas*, *Diomede* is sent from the *Greeks* to bring her from *Troy*; and upon her Arrival at the *Grecian* Camp with him, she receives a Welcome from the Princes.

Agam. *Is this the Lady* Cressida?
Diom. -------------- *Ev'n She.*
Agam. *Most dearly wellcome to the* Greeks, *sweet Lady.* *
Diom. *Lady, a Word,* --- *I'll bring you to your Father.*
Nest. A Woman of quick Sense.
[Diomede *leads out* Cressida, *then returns.*]

If I am not deceiv'd, no less than *Three* Blunders are committed in this Scene on Account of *Cressid.* To set them right methodically, we must go back to the Beginning of the Scene, and examine the Parties entring.

Page 86. Scene VIII.

The GRECIAN *Camp.*

Enter Ajax *arm'd*, Agamemnon, Achilles, Patroclus, Menelaus, Ulysses, Nestor, CALCHAS, *&c.*

Now here the *Editor*, for want of due Care, runs into an Error with the printed Copies. If *Diomede* leads *Cressid* off, as the Poet certainly means he should, in order to deliver her up to her Father, 'tis plain, as the Sun at Noon-day, that *Calchas* cannot be supposed upon the Stage: His Name therefore must be expung'd from among the Names of Those that are said to enter.

In the second Place, is it not very absurd for *Diomede* to bring her on where so many Princes are present, and preparing to give her a Welcome, and then to lead her off abruptly, so soon as ever *Agamemnon* has said a single Line to her? But it is still more absurd, when *Cressid* is made to be led off without uttering one single Syllable, for NESTOR to observe, that *She is a Woman of quick Sense*; as if she had said several witty Things. The Truth is, in the old Copies, *Agamemnon*, *Nestor*, *Achilles*, *Patroclus*, and *Menelaus*, all kiss *Cressid*; and, after the Line at which the *Asterisk* is plac'd, there follows the Quantity of a Page of Repartee betwixt *Menelaus*, *Patroclus*, *Ulysses* and *Cressid*; in which *Cressid* bears her full Share. Indeed, the Matter of the Dialogue is but poor, and consists of Conundrums and low Conceits; yet it contains so much Raillery on the Part of *Cressid*, that there is some Colour for *Nestor* to say, *She is a Woman of quick Sense.* This Dialogue therefore, mean as it is, must be restor'd, or *Nestor*'s Character of her *Wit*, from her saying *Nothing*, will be as extraordinary as the two Kings of *Brentford hearing* the *Whisper*, tho' they are not present, in the REHEARSAL.

And, in the third Place, *Diomede* is said to lead out *Cressid*, and then return. Now, no *Re-entry* of him being mark'd in the Books, this Note, according to the Custom of the Stage, implies, that He only goes with *Cressid* to the Scene, and comes back immediately; but it is intended that he should surrender her to her Father's Hand at his Tent; which, let it have been ever so near to that of *Agamemnon*, must take up some little Space of Time; and therefore, I think, it ought to be said only thus, ---- *Exit* Diomede, *leading* Cressida: --- and that, immediately before this Verse in Page 89.

Agam. *Here is Sir* Diomede: *Go, gentle Knight*; &c.

the Re-entry of *Diomede* ought to be mark'd: For thus above Thirty Verses are allowed for the Interval of his Absence; and the Beginning of *Agamemnon*'s Speech seems to intimate, that *Diomede* comes back, and joins them, at the very Instant he is uttering his Words.

III. But

III. But if (as in marking the Entrance of *Calchas*, when he ought not to be brought on) Mr. Pope has err'd once by *following* all the printed Copies, I'll produce another Inſtance from the ſame Play, in which, I think, he is as plainly miſtaken by *departing* from the whole Set of Editions.

Troilus *and* Cressida, *Page* 12.

Pand. *Good morrow, couſin* Creſſid: *What do you talk of*? * *How do you, Couſin*? *When were you at* Ilium?

* *Good morrow Alexander*, is added in all the Editions very *abſurdly*, Paris not being on the Stage.

This is the Note Mr. Pope has ſubjoin'd as his Reaſon for throwing *thoſe Words* out of the Text. I confeſs, I want a better Reaſon, before I can think of following the *Editor*'s private Opinion, in this Caſe, againſt the Authority of all the Impreſſions. I am very well perſuaded, notwithſtanding *Paris* is not on the Stage, there is no ſuch Abſurdity as Mr. *Pope* has ſuſpected, but that the Words, *Good morrow*, Alexander, ---- ought to be honeſtly reſtor'd to the Poet's Text. In ſhort, before the Entrance of *Pandarus*, *Creſſid* and her Man are upon the Stage together, diſcourſing about *Hector*'s Reſentment againſt *Ajax*, and for what Cauſe. And why might not *Alexander* be the Name of *Creſſid*'s Man? *Paris* had no Patent, I ſuppoſe, for engroſſing the Name to himſelf. Beſides, *Pandarus* being of a buſy, fiddling, inſinuating Character, 'tis natural for him, as ſoon as he has given his Couſin the good Morrow, to pay his Civilities too to her Attendant. And to this I'll add another Obſervation, which falls out very unluckily for the *Editor*'s Remark; that tho' *Paris* is, for the Generality, in Homer call'd Alexander, yet, in this Play of our Author, by any one of the Characters introduced, he is call'd Nothing but Paris. I gave the Play a freſh Reading all through, on Purpoſe to confirm my ſelf in this Obſervation: And it convinces me that, by *Alexander*, the Poet here intended *Creſſid*'s Man. Reſtore the Paſſage therefore, as all the Editions before read it;

Pand. *Good morrow, Couſin* Creſſid: *What do you talk of*? Good morrow, *Alexander*; --- *How do you, Couſin*? *When were you at* Ilium?

IV. I'll now proceed to conſider a Conjecture of the Editor's, which I am very free to own is *ingeniouſly* urg'd: But there is Something more than *Ingenuity* requir'd, to gueſs for the *Stage* rightly. His Conjecture is grounded upon a marginal Interpolation, that had crept into the Text of ſome later Editions, in Dame *Quickly*'s admirable Deſcription of the Manner in which *Falſtaffe* dy'd. *Conjecture refuted.*

K. Henry V. Page 422.

For after I ſaw him fumble with the Sheets, and play with Flowers, and ſmile upon his Finger's End, I knew there was but one way; for * *his noſe was as ſharp as a Pen.*

* His noſe was as ſharp as a pen, and a table of green fields.

Theſe Words, and a table of green fields, *are not to be found in the old Editions of* 1600 *and* 1608. *This nonſence got into all the following Editions by a pleaſant miſtake of the Stage-Editors, who printed from the common piece-meal written Parts in the Play-houſe. A Table was here directed to be brought in, (it being a ſcene in a tavern where they drink at parting,) and this Direction crept into the text from the margin.* Greenfield *was the name of the Property-man in that time who furniſh'd implements*, &c. *for the actors.* A Table *of* Greenfield's.

So far, the Note of the Editor. Something more than *Ingenuity* is wanting, as I ſaid before, to make theſe Conjectures paſs current; and That is, a *competent Knowledge* of the *Stage* and its *Cuſtoms*. As to the Hiſtory of *Greenfield* being then Property-Man, whether it was really ſo, or it be only a *gratis dictum*, is a Point which I ſhall not contend about. But allowing the marginal Direction, and ſuppoſing that a *Table* of *Greenfield*'s was wanting; I poſitively deny that it ever was cuſtomary (or, that there can be any Occaſion for it) either in the *Promptor's* Book, or piece-meal Parts, where any such Directions are marginally inserted for the *Properties*, or *Implements* wanted, to add the *Property-Man's* Name whose Business it was to provide them. The Stage-Necessaries are always furnish'd between the *Property-Man* and the *Scene-Keeper*; and as the Direction is for the *Promptor's* Use, and issued from him, there can be no Occasion, as I said, for inserting the Names either of the one, or the other.

But there is a stronger Objection yet against this Conjecture of the *Editor's*, in the Manner he supposes it: Which he must have foreseen, had he had that Acquaintance with Stage-Books, which it has been my Fortune to have. Surely, Mr. POPE cannot imagine, that when Implements are wanted in any Scene, the Direction for them is mark'd in the Middle of that Scene, tho' the Things are to be got ready against the Beginning of it. No; the Directions for *Entrances*, and *Properties* wanting, are always mark'd in the Book at about a Page in Quantity before the *Actors* quoted are to enter, or the *Properties* be carried on. And therefore GREENFIELD's *Table* can be of no Use to us for this Scene.

I agree, indeed, with Mr. *Pope*, that these Words might be a *Stage-Direction*, and so crept into the Text from the Margin: But, I insist, that they must be a Direction then for the *subsequent* Scene, and not for the Scene *in Action*. I don't care therefore if I venture my Conjecture too upon the Passage: I'll be sure at least, if it be not altogether right, it shall not be liable to the *Absurdity* of the *Objection* last struck at. I suppose, with the Editor, that over-against the Words of the Text, there might be this Marginal Quotation so close to them, that the Ignorance of the Stage-Editors might easily give them Admittance into the Text.

--------- *his Nose was as sharp as a* *Pen.* — *Chairs*, and a Table off. Green Fields.

The Scene in Action is part of Dame *Quickly*, the Hostess, her House; and Chairs and Table were here necessary: The following Scene carries us into the *French* Dominions. I therefore believe This was intended as a Direction to the *Scene-Keepers*, to be ready to remove the *Chairs* and *Table* so soon as the *Actors* went off; and to shift the Scene, from the *Tavern*, to a Prospect of *green Fields*, representing Part of the *French* Territories.

But what if it should be thought proper to retract both Mr. POPE's and my own Conjecture, and to allow that these Words, corrupt as they now are, might have belong'd to the Poet's Text? I have an Edition of *Shakespeare* by Me with some Marginal Conjectures of a Gentleman sometime deceas'd, and he is of the Mind to correct this Passage thus;

for his Nose was as sharp as a Pen, and a' talked *of green Fields.*

It is certainly observable of People near Death, when they are delirious by a Fever, that they talk of moving; as it is of Those in a Calenture, that they have their Heads run on green Fields. The Variation from *Table* to *talked* is not of a very great Latitude; tho' we may still come nearer to the Traces of the Letters, by restoring it thus;

----- *for his Nose was as sharp as a Pen, and* a' babled *of green Fields.*

To *bable*, or *babble*, is to mutter, or speak indiscriminately, like Children that cannot yet talk, or dying Persons when they are losing the Use of Speech.

Conjecture disputed, *and* supplied.

V. The next Conjecture, which I shall produce of the *Editor's*, is likewise upon a *corrupted* Passage of the Author; but I am afraid his Attempt to cure it is questionable for more than one Reason.

First Part of HENRY IV. Page 211.

I am join'd with no foot-land rakers, no long-staff-sixpenny strikers, none of those mad-mustachio-purple-hued-malt worms; but with Nobility and Tranquillity; Burgomasters *and great* * ONE-EYERS, *&c.*

* *Perhaps*, Oneraires, *Trustees or Commissioners.*

I must

I must own, I am at a Loss about this Conjecture of Mr. Pope's. *Gadshil*, the Highwayman, is here boasting to the Chamberlain of the Inn, that he is in no Fear of hanging; because he is not link'd with a Gang of common little Rogues, but countenanced and born out in his Occupation by the Society of Persons of great Rank; alluding, to Prince *Henry*'s sometimes joining with them in their Robberies. But the *Prince* was no *Trustee* or *Commissioner*; nor had they any such link'd with them in their Gang, as I can find any where hinted by the Poet. Nor can I, indeed, conceive how *Oneraire* comes to signify (or, by Whom besides the *Editor* it is so interpreted) *Trustees* or *Commissioners*. The Word is apparently of *French* Termination; and must have its Derivation from *Onus* of the *Latines:* And accordingly the *French* say *Nefs oneraires*, to signify *Ships of Burthen, for Carriage*, &c. and it is always an *Adjective*, and is only used, as I know, in those Senses. There is another *French* Word, which I think would have much more nearly serv'd Mr. Pope's Purpose, tho' not have amounted directly to his Gloss; and that is, *honoraires*, *i. e.* honourable Persons, Persons worthy of honour; and so *Chevaliers honoraires*, we find, were Such as were Knights by the Priviledge of their Birth, and not in the Right of any Order. But I am of Opinion that not even this Word restores us the Poet's Text. For supposing Shakespeare himself acquainted with the Meaning of the Term, *honoraire*; we have no Reason to think he would have put it in the Mouth of so mean a fellow as *Gadshil:* No other Part of his Dialect savours of so much Politeness, or Knowledge in Language. If I may interpose my Conjecture, I believe the Poet's Word here was One much more vulgarly known, and adopted familiarly into our Tongue; and besides, not greatly differing in the *literal* Part, and much less in the *Sound*, from the present corrupted Reading. I can't help suspecting that he wrote,

> --------- *but with Nobility and Tranquillity*; Burgomasters, *and great* SEIGNIORS, *&c.*

As I have exprest my self desirous, as often as may be, to expound the Author by himself, I espouse this my Conjecture with the more Willingness, because I find him coupling the same Terms in another of his Plays. See,

Merchant of Venice. Page 5.

> *Your Mind is tossing on the Ocean,*
> *There, where your* Argosies *with portly Sail,*
> *Like* SEIGNIORS *and rich* BURGHERS *on the Flood*, &c.

VI. I'll next proceed to examine a few Passages, in which, as I conceive, Mr. Pope has adopted a Various Reading for the *worse*, and rejected the *better* Term. So, in

Various Reading disputed and supplied.

Cymbeline, Page 197.

> ----------- *I do note,*
> *That Grief and Patience,* rooted *in him Both,*
> *Mingle their* * POW'RS *together.*

* Spurs.

I must own, I cannot tell for what Reason, unless he did not remember the Signification of the Term, Mr. Pope has degraded *Spurs* here, and substituted *Powers* in its Place. I am sure, there is much greater Consonancy of the Metaphors, in *rooted* and *Spurs*; than in *rooted* and *Powers*. For *Spurs* do not only signify those sharp Irons which we wear at our Heels to make a Horse mend his Pace; and those horny Substances upon a Cock's Legs, with which he wounds his Antagonist in fighting; but likewise the *Fibres*, or *Strings*, which shoot out from the Roots of *Plants* and Trees, and give them a Fixure and Firmness in the Earth. Neither *Skinner*, *Cotgrave*, nor *Baily*, remember to mention the Word in this Sense; but Shakespeare knew the Propriety of the Term, and, as Mr. Pope might have observed, has used it in this Signification in his very first Play.

U 2 The

The TEMPEST, Page 66.

------ The strong-bas'd Promontory
Have I made shake; and by the SPURS *pluck'd up*
The Pine and Cedar.

I think This therefore a sufficient Authority to restore this Term in the Passage now before us, as the most proper, and expressive of the Poet's Meaning.

The Like.

VII. K. LEAR. Page 47.

-------- Strike her young Bones,
† INFECTING *Airs, with Lameness.*

† *You* taking Airs.

Here again, I think, the *Editor* has espoused the worse Reading, and degraded a Term, that has the Authority of most of the Copies, as well as is peculiar to the Author's Sense, and frequently used by him to signify, *blasting*, *bewitching*, &c.

So, afterwards, in the very Play before us, *Page* 61.

Edg. *Bless thee from Whirlwinds, Star-blasting, and* TAKING!

So, in the MERRY WIVES OF WINDSOR, *Page* 300.

And there he blasts the Tree, and TAKES *the Cattle.*

And so in HAMLET, Page 351.

The Nights are wholesome, then no Planets strike,
No Fairy TAKES, ------

And in several other Places: From which it is plain, that *to take*, of old, not only signified to *receive*; but was equivalent to the *attaquer* of the *French*, and *invadere* of the *Latins*; to *lay hold on*, *attack*, *invade*.

The Like.

VIII. K. LEAR, Page 55.

I tax not You, you Elements, with Unkindness;
I never gave you Kingdom, call'd you Children,
You owe me no ‡ SUBMISSION.

‡ Subscription.

Here again the *Editor* has degraded a Term, which takes Possession of the greatest Part of the printed Copies; and one which the Poet chuses to use in other Places, at least the *Verb* of it, rather than the more common Word *submit*.

So afterwards in this very PLAY, *Page* 71.

If Wolves had at thy Gate howl'd that stern time,
Thou should'st have said, Good Porter, turn the Key; ---
All Cruels else SUBSCRIBE.

So in TITUS ANDRONICUS, Page 485.

Advise thee, Aaron, *what is to be done,*
And we will All SUBSCRIBE *to thy Advice.*

And

And so, in TROILUS and CRESSIDA, Page 90.

For Hector *in his Blaze of Wrath* SUBSCRIBES
To tender Objects; but † He *in Heat of Action*
Is more vindicative than jealous Love.

† Troilus

IX. LEAR, Page 26. *The Like.*

---------- *Blasts and Fogs upon Thee!*
Th' * UNTENDER *Woundings of a Father's Curse*
Pierce ev'ry Sense about thee!

* Untented.

I cannot help thinking here again, but that the *degraded* Word, which is likewise in most of the Copies, is the most expressive, and conveys an Image exactly suiting with the Poet's Thought. 'Tis true, *untender* signifies *sharp*, *severe*, *harsh*, and all the Opposites to the Idea of *tender*. But as a Wound *untented* is apt to *rankle* inwards, smart, and *fester*, I believe, *Shakespeare* means to intimate here, that a Father's Curse shall be a Wounding of such a *sharp*, *inveterate* Nature, that Nothing shall be able to *tent* it, *i. e.* to search the Bottom, or assist in the Cure of it.

X. K. LEAR, Page 109. *The Like.*

Kent. *No, my good Lord, I am the very man* ---
Lear. *I'll see that strait.*
Kent. *That from your Life of Difference, and Decay,*
Have follow'd your sad Steps.
Lear. ------- *You're welcome hither.*
Kent. * 'TWAS no man else; *all's cheerless, dark, and deadly;*

* Nor.

I am mightily deceiv'd if Mr. POPE here again, by espousing this Reading, enters into the Poet's Thought, which seems to me to be This. *Kent* having convinced the old King first that he was *Kent*, and then that he had attended him in Disguise under his Misfortunes, as his Servant *Caius*; *Lear*, pleas'd with the Information, says, You're welcome hither; but *Kent*, reflecting on the dismal Accidents that surrounded them, says;

NOR no Man else; ---

i. e. Neither I, nor any Man, can be said to be welcome hither, where the Scene is all Calamity. And I want no better Proof to persuade Me this is the Genuine Meaning, than the Reasons which *Kent* immediately subjoins for his saying so: There can be no such Thing as Welcome *here*; for

------------ *all's cheerless, dark, and deadly;*
Your eldest Daughters have fore-done themselves,
And desp'rately are dead.

XI. MIDSUMMER-NIGHT'S DREAM. Page 145.

Thes. *Now is the* † MOON *used between the two Neighbours.*
Dem. *No Remedy, my Lord, when* Walls *are so wilful to hear without Warning.*

† Now is the ‡ Moral down between the two Neighbours. Old Edit.
‡ mural.

A Burlesque Representation is made, in this odd Play, of the Loves of *Pyramus* and *Thisbe*; and one *Flute* a Bellows-mender, properly equipp'd, plays the Part of the Wall, thro' a Cranny of which the two Lovers were used to whisper their Passion. This Part of the Interlude being over, the *Wall*, for which there was no further Occasion, goes decently off; upon which, the Passage now under Consideration immediately follows. But how can *Theseus* be be supposed to speak of the *Moon*, which has never yet entred? Or, what Relation has *Demetrius*'s Reply, concerning *Wall*'s being wilful, to *Theseus*'s Speech about the *Moon*? Sure, this would be playing at Cross-purposes. But I am very apt to think the Poet wrote the Passage thus;

Thes. *Now is the* MURE ALL *down between the two Neighbours.*

And then *Demetrius*'s Reply is apposite enough. What confirms me that it should be restor'd thus, is another Passage afterwards in Page 149.

Thes. Moonshine *and* Lion *are left to bury the dead.*
Dem. *Ay, and* Wall *too.*
Bot. *No, I assure you, the* WALL *is* down, *that parted their fathers.*

The *Mure* (or, Wall) perhaps is a Substantive of the Poet's own coining from *murus* of the *Latines*. But whether he first employ'd this Word in *English*, or no, 'tis certain he has used it in another of his Plays; and, possibly oftner than once.

Second Part of K. HENRY IV. Page 366.

Th' incessant Care and Labour of his Mind
Hath wrought the MURE *that should confine it in,*
So thin, that Life looks through, and will break out.

And so, in the Prologue to TROILUS and CRESSIDA, he stiles the Walls of *Troy*, the *Immures*.

------------- *and their Vow is made*
To ransack Troy, *within whose strong* IMMURES
The ravisht Helen, Menelaus' *Queen,*
With wanton Paris *sleeps: and That's the Quarrel.*

Various Reading restor'd.

XII. OTHELLO, Page 490.

Of being taken by the insolent Foe,
And sold to Slav'ry; of my Redemption thence,
And WITH IT ALL *my Travels History:* *

* *This Line is restored from the old Edition: It is in the rest,* ------- And PORTANCE in my Travel's History; *&c.*

If *Portance* be in it self a proper and significant Term, and a Term of our Author's too, as it possesses all the other Editions but the first, we have great Reason to believe it was an Alteration of the Poet's own, and which he thought better than the first Reading. SHAKESPEARE was a fond Imitator of SPENSER's Diction, who uses this Word in the very Sense requir'd for it in the Passage before Us. See his *Fairy Queen*, Bo. 2. Can. 3. Stanz. 21.

------- *Eftsoon there stepped forth*
A goodly Lady, clad in Hunter's Weed,
That seem'd to be a Woman of great Worth,
And, by her stately PORTANCE, *born of heav'nly Birth.*

Mr. HUGHS, in his *Glossary* upon this Author, very rightly tells us that *Portance* signifies *Behaviour*; from the *French*, *se porter*, to *behave one's self*. What does *Shakespeare* make his *Othello* say more than this, that he told his Mistress of his being taken a Prisoner, his Redemption, and his *Behaviour* in the whole History of his Travels? In the like Signification we find him using this Word in Another of his Plays.

CORIO-

CORIOLANUS, Page 142.

> *With what Contempt he wore the humble Weed;*
> *How in his Suit he scorn'd You! But your Loves,*
> *Thinking upon his Services, took from You*
> *The Apprehension of his present* PORTANCE, *&c.*

I think therefore *Portance* ought to be restor'd, as a Reading of the Poet's own Choice.

XIII. I cannot say that in the Passage, which now comes under Consideration, the *Editor* has designedly chose the *worse* Term; for, though there be a Various Reading, as he has taken no Notice of it, we cannot say certainly whether he overlook'd or despised it: But whichever was the Case, I think, we may affirm, without Scruple, that it ought to be restor'd to our Author's Text. *The Like.*

TROILUS and CRESSIDA, Page 9.

> *When I do tell thee, there my hopes lye* drown'd,
> *Reply not in how many fathoms deep*
> *They lye* INTRENCH'D.

Besides that, to *intrench by Fathoms*, is a Phrase which we have very great Reason to suspect; what Agreement in Sense is there betwixt *drown'd*, and *intrench'd*? The first carries the Idea of Destruction, and the latter of Security: And this Discordance, if I at all understand the Author, absolutely destroys his Meaning. All the Editions, that I have seen, read the Passage, as there is no Question but it ought to be restor'd;

> *When I do tell thee, there my Hopes lye* drown'd;
> *Reply not, in how many Fathoms deep;*
> *They lye* INDRENCH'D.

Indrench'd corresponds exactly with *drown'd*, and signifies *immers'd* in the Deep, or, as the Poet in another Place calls it, *ensteep'd*.

OTHELLO, Page 502.

> *The gutter'd Rocks, and congregated Sands,*
> (*Traitors* ensteep'd *to clog the guiltless Keel*;)

The Editor, here, I don't know for what Reason, subjoins a Doubt whether it ought not to be --- *Traitors* enur'd *to clog*, &c. I cannot see that there is any Need to disturb the Poet's Text; his own Word is very expressive, and his Meaning as obvious, to wit, That Rocks, and Shoals, lurk under, and lye cover'd by the Deep, treacherously to destroy Vessels which happen to be thrown upon them.

XIV. I shall now address my self to consider a few of the Editor's *Glosses*, in which he has either mistaken the Meaning of the Words he would explain, or, where they are *equivocal*, has taken the wrong Interpretation to the Prejudice of the Author's Sense. Mistaken *Glosses and* Emendation.

MERCHANT of VENICE, Page 8.

> *O my* Anthonio, *I do know of Those,*
> *That therefore only are reputed wise,*
> *For saying Nothing; who, I'm very sure,*
> *If They should speak, would almost* † DAMM *those Ears,*
> *Which, hearing them, would call their Brothers Fools.*

† daunt

I cannot pretend to account where Mr. POPE has met with the Word **damm** to signify, *daunt.* I cannot find it ever so interpreted: But granting it should be ever used in that Acceptation

ceptation, I dare affirm that neither the Word itself, nor its Gloss, ought to have a Place here. Why should one Man's speaking foolishly be presum'd to *daunt* another's Ears? The Discourse of a Fool naturally makes us laugh at, or despise him, but does not, as I conceive, put a Damp upon our Spirits. I cannot but wonder the Editor did not trace the Author's Thought in this Place, as it is evident he did not, both by the Text, and Gloss upon it; but it leaves me the Pleasure of explaining, beyond Exception, a Passage, which this ingenious Gentleman did not so much as guess at. Upon the first Reading, I immediately suspected it should be restor'd, as I since find the fourth folio Edition, and some other more modern Ones, happen to exhibit it;

> ------------- *who, I'm very sure*
> *If They should speak, would almost* DAMN *those Ears,*
> *Which, hearing them, would* call their Brothers Fools.

The Author's Meaning is directly this; That some People are thought wise, whilst they keep Silence; who, when they open their Mouths, are such stupid Praters, that their Hearers cannot help calling them *Fools*, and so incur the Judgment denounced upon them in the *Gospel*. It is very familiar with *Shakespeare* to allude to Passages of Scripture; and it is plain to me, even to Demonstration, that he had here before his Eye this Text of St. MATTHEW, *Ch. 5. v. 22. And whosoever shall say to his Brother*, Raca, *shall be in danger of the Council: But whosoever shall say, thou* Fool, shall be in danger of Hell-fire.

Because I would not assert any Thing, but what I would be willing to second with a Proof, I'll subjoin a few Instances, out of a great Number that may be collected, in which our Poet has an Eye to *Scripture-History*; and Others, in which he both alludes to, and quotes the very *Texts* from *Holy-Writ*.

In *All's well that ends well*, Page 445. he talks of *Nebuchadnezzar*'s eating Grass; in *Love's Labour lost*, Page 104. of *Sampson*'s carrying the City Gates on his Back; in the *Merry Wives of Windsor*, Page 308. of *Goliah*, and the Weaver's Beam; in K. *Richard* II. Page 162. of *Pilate*'s Washing his Hands; in the *First* Part of K. *Henry* IV. Page 261, 262. *Falstaffe*'s Soldiers are compar'd to *Lazarus*, and to the *Prodigal Son*; and in the third Part of *Henry* VI. Page 7. and in *Hamlet*, Page 391. there is an Allusion to *Jephthah*'s Daughter.

I'll now quote a few Passages, in which Texts are either, as I said, evidently alluded to, or literally quoted.

(1.) ALL'S WELL THAT ENDS WELL, Page 445.

S. Mat. vii. 13, 14. *I am for the House with the* narrow Gate, *which I take to be too little for Pomp to enter: Some, that humble themselves, may; but the Many will be too chill and tender, and they'll be for the flowry way that leads to the* broad Gate, *and the great Fire.*

(2.) MUCH ADO ABOUT NOTHING, Page 548.

Genes. iii. 8. *All, all; and moreover,* God saw him when he was hid in the Garden.

(3.) LOVE'S LABOUR LOST, Page 136.

You found his Mote, *the King your* Mote *did see;*
S. Matt. vii. 2. *But I a* Beam *do find in Each of Three.*

(4.) K. RICHARD II. Page 180.

It is as hard to come, as for a Camel
S. Matt. xix. 24. *To thread the Postern of a* Needle's Eye.

(5.) *First* Part of K. HENRY IV. Page 195.

Prov. i. 20. *Thou didst well, for* Wisdom cries out in the Street, and no Man regards it.

(6.) K. HENRY. V. Page 448.

Prov. xxvi. 11. and 2 Pet. ii. 22. Le chien est retournè à son propre vomissement, and la truie lavée au bourbier.

(7.) HAM-

(7.) HAMLET, Page 464.

There's special Providence in the Fall of a Sparrow. S. Matt. x. 29

XV. *First Part of K.* HENRY IV. Page 270. *The Like.*

Worc. ----------- *For I do protest,*
I have not sought the Day of this Dislike.
King. *You have not sought it, Sir? how comes it then?*
Falf. *Rebellion lay in his Way, and he found it.*
Prince. *Peace,* * CHEVET, *peace.*

* Chevet, *a bolster.*

I entirely accord with Mr. POPE, that *Chevet* is the *French* Word for a Bolster; but I can't so easily agree that *Chevet* is SHAKESPEARE's Word here. Why should Prince *Harry* call *Falstaffe* Bolster, for interposing in the Discourse betwixt the King and *Worcester*? With Submission, He does not take him up here for his unreasonable Size, but for his ill-tim'd, unseasonable Chattering. I much rather think it ought to be restored, as the Generality of the Editions have it, and as the Gentlemen of the Stage, I know, constantly repeat it;

Prince. H. *Peace,* CHEWET, *Peace.* ---

A Chewet, or Chuet, is a noisy chattering Bird; That sort of *Pie* which by the *French* is call'd *Goubelet.* This carries a proper Reproach to *Falstaffe* for his meddling and impertinent Jest; and besides, if the Poet had intended that the Prince should fleer at *Falstaffe* on Account of his Corpulency, I doubt not but he would have call'd him Bolster in plain *English*, and not have wrapp'd up the Abuse in the *French* Word *Chevet.*

XVI. K. HENRY VIII. Page 478. *The Like.*

---------- *and which gifts*
(Saving your mincing,) the Capacity
Of your soft * CHIVEREL *Conscience would receive,*
If you might please to stretch it.

* i. e. *Tender, from* Cheverillus, *a young* Cock, *a* Chick.

It ought to be restored --- Cheveril *Conscience.* --- This Word recurrs in another Place of our Author concerning a wanton, playing Wit.

ROMEO and JULIET, Page 281.

Oh, here's a Wit of CHEVERIL, *that stretches from an Inch narrow to an Ell broad.*

But in neither of these Passages is *Cheveril* deriv'd as the Editor supposes. 'Tis true, in BAILY's Dictionary, we are told that *Cheverillius* was an old *Latine* Word for a Cockling, or young Cock. I don't know from what Authority he says This; for neither *Calepine*, *Stevens*, *Vossius*, *Martinius*, *Decimator*, *Buchner*, (the old Glossaries, nor the modern Dictionaries that I have look'd into,) take any Notice of such a Word. And to this I'll produce a third Passage from our Author, which I presume will make it evident beyond a Doubt, that *Cheveril* must have a different Derivation.

TWELFTH-NIGHT. Page 505.

A Sentence is but a CHEVERIL *Glove to a good Wit; how quickly the wrong Side may be turn'd outward.*

I never yet heard of any Leather made of a *Cockrel*'s Skin, and believe it will hardly come into Experiment in Mr. POPE's, or my Time. In short, *Skinner*, *Cotgrave*, and *Baily* too, might

X

might have inform'd the Editor, as the Truth is, that *Cheveril* Leather is made of the Skin of a *Kid*, or *Goat*; which was call'd by the LATINS *Caprillus*, *Caprellus*, and *Capreolus*; by the ITALIANS, *Ciaverello*; and by the FRENCH, *Chevereul*; from which last, our Word *Cheveril* is immediately deduced; so that *Cheveril* is tender, or stretching, from *Chevereul*, a Kid, or wild Goat.

The Like.

XVII. This Appendix insensibly stretches out to such a Compass, that I must be obliged to pass over from mistaken *Glosses*, to Faults of other Kinds. I shall produce one more, however, which is made upon a Word of a double Signification, and where the Editor has happen'd to take it in a Sense, which I believe is very contrary to the Poet's Intention.

Second Part of K. HENR. IV. Page 326.

Falſ. Pistol, *I would be quiet.*
Pist. *Sweet Knight, I kiss thy* † NEIF.

† neif, *from* nativa, i. e. *a Woman Slave that is born in one's house.*

I admit, with Mr. POPE, that This is one of the Constructions of the Word *neif*; and, admitting it to be the proper One here, Mr. POPE must understand that *Pistol* would kiss *Falstaffe*'s domestick Mistress, *Dol Tearsheet*. But I appeal to every One that shall but read the Scene over, whether This could possibly be the Poet's Meaning. There is a perfect Fray betwixt *Dol* and *Pistol*; She calls him an hundred the worst Names She can think of; He threatens to murther her Ruff, and says, He could tear her: *Bardolfe* would have him begone; but He says, he'll see her damn'd first: and *Dol*, on the other Hand, wants him to be thrust down Stairs, and says, She cannot endure such a Fustian Rascal. I should very little expect that these Parties, in such a Ferment, should come to kissing: And I am persuaded SHAKESPEARE thought of no Reconciliation: For the Brawl is kept on, till it rises to drawing Swords; and *Pistol*, among 'em, is hustled down Stairs.

I cannot think any more is intended by the Poet than This; that *Falstaffe*, weary of *Pistol*'s wrangling, tells him He would be quiet; and that *Pistol*, who had no Quarrel with Sir *John*, but a Sort of Dependance on him, speaks the Knight fair and tells him, *that he kisses his* Fist; for so, it seems, the Word *Neif* likewise signifies. * I wonder Mr. POPE did not remember This, when the same Word (with a small Variation in the Orthography) had past him in the second Play of our Author, the *Midsummer Night's Dream*, Page 129.

* *See* Ray *of* North *and* South *Country Words.*

Bott. *Give me thy* NEAFE, *Monsieur Mustard-Seed*; ---

And the Editor there tells us, that *Neafe*, was a *Yorkshire* Word for *Fist*.

The Identity of Sound may easily deceive us in the Sense of two *English* Words so almost the Same; as well as the different Termination of any two similar Words, in any other Language, may, without a particular Care, and Application to the Context. For Want of this Caution and Guard, I believe, I can name a signal Instance, in which Mr. POPE has suffer'd himself to be deceiv'd in his Translation of HOMER.

In the *Eighth* Book of the ILIAD, just as *Teucer* has drawn his Arrow to the Head, and is going to let it fly, *Hector* discharges a large Stone at him, which both prevents its Flight, and disables the Archer:

---------- τὸν δ' αὖ κορυθαιόλος Ἕκτωρ
Αὖ ἐρύοντα, παρ' ὦμον, ὅθι κληῒς ἀποέργει
Αὐχένα τε, στῆθός τε, μάλιστα δὲ καίριόν ἐστι,
Τῇ ῥ' ἐπί οἱ μεμαῶτα βάλεν λίθῳ ὀκριόεντι,
ῬΗ͂ΞΕ ΔΈ ΟἹ ΝΕΥΡΉΝ· νάρκησε δὲ χεὶρ ἐπὶ καρπῷ.

Which Passage Mr. POPE has thus translated;

There, where the Juncture knits the Chanel-bone,
The furious Chief discharg'd the craggy Stone:
The TENDON burst *beneath the pond'rous Blow,*
And his numb'd Hand dismiss'd his useless Bow.

Eust-

Euſtathius, *Spondanus*, *Barnes*, and all the learned World, concurred in a different Conſtruction of the Paſſage, *viz.* that *Hector* with the Stone broke *Teucer*'s Bowſtring, and numb'd his Hand violently into the Bargain. And, indeed, when I firſt read Mr. POPE'S Tranſlation, I imagin'd that by a Poetical Licence he had call'd the *Bowſtring* the *Tendon*, as in another Place he takes the Liberty to call it the *Nerve*: But his Note, ſubjoin'd to ſhew that *Hector* ſtruck *Teucer* juſt about the Articulation of the Arm with the Shoulder, which *cut the Tendon*, or wounded it ſo, that it loſt its Force, ſoon convinced me that the Tranſlator had miſtaken the Meaning of his Original.

It happens very unluckily, for the Diſcovery of this Miſtake, that the ſame Accident again happens to *Teucer* in the fifteenth Book of the ILIAD: His Bowſtring, indeed, is not broke by the Stroke of a Stone; but as he is directing his Shaft againſt *Hector*, *Jupiter*, by an inviſible Means, cauſes it to burſt, and the Bow to fly out of his Hand.

> Ὅς ʽΟΙ ἐΰϛρεφέα ΝΕΥΡΗ῍Ν ἐν ἀμύμονι τόξῳ
> ʽΡΗ͂Ξ᾽ ἐπὶ τῷ ἐρύοντι·

Here again the very ſame Words -- ῥῆξε οἱ νευρὴν -- are repeated, but the Tranſlator has render'd them as they ought to be.

> *At his full Stretch as the tough* STRING *he drew,*
> *Struck by an Arm unſeen* IT *burſt in two.*

Teucer, immediately diſhearten'd at the Diſaſter, complains of the Loſs of a Bowſtring, with which he hop'd to do ſo much Execution, and which he had but that Morning affix'd for the Service of the Day:

> ------------------ ἥν οἱ ἔδησα
> Πρώϊον.

Euſtathius ſays Something ſo remarkable upon this Place, that Mr. POPE could not poſſibly have made the Miſtake upon the former Paſſage, if he had attended to the Commentator's Words here. Teucer *obſerving that he had new-ſtrung his Bow that morning*, ſays he, *calls to his Remembrance his* former Miſfortune *of having his* Bowſtring burſt *by the* Stroke of a Stone.

Τὸ δὲ πρώϊον, εἰς μνήμην ἄγει καὶ ἑτέρας δυϛυχίας τὸν Τεῦκρον. δῆλον γὰρ, ὅτι πρώϊον ἐνέδησε τὴν νευρὰν, διὰ τὸ προῤῥαγῆναι τὴν ἑτέραν λίθου βολῇ. Euſtath. Romæ. Pag. 1025.

It is plain in the firſt Paſſage Mr. POPE underſtands νευρὴν in the Senſe of νεῦρον or the Nerve of the Body. I cannot remember that it is ever employ'd in that Signification by any Author whatſoever: But This I know well and can aſſure Mr. POPE, if he has not yet obſerv'd it, that, as often as HOMER has uſed νευρὴ either in the *Iliad* or *Odyſſey*, it ſignifies in Him nothing but a *Bowſtring*.

This is a Digreſſion from the *Buſineſs* of SHAKESPEARE, but One that a Sameneſs of Error naturally introduc'd; and I hope it will be pardonable, as it ſets right a Paſſage, in which Many may be miſled by the Authority of the Tranſlator's Name.

XVIII. I ſhall now proceed to give a Specimen of ſome few Paſſages, in which the *Pointing* is ſo unſufferably bad, that the Poet's Senſe is not only maim'd, but quite ſtifled. And yet as the Editor in Theſe has follow'd the Pattern ſet him in the old Editions, the Continuation of Error cannot be ſuppoſed thro' Negligence, but becauſe he would not pleaſe either to ſuſpect a Fault, or to indulge his private Senſe in curing it. There are ſo many ſignal Blots of this Sort left, that, to point at them all, would be to extend this Work to ten Times the Compaſs it has already taken up: I ſhall therefore only cull out ſuch a Parcel, as may demonſtrate how far SHAKESPEARE wants reſtoring in this Particular.

Bad Pointings rectified.

TROILUS and CRESSIDA, Page 74.

> Æne. *And thou ſhalt hunt a Lion that will flie*
> With his Face back in human gentleneſs:
> *Welcome to* Troy --- *Now, by* Anchiſes' *Life,*
> *Welcome indeed ---*

Thus this Passage has all along been read, and never understood, as I suppose, by any of the Editors. The second and fourth *Folio* Editions make a small Variation of the Pointing, but do not at all mend the Matter. I don't know what Conception the Editors have had to themselves of *a Lion's flying in humane Gentleness*: To Me, I confess, it seems strange Stuff. If a Lion fly with his Face turn'd backward, it is fighting all the Way in his Retreat: And in this Manner it is *Æneas* professes that He shall fly, when he's hunted. But where then are the Symptoms of *humane Gentleness*? Mr. DRYDEN, in his Alteration of this Play from SHAKESPEARE, has acted with great Caution upon this Passage: For not giving himself the Trouble to trace the Author's Meaning, or to rectify the Mistake of his Editors, he closes the Sentence at --- *with his face backward*; and entirely leaves out, *in humane Gentleness*. In short, the Place is flat Nonsense as it stands, only for Want of true Pointing. I think, there is no Question to be made, but that SHAKESPEARE intended it thus;

And Thou shalt hunt a Lion, that will flie
With his Face back. --- In humane Gentleness,
Welcome to Troy; --- *Now, by* Anchises' *Life,*
Welcome indeed: ---

Æneas, as soon as ever he has return'd *Diomede*'s Brave, stops short and corrects himself for expressing so much Fury in a Time of Truce; from the fierce Soldier becomes the Courtier at once; and, remembring his Enemy as a Guest and an Ambassador, welcomes him as such to the *Trojan* Camp. This Correction, which I have here made, slight as it is, not only restores good Sense, but admirably keeps up the Character, which *Æneas* had before given to *Agamemnon* of his *Trojan* Nation, Page 27.

Courtiers as free, as debonair, unarm'd,
As bending Angels; that's their Fame in peace:
But when they would seem Soldiers, they have Galls,
Good Arms, strong Joints, true Swords, and Jove'*s Accord,*
Nothing so full of Heart.

Occasional Correction. This Quotation obliges me to make a short Stop, to set right the latter Part of this Passage; whose Sense is likewise bad, thro' a small Defect in the Pointing. Can the Poet be supposed to mean, that the *Trojans* had *Jove*'s Accord, whenever they would seem Soldiers? No; certainly he would intimate, that Nothing was so full of Heart as They, when that God did but shew himself on their Side. This Circumstance added, brings no Impeachment to their Courage: Valour would become Presumption and Impiety in them, if they trusted to it, when *Jove* manifestly declared himself on the other Side. It ought to be pointed and understood thus;

But when They would seem Soldiers, they have Galls,
Good Arms, strong Joints, true Swords; and, Jove'*s Accord,*
Nothing so full of Heart.

i. e. Jove's Accord, and Concurrence, seconding them, Nothing so full of Heart as They.

The Like. XIX. TROILUS and CRESSIDA, Page 9.

--------- *I tell thee, I am mad*
In Cressid'*s love. Thou answer'st, she is fair,*
Pour'st in the open ulcer of my Heart;
Her eyes, her hair, her cheek, her gate, her voice
Handlest in thy discourse --- O that! *her hand!* --

Any Body with half an Eye must perceive the Pointing to be disturb'd here; and that the Semicolon at the End of the third Verse quite destroys the Meaning of the Passage. Restore it thus;

--- I

-------- *I tell thee, I am maa*
In Creſſid'*s Love: Thou anſwer'ſt, She is fair;*
Pour'ſt in the open Ulcer of my Heart
Her Eyes, her Hair, her Cheek, her Gate, her Voice;
Handleſt in thy Diſcourſe -- O that! *her Hand!*

i. e. When I am already wounded to the Heart with her Beauties, you inflame my Wound with the Repetition and Praiſe of their Particulars; or to uſe the Poet's own Words in the Cloſe of the Speech;

But ſaying thus, inſtead of oil and balm,
Thou lay'ſt, in ev'ry Gaſh that Love has giv'n me,
The Knife that made it.

But I cannot diſmiſs the Paſſage, whoſe Pointing I have cur'd, without ſubjoining a Conjecture on the laſt Line of it.

Handleſt in thy Diſcourſe -- O that! *her hand!* *Occaſional Conjecture.*

I have always (notwithſtanding the whole Set of printed Copies ſupport the Reading;) ſuſpected this odd *Interjection* of Rapture, -- *O that!* and cannot help thinking it is an inelegant Break, as I am ſure it is an ill-ſounding one. Without departing very widely from the Letters of the Text, I muſt own I ſhould like it better, if it ſtood thus;

Handleſt in thy Diſcourſe -- how white *her hand!*

And then, methinks, by the Repetition of the Term, the Verſe immediately following acquires a double Beauty.

In whoſe Compariſon all whites *are Ink,*
Writing their own Reproach!

XX. Cymbeline, Page 170. *The Like.*

----------- *You good Gods,*
Let what is here contain'd reliſh of Love,
Of my lord's health, of his content, yet not
That we two are aſunder; let that grieve him:
Some Griefs are medicinable, that is one of them,
For it doth phyſick love of his Content,
All but in that.

Certainly this Paſſage could not be underſtood by the Editor, or he would never have pointed it thus: The Foundation of the Speech is this: *Imogen*, a young Princeſs, receiving a Letter from her baniſh'd Lord whom ſhe paſſionately lov'd, before ſhe opens it, prays that the Contents of it may ſhew that her Lord ſtill loves her, that he is in Health, and that he taſtes Content: Yet, ſays She, as it were recollecting her ſelf, let him not taſte a full and abſolute Content; let it give him ſome Grief, that Fate has divided Him and Me; for That's a Grief which will exerciſe and ſupport his Love; but in every other Circumſtance let him enjoy Content at Heart. This, I dare ſay, is directly the Author's Meaning; and that the Pointing ought to be reſtored thus.

--- *You*

-------- You good Gods,
Let What is here contain'd relish of Love,
Of my Lord's Health, of his Content, -- (yet not,
That We Two are asunder; let That grieve Him:
Some Griefs are med'cinable; That is One of Them,
For it doth physick Love.) -- of his Content,
All but in That!

Imogen, as it is very frequent with our Poet upon other Occasions, breaks in upon the Thread of her own Address to the Gods, interposes a Reflection, and moralizes upon it; and then resumes the Substance of her Prayer at the very Words where She left it off. She catches herself up in the same manner in the very next Page.

-------- Then, true Pisanio,
Who long'st like Me *to see thy Lord*; who long'st,
(*Oh! let me bate*) -- *but not* like Me; *yet* long'st,
But in a fainter kind: -- Oh! not like Me.

The Like. XXI. Timon of Athens, Page 52.

You Fools of Fortune, trencher-friends, time-flies,
Cap-and-knee Slaves, vapours, and minute-jacks
Of man and beast; *the infinite malady*
Crust you quite o'er! ---

I always suspected the Pointing of this Passage; Mr. Shadwell, who alter'd this Play, seems not to have understood it, and therefore has left out Part. But in what Sense were these ungrateful Senators *Minute-Jacks* of *Man* and *Beast*? The Poet just before calls them Vapours, and I dare say means to inforce that Image, by saying they were *Jacks* not of a Minute's Trust, or Dependance. Then what does *the infinite Malady* signify, without Something following to give us a clearer Idea of it? I am in no Doubt, but the Poet ought to be restor'd thus;

You * Fools *of Fortune, Trencher-friends, Time-flies,*
Cap-and-knee Slaves, Vapours, and Minute-jacks, --
Of Man and Beast the infinite Malady
Crust You quite o'er!

* *Perhaps,* Tools.

i. e. May the whole Catalogue, the infinite Number of Distempers that have ever invaded either Man or Beast, all be join'd to plague You.

The Like, XXII. *Ibid.* Page 54.

------- Slaves and fools
Pluck the grave wrinkled Senate from the bench,
And minister in their steads to general filths.
Convert o'th'instant, green, Virginity,
Do't in your parents eyes.

This Passage is so disfurnish'd of all Sense by the bad Pointing, that I am willing to think it One of Those which were never revised by the Editor. 'Tis true, the old Copies are faulty too in the Pointing; but if Mr. Pope had cast his Eye on Mr. Shadwell here, he would not have wanted Direction for reforming it in Part. Restore the whole thus;

--- *Slaves*

--------- Slaves and Fools,
Pluck the grave wrinkled Senate from the Bench,
And minister in their Steads. -- To gen'ral Filths
Convert o'th'instant, green Virginity;
Do't in your Parents Eyes.

i. e. You Virgins, that are scarce ripe for Man, turn at once such shameless Prostitutes, as to commit Whoredom even before your Parents faces.

XXIII. Coriolanus, Page 107. *The Like.*

All the contagion of the south light on you,
You shames of Rome; you herds; of boils and Plagues
Plaister you o'er, *that you may be abhorr'd*
Farther than seen, ---

Here, again, the old Copies are defective in the Pointing, by which the Sense is so maim'd, that this too must be a Passage which either was not revis'd by Mr. Pope, or in which he would not indulge his private Sense to make it intelligible. Mr. Dennis, who has alter'd this Play, was obliged, by a different Disposition of the Fable, to leave out this Passage, otherwise, I am persuaded, there would have been no Room for my making a Correction upon it. The meanest Judges of *English* must be aware, that no Member of any Sentence can begin with a *Genitive* Case, and a preceding *Nominative* be wanting to govern That and the *Verb*. Where, therefore, is the Nominative to -- *of Boils and Plagues plaister You o'er*? Or what Sense or Syntax is there in the Passage, as it now stands? Restore it without the least Doubt,

All the Contagion of the South light on you,
You Shames of Rome, *You! -- Herds of Boils and Plagues*
Plaister you o'er, that you may be abhorr'd
Farther than seen! ---

It is not infrequent with Shakespeare to redouble his Pronouns, as in this Place; So,

Andronicus, Page 513.

Oh, why should Wrath be mute, and Fury dumb?
I *am no Baby,* I; *that with base Pray'rs*
I should repent the Evil I have done:

So, Romeo and Juliet, Page 290.

Mens Eyes were made to look, and let them gaze;
I *will not budge for no Man's Pleasure,* I.

And so in a Number of Instances more.

XXIV. *Ibid.* Page 128. *The Like.*

--------- This, *as you say, suggested*
At some time, when his soaring insolence
Shall teach the people, which (*time shall not want,*
If he be put upon't, and that's as easie,
As to set dogs on sheep) will be the fire
To kindle their dry stubble; and their blaze
Shall darken him for ever.

As

As in the last Instance a Nominative was wanting to the Verb, so, on the other hand, as this Passage is pointed, we have a Redundance; for Both the Pronouns, *this* and *which*, stand as Nominatives to *will be*. The whole Passage ought to be rectified thus;

----- This, as you say, suggested
At some Time, when his soaring Insolence
Shall teach the People, (which Time shall not want,
If He be put upon't; and That's as easy
As to set Dogs on Sheep:) will be the Fire
To kindle their dry Stubble; and their Blaze
Shall darken him for ever.

Occasional Conjecture.

There is one Word, however, still in this Sentence, which, notwithstanding the Concurrence of the printed Copies, I suspect to have admitted a small Corruption. Why should it be imputed as a Crime to *Coriolanus*, that he was prompt to *teach* the People? or how was it any soaring Insolence in a *Patrician* to attempt this? I believe rather that the Poet wrote;

----- When his soaring Insolence
Shall reach *the People,*

i. e. When it shall extend to impeach the Conduct, or touch the Character of the People.

The Like.

XXV. Antony *and* Cleopatra, *p.* 410.

------- Look you, sad friends:
The Gods rebuke me, but it is a tiding
To wash the eyes of Kings.

This Speech is made by *Octavius Cæsar*, on * *Dercetas*'s bringing him Word of *Antony*'s Death, and bringing the Sword which he had drawn forth from his Wounds. Is there any Reason in This, why *Octavius* should call his Friends *sad friends*? The Poet's Sense, methinks, is very obvious, and the Cure easy. *Octavius* enjoins his Friends to be concern'd at the News; and tells them it is a Calamity, that ought to draw Tears even from the Eyes of Princes. Correct therefore,

------ Look You sad, Friends: ---
The Gods rebuke me, but it is a Tiding
To wash the Eyes of Kings.

* *From* Plutarch *we ought to write it* Dercetaeus. *But this Play is very faulty in the proper Names: We meet with* Thidias *for* Thyreus, Torus *for* Taurus, Sosius *for* Sossius, Hiparchus *for* Hipparchus, Bochus *for* Bocchus, Polemen *for* Polemon, *&c.*

XXVI. Julius Cæsar, *p.* 263.

Our reasons are so full of good regard,
That were you Antony *the Son of* Cæsar,
You should be satisfied.

The Like.

The true Pointing of this Place must likewise be obvious at the first View, but the Neglect of it puts such a Change upon our Poet's Sense, that it makes him suppose *Cæsar* had a Son whose Name was *Antony*; a Point of History altogether new to the World. It must be restored;

That were You, Antony, *the Son of* Cæsar,
You should be satisfied.

The Like.

XXVII. Another Negligence of this Sort occurs in the Merchant *of* Venice, by which a Civilian and Pleader is turn'd into a Lord, *p.* 68.

Duke. *Came You from* Padua, *from* Bellario?
Ner. *From both: my Lord* Bellario *greets your Grace.*

The

The Duke within half a Page above tells us the Profession of this *Bellario*, and that, unless he comes, he may by his own Power put off the Tryal.

Upon my Power I may dismiss this Court,
Unless Bellario, *a* learned DOCTOR,
Whom I have sent for to determine This,
Come here to day.

The Passage before Us, therefore, must be restored thus;

Duke. *Came You from* Padua, *from* Bellario?
Ner. *From Both, my Lord: ---* Bellario *greets your Grace.*

XXVIII. As in the last Passage, by the false Pointing, a Doctor of Laws was promoted to the Peerage; so in King LEAR, by the same Accident, a Physician rises to the same Honour, *p*. 93. *The Like.*

Cordel. ------ *Then be it so.*
My Lord, how does the King?
Phys. *Madam, sleeps still.*

Cordelia entring with the Earl of *Kent* and the King her Father's Physician, desires *Kent* to shift out of his Disguise of Servitude; who begging to go his own way a little longer, *Cordelia* consents it shall be as his Lordship pleases; and then addressing herself to the Physician, enquires after her Father's Health. It ought to be restor'd thus;

Cord. ----- *Then be it so,*
My Lord. --- How does the King?
Phys. ------ *Madam, sleeps still.*

XXIX. But before I dismiss the Errors of false Pointing, I'll produce one Instance of more Importance; because it is plain the Editor has not made common Sense of it; and because, I believe, it has never yet been understood by any body, since the first Corruption of it in the old Copies. *The Like, and Emendation.*

CYMBELINE, *p*. 181.

------- *Would you in their serving,*
And with what imitation you can borrow
From youth of such a season, before Lucius
Present yourself, desire his service; tell him
Wherein you're happy, *which will make him* KNOW,
If that his head have ear in musick, doubtless
With joy he will embrace you;

It is evident, I say, that this Passage is faulty both in the Pointing and the Text. *Which will make him know* --- What? --- What Connection has This with the rest of the Sentence? Surely, SHAKESPEARE can't be suspected of so bald a Meaning as This; *If you'll tell him wherein you're happy, that will make him know wherein you're happy:* --- and yet This is the only Meaning, I think, the Words can carry, as they now stand. In short, I take the Poet's Sense to be This. *Pisanio* tells *Imogen*, if she would disguise herself in the Habit of a Youth, present herself before *Lucius* the *Roman* General, offer her Service, and tell him wherein she was happy, *i. e.* what an excellent Talent she had in Singing, he would certainly be glad to receive her. Afterwards in *p*. 196, 7. *Bellarius* and *Arviragus*, talking of *Imogen*, give this Description of her.

Bell. *This Youth, howe'er distress'd, appears to have had*
Good Ancestors.
Arv. -- *How* Angel-like *he* sings!

I doubt not therefore but, upon this Foundation, the entire Passage ought to be restored thus;

> -------- *Would you in their Serving,*
> *And with what Imitation you can borrow*
> *From Youth of such a Season, before* Lucius
> *Present your self, desire his Service, tell him*
> *Wherein You're happy; (which will make him* SO,
> *If that his Head have Ear in Musick,) doubtless*
> *With Joy he will embrace You:*

Transpositions. XXX. I must now pass over to another Species of Errors, not infrequent in this Edition, which I cannot otherwise distinguish than by the Title of Transpositions; that is, either where the Verses are so transposed and taken to Pieces, that the Numbers are unnecessarily disjointed; where wrong Names have been prefix'd to the Parties speaking, or Parts of Sentences plac'd to one Speaker, that ought to belong to the Person answering; or where Stage-Directions are either misplac'd, or erroneously adopted into the Text. I shall content my self with very few Instances, in present, of each Sort, because I am hastening to conclude; and because this Work has already swell'd beyond the Size of a reasonable Specimen.

Transposition of Numbers. The dismounting a few Verses, indeed, where the Sense of them remains unbroken, is not a matter of the greatest Consequence; yet, I think, ought not to have been done, where it is altogether unnecessary, and might easily be prevented. I shall quote but two Examples, and Both of them out of the same Play; where 'tis plain there was no Occasion for breaking the Numbers.

TROILUS and CRESSIDA, Page 38.

> Hector. *Brother, She is not worth*
> *What She doth cost the holding.*
> Troil. *What's ought, but as 'tis valued.*

Here are three Hemistichs made out of Words that, with a very slight Variation, naturally fall into two compleat Verses.

> Hect. *Brother, She is not worth what She doth cost*
> *The holding.*
> Troil. ----- *What is aught, but as 'tis valued?*

So again, afterwards, Page 89.

> *'Tis done like* Hector, *but securely done,*
> *A little proudly, and great deal misprizing*
> *The Knight oppos'd.*
> Æne. *If not* Achilles, *Sir, what is your Name?*
> Achil. *If not* Achilles, *nothing.*

Here two Hemistichs are made by a Break in the Versification altogether unnecessary: Restore the Numbers thus;

> *'Tis done like* Hector, *but securely done,*
> *A little proudly, and great deal misprizing*
> *The Knight oppos'd.*
> Æne. --- *If not* Achilles, *Sir,*
> *What is your Name?*
> Achil. --- *If not* Achilles, *nothing.*

XXXI.

XXXI. TIMON of ATHENS, Page 68, 9. Transpositions *of* Persons Names.

Tim.	*Would thou wert clean enough to spit upon.*
Apem.	*A Plague on thee. Thou art too bad to curse.*

It seems clear to Me that the Division of these Speeches is mistaken: There is such a Contradiction in Sense in the second Line. If *Timon* was too bad to curse, why then does *Apemantus* curse him? I think, it would be more reasonable to split the Speeches thus;

Tim.	*Would Thou wert clean enough to spit upon.*
	A Plague on Thee! ---
Apem.	----- *Thou art too bad to curse.*

XXXII. TITUS ANDRONICUS, Page 497. *The Like.*

Aaron.	*Touch not the Boy, he is of royal Blood.*
Luc.	*Too like the Sire for ever being good.*
	First hang the Child, that he may see it sprall,
	A Sight to vex the father's Soul withal.
Aaron.	*Get me a Ladder,* Lucius, *save the Child*; &c.

Why should *Aaron*, the Moor, here ask for a Ladder, who earnestly wanted to have his Child sav'd? Unless the Poet is suppos'd to mean for *Aaron*, that if they would get *him* a Ladder, he would resolutely hang himself out of the Way, so they would spare the Child. But I much rather suspect there is an old Error in prefixing the Names of the Persons, and that it ought to be corrected thus;

Aar.	*Touch not the Boy, he is of royal Blood.*
Luc.	*Too like the Sire for ever being good.*
	First hang the Child, that he may see it sprall,
	A Sight to vex the Father's Soul withal.
	Get me a Ladder. ---
Aar.	------ Lucius, *save the Child*; &c.

XXXIII. TROILUS and CRESSIDA, Page 89. *The Like.*

Agam.	----- *Which way would* Hector *have it?*
Æne.	*He cares not; He'll obey Conditions.*
AGAM.	*Tis done like* Hector, *but securely done,*
	A little proudly, and great deal misprizing
	The Knight oppos'd.
Æne.	----- *If not* Achilles, *Sir,*
	What is your Name?
Achil.	----- *If not* Achilles, *Nothing.*
Æne.	*Therefore,* Achilles; *but whate'er, know this,*
	In the Extremity of great and little
	Valour and Pride excel themselves in Hector.

I must confess I could not read this Passage at first without stopping, and a Suspicion that the Names of the Characters were not all rightly prefix'd to these Speeches. It seem'd very absurd to Me, however the Editor has taken it upon Content, that *Agamemnon* should make a Remark to the Disparagement of *Hector* for Pride, and that *Æneas* should immediately say, If not *Achilles*, Sir, what is your Name? and then desire him to take Notice that *Hector* was as void of Pride as he was full of Valour. Why was *Achilles* to take Notice of This, if it was *Agamemnon* that threw this Imputation of Pride in *Hector*'s Teeth? I was fully satisffied that this Reproach on *Hector* ought to be plac'd to *Achilles:* And consulting Mr. DRYDEN's Alteration of this Play, (which, I suppose, Mr. POPE did not look into, while he was publishing *Shakespeare*,) I was not a little pleas'd to find that I had but seconded the Opinion of That Great Man in this Point: Correct the Passage therefore,

Agam. ----- *Which Way would* Hector *have it?*
Æneas. *He cares not; He'll obey Conditions.*
ACHIL. *Tis done like* Hector, *but securely done;*
A little proudly, &c.

The Like. XXXIV. MEASURE for MEASURE, Page 325.

Lucio. *Behold, behold, where Madam* Mitigation *comes.*
I have purchas'd as many Diseases under her Roof
As come to ---
2d. Gent. *To what, pray?*
Lucio. *Judge. ---*
2d. Gent. *To three thousand Dollars a Year.*
1st. Gent. *Ay, and more.*
Lucio. *A* French *Crown more.*
1st. Gent. Thou art always figuring Diseases in Me; but Thou art full of Error; I am sound.

Not to dwell upon Explanation here, whoever reads this Passage but once over, I dare say, will be convinc'd from the last Speech in it quoted, that all which is plac'd to *Lucio* in his first Speech could never be intended to belong to him. It must be restor'd, as the Sense of the Context requires.

Lucio. *Behold, behold, where Madam* Mitigation *comes.*
1st. Gent. *I have purchas'd as many Diseases under her Roof,*
As come to, &c.

The Like. XXXV. TAMING of the SHREW, Page 317.

Hort. ----- *I'll watch you better yet.*
In time I may believe, yet I mistrust.
Bian. *Mistrust it not: For sure* Æacides
Was Ajax, *call'd so from his Grandfather.*
I must believe my Master, else I promise You, &c.

Here, indeed, the Names are so shuffled and displaced, that I must be obliged to explain the Business of the Scene, before I can convince that there has been a manifest *Transposition. Bianca* is courted by two Gentlemen, *Hortensio* and *Lucentio*, who make Way for their Addresses under the Disguise of Masters, the One to instruct her in *Latine*, the other in Musick. *Lucentio*, as he is teaching her Language, informs her who he is, and to what Purpose he comes: She says, She'll construe the Lesson her self, and, in so doing, she tells him, She does not know him, does not trust him, bids him take Heed that *Hortensio* do not overhear them, and neither to presume, nor to despair. *Hortensio* is jealous that *Lucentio* is, like himself, a Lover in Disguise, and says he'll watch Him. After this, *Bianca* and *Lucentio* proceed in their Discourse, under Colour of continuing the Lesson; and there is no doubt but that the Speeches ought to be distinguish'd thus;

Hort

Hort. ------- *I'll watch You better yet.*
BIAN. *In Time I may believe; yet I mistrust.* [*To* Luc.
LUC. *Mistrust it not: ---- for sure* Æacides
Was Ajax, *call'd so from his Grandfather.*
BIAN. *I must believe my Master, else* &c.

XXXVI. Antony and Cleopatra, Page 311. *The Like.*

Char. *Our worser thoughts heav'n mend.*
ALEX. *Come, his fortune, his fortune. O let him marry a Woman that cannot go, sweet* Isis, *I beseech thee, and let her die too, and give him a worse,* &c.

This I dare pronounce to be so palpable, and signal a *Transposition*, that I cannot but wonder it should slip the Editor's Observation. *Alexas* brings a Fortune-Teller to *Iras* and *Charmian*, *Cleopatra*'s Women, and says himself, *We'll know all our Fortunes.* Well; the Soothsayer begins with the Women, and some Joakes pass upon the Subject of Husbands and Chastity; after which, as I apprehend, the Women hoping for the Satisfaction of having Something to laugh at in *Alexas*'s Fortune, call to him to hold out his Hand, and wish heartily he may have the Prognostication of Cuckoldom upon him: Restore therefore the Passage:

Char. *Our worser Thoughts Heav'n mend!* Alexas, -- *come, his fortune, his fortune.*

I think, there needs no stronger Proof of this being a true Correction, than this Observation which *Alexas* immediately subjoins on their Wishes and Zeal to hear him abused.

Alex. *Lo now! if it lay in their hands to make me a Cuckold, they would make themselves Whores, but they'd do't!*

XXXVII. The Editor has complain'd in his *Preface*, Page 18. that, often in the old Impressions, the Notes of *Direction* to the *Property-Men* for their *Moveables*, and to the *Players* for their *Entries*, are inserted into the Text, thro' the Ignorance of the Transcribers. I am afraid, he has not taken Care to remove all these wrong Insertions; and I believe the Instance I am about to subjoin will be determined One of Those which ought not to have escap'd his Observation. Stage-Direction *crept into the Text.*

Macbeth, Page 594.

I'gin to be a weary of the Sun,
And wish the State o'th'World were now undone.
Ring the alarum-bell, *blow wind, come Wrack,*
At least we'll dye with Harness on our Back.

Macbeth, seeing that he cannot be safe within his Fortifications, resolves to issue out upon the Enemy. But in a besieg'd Town, is it ever customary to order an Alarum, or Sally, by the ringing of a Bell? Or rather is not this Business always done by Beat of Drum?

Hieronymus Magius, I know, in an accurate and scarce Tract of his upon the Antiquity and various Use of Bells, speaks, among the rest, of a *Tintinnabulum Castrense*, or Great Bell used in Camps. " Within the Period of Christianity, *says He*, and after Great Bells " obtain'd in Churches, the Commanders of Armies employ'd Such a One flung in a Wood- " en Turret at the Top of a large Chariot; which Chariot was always plac'd near the Pa- " vilion, and every day, at the Rising and Setting of the Sun, this Bell was rung out as a " Notice to the Army to perform their Devotions; instead of Sounding the Charge, likewise, " the Soldiers were call'd to Arms by this Bell; and in the Battle, it was placed in the " Middle of the Army, and defended with the same Care as they are used to do a Standard." The Author concludes his Account of this Military Bell, with saying, *That if any other Na-*

tions

tions, besides the Italians, *made use of such a Machine in their Camps, it was more than he knew.* * We may dare assert, at least, that it never found an Introduction into *Scotland*; and that therefore the Poet could not make *Macbeth* employ it, instead of the customary Way of directing a Charge upon the Enemy.

In short, I believe these Words were a *Stage-Direction* crept from the Margin into the Text, thro' the last Line but One being deficient without them; occasion'd probably by a Cut that had been made in the Speech by the Actors. They were a Memorandum to the Promptor to ring the *Alarum-bell*, i. e. the Bell, perhaps at that Time used, to warn the *Tragedy-Drum* and *Trumpets* to be ready to sound an Alarm: And what confirms me in this Suspicion, is, that for the four Pages immediately following, it is all along quoted in the Margin, *Alarum*; *Fight*, and *Alarum*; *Alarums continued.*

It may be objected, indeed, to this Observation of mine, that the same Expression is to be met with before in this very Play; and therefore we must examine that Passage;

Ibid. Page 543.

Macd. Ring the Alarum Bell --- *Murther, and Treason!*
Banquo, *and* Donalbaine! Malcolme! *awake!*

I do not dispute these Words here being a genuine Part of the Text; because the Reason for them is very different. The Scene is in *Macbeth*'s Castle at *Inverness*; whither the King goes to pay a Visit. *Macduff* rises early, being so order'd, to call up the King; and discovering him to be murther'd, orders the Bell to be rung out, to wake his Master's Sons, and the rest of the Court, to apprize them of the dismal Accident. The Bell was entirely proper upon this Occasion; as it is, to this day, employ'd in great Houses to call together Assistance in Cases of *Thieves* or *Fire*.

Stage-Direction *transpos'd.*

XXXVIII. We come now to a *Stage-Direction* very unluckily misplaced; in which the *Editor* seems to have been misled by the small Edition, formerly publish'd by Mr. *Tonson*, for want of a competent Knowledge of the *Customs* of the *Stage*.

Second Part of K. HENRY VI. *Page* 120.

FLOURISH. *Enter Mother* Jordan, Hume, Southwel, *and* Bolingbroke.

This is the first Instance, as I take it, where Conjurers and common Witches are supposed to be usher'd into the Scene by the Sound of Trumpet; which is signified by the Word *Flourish*. The Truth of the Case is this; whenever a King enters or goes off with his Court it is the constant Practice of the Stage to *flourish* him *on* and *off*. In the Scene immediately preceding This of the Conjurers, K. *Henry* VI. and his Court are upon the Stage; and when they quit it, in the second *folio* Edition, and other old Books, we find it mark'd thus, as it most certainly ought to be restor'd;

Flourish. Exeunt.
Enter Mother Jordan, Hume, Southwel, *and* Bolingbroke.

As the *Editor*, in the above Instance, committed a Mistake by departing from the older Copies; I believe, I can point out another Place, in which he has err'd with some of those Copies, by prefixing the Word *flourish* where it ought by no Means to be admitted.

K. RICHARD III. Page 349. The Court.

FLOURISH. *Enter King* Edward SICK, *the Queen*, &c.

This is one prevailing Instance of the *Theatrical* Custom, as I above hinted, of *flourishing* their Kings *on* and *off*. But certainly this Custom is most absurdly maintain'd in this Place. The King is here brought in *sick*, nay, and to such a Degree, that upon his very Entrance, he says, he expects every day to be releas'd from Life. Can *Trumpets* be proper under this Circumstance? The Stage generally takes its Rules from the World, and 'tis known, whenever

* *An aliæ Nationes, præter* Italos, *hujusmodi Curru in Castris uterentur, mihi adhuc est incognitum.*

ever a King is sick, all *Martial* Sounds are forbid at Court, and even the Guard are reliev'd without Beat of Drum.

XXXIX. The Editor (who tells us, that in the oldest *Folio* Edition, where the *Acts* and *Scenes* are first distinguish'd, they were divided according as they play'd them, often where there was no Pause in the Action, or where they thought fit to make a Breach in it) has sometimes taken Care to regulate the *Shufflings* and *Transpositions* of the *Scenes*, and rectify the injudicious Divisions of the *Acts*: But this Part of Criticism does not display itself thro' the whole Work. I shall subjoin one Passage, for Example, in which he seems to have employ'd none of this Skill in marking the Division of an *Act*, viz. the End of the Second *Act* of King JOHN, Page 145. 'Tis true, he errs here in following the old Copies; as he did, in the last Instance but one, by contradicting them. The Lady *Constance*, her Son *Arthur*, and Lord *Salisbury*, are upon the Scene; *Constance* bids *Salisbury* be gone, and leave her to her Woes: He tells her, he must not go without her to the two Kings of *England* and *France*. She absolutely refuses to go with him; says, her Sorrow shall keep its State, and the Kings may come to it. Her concluding Lines are these;

Division *of an* Act *mistaken.*

> --------- *For my Grief's so great,*
> *That no Supporter, but the huge firm Earth,*
> *Can hold it up. Here -- I and Sorrow sit;*
> *Here -- is my Throne; bid Kings come bow to it.*

It is evident, I think, beyond Contradiction, that *Constantia* here, in her Despair, seats her self upon the Floor of the Stage: And can she be supposed immediately to *rise* again, only to *go off* and *end* the Act decently? And if she does not, how can the Act end here? There is but one other Method for it; and that is, of the foremost *flat-scene* shutting her in from the Sight of the Audience, an Absurdity never once practised by SHAKESPEARE. In the very next Scene which follows, and stands as the *first* Scene of the *Third* Act, the Kings are introduc'd, and *Constantia* is likewise upon the Stage, and speaks within eight Lines of the Scene's beginning. We must therefore either suppose an *Unity* of the *two* Scenes, and that They come in to her so soon as she sits down on the Floor; or rather, (which I think has been an Opinion of long Standing,) that an *intermediate* Scene or two have been lost, whereby we cannot now be certain how the Act ended; and that an *Hiatus in Manuscripto* ought to be mark'd to signify the Imperfection.

XL. The faulty Passages which I have hitherto alledged, I think, are mostly such, as called for the Assistance of *Judgment* to set them right: There are other Places again, which are corrupted in our Author, that are to be cur'd by a strict Attention to the Author himself, and by taking *History* along with us, wherever his Subject is *historical*. Diligence in this Respect is certainly the Duty of an Editor: And yet that a due Care, even in this Part, has been hitherto wanting, the Instances I am now going to subjoin will manifestly prove.

Faults of Inadvertence.

MIDSUMMER NIGHT'S DREAM, Page 95.

> *Did'st Thou not lead him thro' the glimm'ring Night*
> *From* PEREGENIA, *whom he ravished?*

Mr. POPE confesses in his *Preface*, * that *No one is more a Master of the* Poetical *Story, or has more frequent* Allusions *to the various Parts of it than* SHAKESPEARE. It must be own'd; and the Passage before us is a signal Instance. He touches upon a minute Circumstance in the Story of *Theseus*; but, indeed, None of the old Classicks tell us of such a Person as *Peregenia*, with whom that Hero had an Affair: Restore therefore the Place, from the Authority of the *Greek* Writers.

* *Page* 10.

> *Did'st thou not lead him thro' the glimm'ring Night*
> *From* PERIGUNE, *whom he ravished?*

Here

Here we have the Name of a famous Lady, by whom *Theseus* had his Son *Melanippus*. She was the Daughter of *Sinnis*, the cruel Robber, and Tormentor of Passengers in the *Isthmus*; and PLUTARCH and ATHENÆUS are Both express in the Circumstance of *Theseus*'s ravishing her, which is so exactly copied by our Poet. The former of Them adds, (as *Diodorus Siculus*, *Apollodorus*, and *Pausanias*, likewise tell us,) that he kill'd her Father into the Bargain.

The Like. XLI. K. JOHN, Page 139.

> *For* ANGIERS, *and fair* Touraine, Maine, Poictiers,
> *And all that We upon this Side the Sea,*
> Except this City *now by us* besieg'd,
> *Find liable*, &c.

Here we have an Instance of the like Carelesness in a Point of *English* History. King *John* consenting to match the Lady *Blanch* with the *Dauphin*, agrees, in Part of her Dowry, to give up all he held in *France*, except the City of *Angiers*, which he now besieg'd, and laid Claim to. How can it be thought then, that he should at one and the same Time give up all except *Angiers*, and give up *That* too? The Error is transmitted from the old Copies, and must be corrected thus;

> *For* ANJOU, *and fair* Touraine, &c.

This was one of the Provinces, as Mr. *Pope* might have remember'd, which the *English* held in *France*, and which the *French* King by *Chatilion* claim'd of K. *John* in Right of Duke *Arthur*, at the very opening of the Play, *Page* 116.

> ------ *Poictiers*, ANJOU, *Touraine*, *Maine*.

Occasional Emendations. But *Angiers*, instead of *Anjou*, has been printed in more Places than That already quoted; and some other Errors been transmitted down to boot. See *Page* 129.

> Aust. *King* LEWIS, *determine what we shall do streight.*
> LEWIS. *Women and Fools, break off your Conference.*
> *King* John, *this is the very Sum of All:*
> England *and* Ireland, ANGIERS, Touraine, Maine,
> *In right of* Arthur *do I claim of thee:*
> *Wilt Thou resign them, and lay down thy Arms?*
> K. John. *My Life, as soon. I do defy thee*, FRANCE.

Here again, instead of *Angiers*, we must restore ANJOU. But who is it makes this Claim upon the *English* King? 'Tis plain, both from the Verse quoted of the Duke of *Austria*'s Speech, and from the other of K. *John*'s, that the King of *France* was the Demandant. But the King of *France*'s Name was not *Lewis*. In both Lines therefore where *Lewis* is printed, it must be restor'd PHILIP.

The Like. XLII. Will. *Under what Captain serve you?*

> K. Hen. *Under Sir* JOHN Erpingham.
> Will. *A good old Commander*, &c.

Here again History and our Poet's Text are made to disagree; nor was there any such Gentleman as Sir *John Erpingham* in Being in K. *Henry* Vth's Reign: Restore it, as it ought to be;

> Will. *Under what Captain serve you?*
> K. Hen. *Under Sir* THOMAS Erpingham, &c.

This

This is one of the Characters introduc'd in the Play; and he entring but three Pages before, the King salutes him thus;

> *Good Morrow, old Sir* THOMAS Erpingham:
> *A good soft Pillow for that good white Head*
> *Were better than a churlish Turf of* France.

That this was his Name, we have the Authority of our Chronicles; and They, and our Poet from them, in his *Richard* II. Page 121, tell us, that Sir *Thomas Erpingham* was One of those who embark'd from *Bretagne* to espouse the Interest of *Bolingbroke* the Father of K. *Henry* V.

XLIII. *Ibid.* Page 475. *The Like.*

Alarum. *Enter K.* Henry *and* BOURBON *with Prisoners, Lords,* &c.

This is likewise an Error transmitted from the Old to the Modern Editions; *Bourbon* was one of the *French* Party, and therefore could not make a Part of K. *Henry's* Train. Restore it;

Alarm. *Enter K.* Henry, *ana* GLOUCESTER, *with Prisoners,* &c.

But may it not be said, that *Bourbon* is brought in here amongst the *French* Prisoners? To This, I reply, that our Poet would hardly have introduc'd a Character of that Dignity, crowded him amongst the common Prisoners, and neither made him speak to the King, nor the King to him. Besides, I have another Exception yet stronger to add, why *Bourbon* cannot be supposed to enter here: In a few Pages after, (*viz.* Page 481.) the King asks the Duke of *Exeter* (who enter'd with him, and had been all along in the Presence) what Prisoners of Rank were taken, and *Exeter* replies;

> Charles *Duke of* Orleans, *Nephew to the King*;
> John *Duke of* BOURBON, *and Lord* Bouchiquald.

I submit it therefore to the most common Judgments, whether 'tis probable, if *Bourbon* was among the Prisoners introduc'd in the King's Train, that the Duke of *Exeter* could have been guilty of such an Absurdity, to tell the King that *Bourbon* was taken Prisoner.

XLIV. *First Part of* K. HENRY VI. Page 17. *The Like.*

Winch. *How now, ambitious* UMPIRE, *what means This?*

These Words are spoken by the Bishop of *Winchester* to the Duke of *Gloucester*, who is forcing his Way into the Tower to survey it. But why, *Umpire*? or, of what? *Gloucester* was *Protector* of the Realm in the King's Minority; but not an *Umpire* in any particular Matter that We know of. I am persuaded the Duke's Christian Name lurks under this Corruption, and the very Traces of the Letters convince me that our Poet wrote, as it ought certainly to be restor'd.

Winch. *How now, ambitious* HUMPHREY, *what means This?*

XLV. *Second Part of* K. HENRY VI. Page 127. *The Like.*

> Sim. *God knows of pure Devotion, being call'd*
> *A hundred Times, and oftner, in my Sleep,*
> *By good St.* Alban; *who said,* SIMON, *come,*
> *Come, offer at my Shrine, and I will help thee.*

The Editions here again are at Odds with the Hiſtory. Why, *Simon*? The Chronicles, that take Notice of the Duke of *Glouceſter*'s detecting this pretended Miracle, tell us, that the Impoſtor, who aſſerted Himſelf to be cur'd of Blindneſs, was call'd *Saunder Simpcox.* --- *Simon* is therefore a Corruption, thro' the Negligence of the Copyiſts; and we muſt reſtore it,

------- *Who ſaid*, SIMPCOX, *come*,
Come, offer at my Shrine, and I will help thee.

But we have no need of going back to *Chronicles* to ſettle this Point, ſince our *Poet*, in the very next Page, gives us the Fellow's Names, which correſpond with the Hiſtory.

Glouc. *What's thine own Name?*
Simp. Saunder Simpcox, *an' if it pleaſe you, Maſter.*
Glouc. Saunder, *ſit there*, &c.

The Like. XLVI. *Ibid.* Page 132.

The Fifth was EDWARD Langley, *Duke of* York.

Having an Eye to Hiſtory, as I hinted before, would eaſily have diſcover'd an Error in the Copies here, and that the Paſſage ought to be reſtor'd;

The Fifth was EDMOND Langley, *Duke of* York.

The Poet is here enumerating the Iſſue Male of K. *Edward* III. and the whole Tenour of Hiſtory is expreſs, that his fifth Son was *Edmond* of *Langley*, and created Duke of *York*.

The Like. XLVII. *Ibid.* Page 155.

Marg. *God forbid, any Malice ſhould prevail,*
That faultleſs may condemn a Nobleman:
'Pray God, he may acquit him of Suſpicion.
K. Hen. *I thank thee*, NELL, *theſe Words content me much.*

I remember, our Poet, in his King JOHN, makes *Falconbridge* the Baſtard, upon his firſt ſtepping into Honour, ſay, that he will ſtudy to forget his old Acquaintance;

And if his Name be George, *I'll call him* Peter;
For new-made Honour doth forget Mens Names.

But, ſurely, this is wide of K. HENRY's Caſe, and it can be no Reaſon why he ſhould forget his own Wife's Name, and call her *Nell* inſtead of *Margaret*. Perhaps, it may be alledg'd, that the Blunder was Original in the Poet; that his Head was full of another Character, which he introduces in this Play, *Eleanor* Dutcheſs of *Glouceſter*, whom her Husband frequently calls *Nell:* and thence thro' Inadvertence he might ſlip into this Miſtake. Were this to be allow'd the Caſe, is not the Miſtake therefore to be rectified? As the Change of a ſingle Letter ſets all right, there's very little Reaſon to accuſe our Poet of ſuch an Inadvertence: I am much more willing to ſuppoſe it came from his Pen thus;

K. Hen. *I thank thee.* -- WELL; *theſe Words content me much.*

K. *Henry* was a Prince of great Piety and Meekneſs, a great Lover of his Uncle *Glouceſter*, whom his Nobles were rigidly perſecuting, and to whom he ſuſpected the Queen bore no very good Will in her Heart: But finding her, beyond his Hopes, ſpeak ſo candidly in the Duke's Caſe, he is mightily comforted, and contented at her impartial Seeming. I believe, Every body in their Converſation muſt have obſerv'd, that the Word, *Well*, -- is uſed to expreſs an Air of Satisfaction, when any Incident in Life goes to our Wiſh; or any Purpoſe, that was dreaded, happens to be diſappointed.

XLVIII.

XLVIII. K. Richard III. Page 432. *The Like.*

And who doth lead them but a paltry Fellow,
Long kept in Britaine *at* OUR *Mother's Cost?*

This is ſpoken by *Richard* III. of *Henry* Earl of *Richmond*; but They were far from having any *common* Mother, but *England*; and the Earl of *Richmond* was not ſubſiſted abroad at the Nation's publick Charge. He fled with the Earl of *Pembroke* into *Bretagny* in K. *Edward* IVth's Reign: And many Artifices were tried both by That King firſt, and K. *Richard* afterwards, to get him deliver'd up by the *French* King, and Duke of *Bretagny*: But he happily eſcap'd all the Snares laid for him. But during the greateſt Part of his Reſidence abroad, he was watch'd and reſtrain'd almoſt like a Captive, and ſubſiſted by Supplies convey'd from the Counteſs Dowager of *Richmond*, his Mother: Reſtore therefore the Poet thus;

And who doth lead them but a paltry Fellow,
Long kept in Bretagne *at* HIS *Mother's Coſt?*

XLIX. K. Henry VIII. Page 448. *The Like.*

-------- *Here is a Warrant from*
The King t'attach Lord Montague, *and the Bodies*
Of the Duke's Confeſſor, John de la Car,
ONE Gilbert Peck, *his* COUNSELLOR.

Beſides a ſlight Corruption in the Beginning of the laſt Line, which makes the Connection faulty, this Paſſage labours with another Error, which the Editor might have amended either from having an Eye to the real Hiſtory, or to the Words of the Poet afterwards: Correct the Whole thus;

-------- *Here is a Warrant from*
The King t'attach Lord Montague, *and the Bodies*
Of the Duke's Confeſſor, John de la Car,
AND Gilbert Peck, *his* CHANCELLOR.

Sir *Gilbert Peck*, (or *Perk*, as it is in ſome Copies,) the Chronicles tell us, was *Chancellor* to the Duke of *Buckingham*; and ſo we afterwards find him ſtyled by our Author in the Play before us, Page 466.

At which appear'd againſt him his Surveyor,
Sir Gilbert Peck *his* CHANCELLOR, *and* John Car,
Confeſſor to him, with that Devil-Monk
Hopkins, *that made this Miſchief.*

The Mention of this Monk naturally calls upon me to correct a Paſſage or two, in which all the Copies have hitherto been faulty, with Regard to his Name. See Page 449. *Occaſional* Emendation.

Buck. ---------- *So, ſo,*
Theſe are the Limbs o'th' Plot: No more, I hope.
Brand. *A Monk o'th'* Chartreux.
Buck. ------------ MICHAEL Hopkins?
Brand. *He.*

Here again, from the Concurrence of our Historians, we are warranted to correct the Poet;

Bran. *A Monk o'th'* Chartreux. ---
Buck. ------ NICHOLAS Hopkins?

But what shall we then do with another Passage, where the Duke's Surveyor is under his Examination before the King and Council?

P. 455. Surv. --------- *He was brought to This*
By a vain Prophesie of Nicholas HENTON.
King. *What was that* HENTON?
Surv. ----- *Sir, a* Chartreux *Fryar*, &c.

2d *Occasional* Emendation. 'Tis evident, *Brandon* and the Surveyor are in two Stories, as the Poet's Text now stands; but, I am persuaded, it is corrupt: For in Fact there was but One Monk concern'd with, or Evidence against the Duke; and his Name was *Nicholas Hopkins*. Our Poet therefore must be restor'd;

By a vain Prophecy of Nicholas HOPKINS.
King. *Who was That* HOPKINS?

But how came *Henton* to find a Place at all in the Text? It will be no great Difficulty to account for This, when we come to consider, that *Hopkins* was a Monk of the Convent call'd *Henton* near *Bristol*; and might, according to the Custom of those Times, be call'd as well *Nicholas* of *Henton* by Some of the Historians from the Place, as *Hopkins*, by Others, from his Family. And This, as I take it, is sufficient Ground for the Mistake from the Hands of a negligent Transcriber.

The Like. L. I shall add but one more *Error* at present (but It shall be a signal One) transmitted by the EDITOR thro' *Indiligence*, and a Want of *due Application* to the Meaning of the Author and the Sense of the Passage.

MUCH ADO ABOUT NOTHING, Page 503.

Borach. *Go then find me a meet Hour to draw on* Pedro, *and the Count* Claudio, *alone; tell them that you know* Hero *loves* ME; ------ *Offer them Instances which shall bear no less Likelyhood than to see* Me *at her Chamber Window, hear me call* Margaret, Hero; *hear* Margaret *term me* CLAUDIO; *and bring them to see this the very Night before the intended Wedding.*

I am obliged to give here a short Account of the *Plot* depending, that the *Emendation*, which I am about to make, may appear the more clear and unquestionable. The Business stands thus: *Claudio*, a Favourite of the *Arragon* Prince, is, by his Intercessions with her Father, to be married to the fair *Hero*; *Don John*, a natural Brother of the Prince, and a Hater of *Claudio*, is in his Spleen zealous to disappoint the Match. *Borachio*, a rascally Dependant on *Don John*, offers his Assistance, and engages to break off the Marriage by this Stratagem. " Tell the Prince and *Claudio* (*says He*) that *Hero* is in Love with *Me*, they won't believe " it; offer them Proofs, as that they shall see me converse with her in her Chamber Win- " dow: I am in the good Graces of her Waiting-Woman *Margaret*; and I'll prevail with " *Margaret*, at a dead Hour of Night, to personate her Mistress *Hero*; do you then bring " the Prince and *Claudio* to over-hear our Discourse, and they shall have the Torment to " hear *me* address *Margaret* by the Name of *Hero*, and her say sweet Things to me by the " Name of *Claudio*." ---- This is the Substance of *Borachio*'s Device to make *Hero* suspected of Disloyalty, and to break off her Match with *Claudio*. But, in the Name of Goodness, could it displease *Claudio* to hear his Mistress making Use of *his* Name tenderly? If he saw another Man with her, and heard her call him *Claudio*, he might reasonably think her betray'd, but not have the same Reason to accuse her of Disloyalty. Besides, how could her naming *Claudio*, make the Prince and *Claudio* believe that she lov'd *Borachio*, as He desires *Don John* to insinuate to them that She did. The Circumstances consider'd, I have no Doubt but the Passage ought to be corrected thus;

Borach.

Borach. *Go then, find me a meet Hour to draw on* Pedro, *and the Count* Claudio, *alone; tell them that you know* Hero *loves* ME; ------ *Offer them Instances which shall bear no less Likelihood than to see* Me *at her Chamber-Window; hear* Me *call* Margaret, Hero; *hear* Margaret *term me* BORACHIO; *and bring them to see this the very Night before the intended Wedding.*

LI. But it is high Time now that I turn my Pen to one promised Part of my Task, which is yet in Arrears, *viz.* an Endeavour to restore Sense to Passages, in which, thro' the Corruption of successive Editions, no Sense has hitherto been found: Or to restore, to the best of my Power, the Poet's true Text, where I suspect it to be mistaken thro' the Error of the *Press* or the *Manuscripts.* The utmost Liberty that I shall take in this Attempt, shall generally confine it self to the minute Alteration of a *single* Letter or *two:* An Indulgence which, I hope, I cannot fear being granted me, if It retrieves Sense to such Places as have either escaped Observation, or never been disputed or understood by their Editors. I'll dispatch this remaining Part of my *Appendix* with all the Brevity that the Nature of the EMENDATIONS will admit; as *Such,* they are humbly propos'd: But wherever better Judges are pleased to think *that* Word too peremptory, I am very well content to soften it into CONJECTURES. EMENDATIONS

As the MERCHANT of VENICE happens to furnish three or four remarkable Ones, they shall stand the foremost in this List.

MERCHANT of VENICE, Page 12.

Ner. *First, there is the* Neapolitan *Prince.*

Port. *Ay, that's a* COLT *indeed, for he doth Nothing but talk of his horse, and he makes it a great Appropriation to his own good Parts that he can* shoo *him himself: I am much afraid my Lady his Mother play'd false with a Smith.*

Portia here discoursing with her Waiting-Woman about her Suitors, *Nerissa* runs over the Catalogue of them, with Design to sound the Affections of her Lady. But how does talking of Horses, or knowing how to shoe them, make a Man e'er the more a *Colt*? Or why, if a *Smith* and a *Lady* of *Figure* were to have an Affair together, should a *Colt* be the Issue of that Conjunction? I make no Doubt but this is simply *Portia*'s Meaning: *What do you tell me of the* Neapolitan *Prince? he is such a stupid Dunce, that instead of saying fine Things to me, he does Nothing but talk of his Horses.* ----- Now; This is some Reason for suspecting that his Mother should have play'd false with a *Smith:* People generally talk most in their own Professions, or in Those of their Family; and Farriers, I presume, will be allowed to talk more of Horsemanship than any other Subject. I do not question therefore to restore it;

Port. *Ay, That's a* DOLT *indeed; for he doth Nothing but talk of his Horse, and he makes it a great Appropriation to his own good Parts, that he can* shoe *him himself,* &c.

A *Dolt* is properly one of the most stupid and blockish of the Vulgar; and in this Signification it is used by our Author himself. See his *Anthony* and *Cleopatra,* Page 398.

Follow his Chariot, like the greatest Spot
Of all thy Sex; most monster-like, be shewn
For poor'st Diminutives, for DOLTS ---

i. e. become the Gaze of the most vile *Plebeians,* the most sordid ignorant Rabble.

And so, again, in OTHELLO, Page 583.

-------- *Oh, Gull! Oh,* DOLT!
As ignorant as Dirt;

LII. *Ibid.* Page 24.

VVhat a Beard hast thou got! Thou hast got more Hair on thy Chin, than Dobbin *my* PHIL-*horse has on his Taile.* EMENDATION.

I

I should have pass'd this over as a Literal Error, occasion'd by the Oversight of the Editor, but that I find it is copied from the old Editions: And yet even there originally it is but a literal Error. It must be restor'd;

> ------ *Thou hast got more Hair on thy Chin, than* Dobbin *my* THILL-*horse has on his Tail.*

A *Thill*, as it is very well known, is the Beam or Draught-Tree of a Cart or Waggon; and the *Thill*-Horse, consequently, is that Horse which is put under the *Thill*. SKINNER, indeed, mentions the **Fill**-Horse, *i. e.* the last Horse in the **File**; but he confesses it, a Term, which he derived from the Informationof a learned Clergyman.

EMENDATION. LIII. *Ibid.* Page 21. *Morochius*, a black Prince, among the rest of *Portia*'s Suitors, putting in his Pretensions, and preparing to decide his Fate by the Choice of the Casket, reflects upon the Conditions to which he is subjected: That he, who had slain a *Sophy* with his Scimitar, won three Battles of a *Sultan*, who could outstare and outbrave the sternest and most daring Creatures upon Earth, pluck the Cubs from a She-Bear, and mock the roaring of a hungry Lion, might be baffled and worsted in this Adventure by the Caprice of blind Fortune.

> ------- *But, alas the while!*
> *If* Hercules *and* LYCHAS *play at dice*
> *Which is the better man, the greater throw*
> *May turn by fortune from the weaker hand:*
> *So is* Alcides *beaten by his* RAGE,
> *And so may I, blind fortune leading me,*
> *Miss that which one unworthier may attain,*
> *And die with grieving.*

Tho' the whole Set of Editions concur in this Reading, and it has pass'd wholly unsuspected by the Learned Editor, I am very well assur'd, and I dare say the Readers will be so too anon, that it is corrupt at Bottom. Let us look into the Poet's Sentiment, and the History of the Persons represented. If *Hercules* (says he) and *Lichas* (for so is his Name to be spelt, if we may take *Sophocles*, *Ovid*, &c. for our Guides) were to play at Dice for the Decision of their Superiority; *Lichas*, the weaker Man, might have the better Cast of the Two. But how then is *Alcides* beaten by his Rage? To admit This, we must suppose a Gap in the Poet; and that some Lines are lost in which *Hercules*, in his Passion for losing the Hand, had thrown the Box and Dice away, and knock'd his own Head against the Wall for meer Madness. Thus, indeed, might he be said, in some Sense, to be beaten by his *Rage*. But SHAKESPEARE had no such Stuff in his Head. He means no more than, if *Lichas* had the better Throw, so might *Hercules* himself be beaten by *Lichas*. In short, *Lichas* was the poor unfortunate Servant of *Hercules*, who, unknowingly brought his Master the envenom'd Shirt, dipp'd in the Blood of the Centaur *Nessus*, and was thrown headlong into the Sea for his Pains. The Poet has alluded to some Parts of this Fable in another of his Plays; and there indeed a reasonable Intimation is made of *Hercules* worsting himself thro' his own Rage. See *Anthony* and *Cleopatra*, Page 398.

> Anth. --------------- Eros, *hoa,*
> *The Shirt of* Nessus *is upon Me*; -- *teach me,*
> Alcides, *thou mine Ancestor, thy* Rage:
> *Let me lodge* Lichas *on the Horns o'th' Moon,*
> *And, with those hands that grasp'd the heaviest Club,*
> *Subdue my worthiest Self.*

But to return to the Place before Us: Can we desire more than to know this one Circumstance of *Lichas*'s Quality to set us right in the Poet's Meaning, and put an End to all the present Absurdity of the Passage? Restore it, without the least Scruple, only with cutting off the Tail of a single Letter;

--- *But*

> ---------- *But, alas, the while!*
> *Should* Hercules *and* Lichas *play at Dice*
> *Which is the better Man, the greater Throw*
> *May turn by Fortune from the weaker Hand:*
> *So is* Alcides *beaten by his* PAGE;
> *And so may I, blind Fortune leading me,*
> *Miss That which an* Unworthier *may attain,*
> *And die with grieving.*

It is scarce requisite to hint here, it is a Point so well known, that *Page* has been always used in *English* to signify any Boy-Servant; as well as what latter Times have appropriated the Word to, a Lady's *Train-Bearer*. And so *Falstaffe*'s Boy, in our Poet, is frequently called *his Page*. So much in Explanation of this new-adopted Reading. The very excellent Lord LANSDOWNE, in his Alteration of this Play, tho' he might not stand to make the Correction upon the Poet, seems at least to have understood the Passage exactly as I do: And tho' he changes the Verse, retains the Sense of it in this Manner;

> *So were a* Giant *worsted by a* Dwarf!

Tho' I had made the *Emendation*, before I thought to look into his *Lordship*'s Performance, it is no small Satisfaction to me, that I have the Authority of such a *Genius* to back my Conjecture.

LIV. *Ibid.* Page 71. EMENDATION.

> Port. *Is he not able to discharge the money?*
> Bass. *Yes, here I tender it for him in the Court,*
> *Yea, twice the Sum; if that will not suffice,*
> *I will be bound to pay it ten times o'er,*
> *On forfeit of my hands, my head, my heart.*
> *If this will not suffice, it must appear*
> *That malice bears down* TRUTH. ----

This is a Passage which has ever pass'd unsuspected, and yet, I dare say, does not yield us the Poet's Text. The Case is this; *Shylock*, a Jew, lends *Anthonio*, a *Venetian* Merchant, 3000 Ducats on Bond, with Condition, that if he did not pay them at a Day certain, the Jew might claim the Forfeiture of a Pound of *Anthonio*'s Flesh to be cut from the Parts nearest to his Heart. The Bond becomes forfeited; and the Jew rigidly insists upon the specifick Penalty, and will accept no Sum whatever to remit that. But how does *Malice* bear down *Truth* in this Process? Or what one Circumstance is there in the Cause, whereby *Truth* or *Falshood* can come into the Question? I cannot suppose that by *Truth* the Poet means *Justice*, and the Equity of the Thing; if That had been his Thought, there is a Monosyllable so much more proper and intelligible at hand to answer that Sense, that he would unquestionably have said *That* Malice *bears down* Right. ---- But I am persuaded that SHAKESPEARE intended *Bassanio* should intimate, if the Jew would come to no Terms, nor take his Debt though tender'd with such large Advantage, it was plain, he was so blood-thirsty that his Malice had got the better of his Passion of Interest, and extinguish'd all Sentiments of *Remorse*, *Tenderness*, and *human Charity*. The Stress of the Affair lies betwixt the Jew's Malice, and the Intercessions of the Court to him to be merciful. This is the Tenour of the whole Scene; and consonant to this Meaning, the *Duke* addresses himself to *Shylock*, so soon as he appears at the Bar, in these Words; Page 64.

Shylock,

Shylock, *the World thinks, and I think so too,*
That thou but lead'st this Fashion of thy Malice
To the last Hour of Act, and then 'tis thought
Thou'lt shew thy Mercy *and* Remorse *more strange*
Than is thy strange apparent Cruelty.

The *Duke*'s Speech is directly a Persuasive to *Compassion*, and this Topick is so often reinforced in several Passages of the Scene, that I make not the least Question but our Poet made his *Bassanio* say, the Jew not complying to accept such an extravagant Return for his Debt,

If This will not suffice, it must appear
That Malice *bears down* RUTH. --

i. e. Mercy, and *Compassion*. So this Word is explain'd by the *Etymologists*; and so it is used both by CHAUCER and SPENSER, SHAKESPEARE's two Great Originals in Language. I could quote Instances almost without Number, where our Poet uses *ruthful* and *ruthless*: Nor was the Substantive it self so obsolete, or uncommon, but that he has frequently chose to employ it.

K. RICHARD II. Page 154.

Here did She drop a Tear, here in this Place
I'll set a Bank of Rue, *sow'r Herb of Grace:*
Rue, *ev'n for* RUTH, *here shortly shall be seen,*
In the Remembrance of a weeping Queen.

So TROILUS and CRESSIDA, Page 109.

Let's leave the hermit Pity *with our Mothers;*
And when we have our Armours buckled on,
The venom'd Vengeance ride upon our Swords,
Spur them to rueful *Work, rein them from* RUTH.

And so, CORIOLANUS, Page 97.

Would the Nobility lay aside their RUTH,
And let me use my Sword, &c.

EMENDATION. LV. *Ibid.* Page 68.

Bass. *Why dost thou whet thy knife so earnestly?*
Shyl. *To cut the forfeit from that bankrupt there.*
Grat. *Not on thy* SOUL! *but on thy* SOUL, *harsh Jew,*
Thou mak'st thy knife keen; ---

I don't know what Ideas the *Editor* had affix'd to himself of the Poet's Sense here; for my own Part I can find None, as the Text stands now. I dare venture to restore Him, from the Authority of some of the *Folio* Editions; tho' I am obliged at the same Time to restore such a Sort of Conceit, and Jingle upon two Words, alike in Sound but differing in Sense, as our Author ought to have blush'd for. But be That upon his own Head. If I restore his Meaning, and his Words, he himself is accountable to the Judges for writing them.

Bass.

Baff. *Why doſt thou whet thy Knife ſo earneſtly?*
Shyl. *To cut the Forfeit from That Bankrupt there.*
Grat. *Not on thy* SOLE, *but on thy* SOUL, *harſh Jew,*
Thou mak'ſt thy Knife keen; ---

i. e. Tho' thou thinkeſt that thou art whetting thy Knife on the *Sole* of thy Shoe, yet it is upon thy *Soul*, thy immortal Part, that Thou doeſt it, miſtaken, inexorable Man! The bare Intention of thy Cruelty is ſo unpardonable, that it muſt bring thy very *Soul* into Hazard.

I dare affirm, This is the very *Antitheſis* of our Author; and I am the more confident, becauſe it was ſo uſual with him to play on Words in this manner; and becauſe in another of his Plays he puts the very ſame Words in Oppoſition to one another, and That from the Mouth of one of his ſerious Characters. See ROMEO and JULIET, Page 259, 60.

Merc. *Nay, gentle* Romeo, *we muſt have you dance.*
Rom. *Not I, believe me*; *You have dancing Shoes*
With nimble SOLES, *I have a* SOUL *of Lead,*
That ſtakes me to the Ground, I cannot move.

He is at it again within three Lines after, upon two other Words agreeing in Sound; as we find the Paſſage in the ſecond *Folio*, and ſeveral other Editions, tho' Mr. POPE has not inſerted it.

I am too SORE *enpierced with his Shaft,*
To SOARE *with his light Feathers.* ---

But, as I ſaid, theſe Jingles are perpetual with Him.

LVI. LOVE's LABOUR LOST, Page 133. EMENDATION.

Long. *I fear, theſe ſtubborn lines lack pow'r to move*;
O ſweet Maria, *Empreſs of my love!*
Theſe Numbers will I tear, and write in Proſe.
Bir. *Oh, Rhimes are guards on wanton* Cupid's *hoſe:*
Disfigure not his SHOP. --

This is one of thoſe Paſſages, which, I am very willing to ſuppoſe, never paſs'd Mr. POPE's Reviſal. What Agreement in Senſe is there betwixt CUPID's *Hoſe* and his *Shop*? Or, what Relation can thoſe two Terms have to one Another? Or, what is *Cupid's Shop*? All the Editions happen to concur in the Error; but That ought not to hinder us from correcting it;

Oh! Rhymes are Guards on wanton Cupid's *Hoſe*;
Disfigure not his SLOP. -

Slops are, as SKINNER and others rightly inform us, large and wide-kneed Breeches, now only worn by *Ruſticks* and *Sea-faring* Men: And we have at this Day Dealers, whoſe ſole Buſineſs it is to furniſh the Sailors with Shirts, Jackets *&c.* who are call'd *Slop-Men*; and their Shops, *Slop-Shops:* SHAKESPEARE knew the Term, and has made Uſe of it in more than one Place;

Second Part of K. HENRY IV. Page 299.

What ſaid Mr. Dombledon *about the Sattin for my ſhort Cloak and* SLOPS?

So in ROMEO and JULIET, Page 280.

Signior Romeo, bon jour; --- *there's a* French *Salutation to your* French SLOP.

'Tis true, Mr. POPE has printed it here --- *your* French STOP. But it must be corrected as I have restored it from the second *Folio* Edition, and the other better Copies, or We come at no Sense. Those wide-kneed Breeches were the Garb in fashion in our *Author*'s Days, (as we may observe from old Family-Pictures,) as well off, as upon the Stage: And that they were the Mode in *France* too, is plainly hinted in another of our *Author*'s Plays. See K. HENRY V. Page 448.

Dauph. *Oh, then belike she was old and gentle, and you rode like a* Kerne *of* Ireland, *your* French HOSE *off, and in your* streight Strossers.

Hose and *Slops* were synonymous Terms, and used to signify the self-same Accoutrement. I'll throw in one Instance more of our Author's being acquainted with the Word *Slops*, because the Passage is not to be found in the common Editions; but I'll restore it from an old One in *Quarto*, (publish'd for *Andrew Wise* and *William Aspley*, in 1600) an Edition which Mr. POPE never saw, or at least never *collated*.

MUCH ADO ABOUT NOTHING, Page 516.

There is no Appearance of Fancy in him, unless it be a Fancy that he hath to strange Disguises, as to be a Dutchman *to day, a* Frenchman *to morrow*; or in the shape of two Countries at once, as a *German* from the Waste downward, all SLOPS; and a *Spaniard* from the Hip upward, no Doublet, *&c.*

EMENDATION. LVII. MERRY WIVES of WINDSOR, Page 244.

Fals. *Sometimes the Beam of her Eye* GUIDED *my Foot, sometimes my portly Belly.*

Falstaffe is here talking how Mrs. *Page* look'd upon him, and survey'd him all over, and examin'd his Parts with very good Liking. But how did her Eye *guide* his Foot? *&c.* Certainly, this can never mean, *guided itself towards* his Foot. *Falstaffe* seems to me here to speak as a Man in Love, with much Complaisance; and as comparing his Mistress's Eye to the Sun for Brightness, and for a Power of brightening the Object which it darted on: I therefore question not but it should be corrected thus;

Sometimes the Beam of her Eye GUILDED *my Foot, sometimes my portly Belly.*

It is a poetical Expression to say that her Eye, like the Sun, *gilded* (or, *guilded*, as of old they wrote it) what Part it shone upon; and I am the rather persuaded that my Correction is right, from the immediate Reply of *Pistol*, which keeps up the *Metaphor*;

Then did the SUN *on Dunghill* shine.

EMENDATION. LVIII. *Ibid.* Page 311.

Mrs. Ford. *Mrs.* Page *is come with me, Sweet-heart.*
Fals. *Divide me like a* BRIB'D buck, *each a haunch.*

I must confess, I don't understand the Meaning of a *brib'd Buck*: If I conceive the Author's Sense at all, it ought to be restor'd;

Divide

Divide me like a BRIBE-Buck, *each a Haunch.*

i. e. as a Buck sent for a Bribe betwixt You. So it becomes a Term of Art, and a very proper One; and it brings to my Mind what is recorded in Print concerning my Lord *Chief Justice* HALE; that when he went the Circuit, if any Gentleman, who had a Cause to come before him, sent him Venison, he constantly refused it, saying, -- It is a BRIBE-Buck, and I'll have None of it.

LIX. K. LEAR, Page 9. EMENDATION.

Cordel. -------- *Peace be with* Burgundy,
Since that Respect AND Fortunes *are his Love,*
I shall not be his Wife.

The Duke of *Burgundy* had made his Addresses to *Cordelia*, and was to have her to Wife with a Third Part of her Father's Kingdom in Dowry; but her Father falling out with, and disinheriting her, asks *Burgundy* if he will take her in that Condition, and dowerless: *Burgundy* excusing himself, and that he cannot take her without the propos'd Portion, *Cordelia* thus replies to his Refusal. But what does the Poet mean by *Respect and Fortunes*? What Respect? If *Lear* would have bestowed the third Part of his Dominions, as he had contracted, that was all the Respect which *Burgundy* would have stood upon with her. I would willingly restore it with my *Quarto* Edition, publish'd in 1655, which I presume never came to the Editor's View.

--------- *Peace be with* Burgundy!
Since that Respects OF Fortune *are his Love,*
I shall not be his Wife.

i. e. since his profest Love and Addresses to Me, were only on Account of the Dowry which he hop'd to have with me.

LX. *Ibid.* Page 10. EMENDATION.

Time shall unfold what PLIGHTED *Cunning hides.*

There is no good Sense in this Epithet, *plighted*, here, and therefore there is Reason to suspect it a Corruption. The Meaning of the Poet certainly is, that Time shall discover what intricate, perplex'd, involv'd Cunning labours to conceal. It must be restor'd therefore either thus;

Time shall unfold what * PLEACHED *Cunning hides.*

* i. e. *twisted, intangled*, &c. See MUCH ADO ABOUT NOTHING, Page 512; ANTONY and CLEOPATRA, Page 402; and HENRY V. Page 489.

Or rather,

Time shall unfold *what* PLAITED *Cunning hides.*

Each of the Terms answer the Idea required in this Place; but I prefer the latter, because it signifies *wrapt in Folds*, and is more directly opposite in Sense to *unfolding*. The Word might possibly, according to the old Spelling, be wrote thus, *plaighted*; and so the Mistake arise by an easy Corruption of it into *plighted.*

LXI. *Ibid.* Page 73. EMENDATION.

--------- *World, world, O world!*
But that thy strange Mutations make us HATE *thee,*
Life would not yield to age.

This, I think, is as remarkable a Passage, as has at all fall'n under my Consideration. It has neither been suspected, nor attempted; tho', 'tis evident, it carries a flat Contradiction to the Sentiment which the Poet would infer. If the *Vicissitudes* in the World make us *hate* the World, is that a Reason why we should submit to *live to be old*? -- I should rather have thought it an Argument for the putting an End to a miserable Life. There is so flagrant a *Paradox* in Sense, as the Text now stands, that, tho' all the Editions unhappily countenance it, I conceive, Mr. POPE might very safely have indulg'd his private Sense here. I communicated my Objections upon this Place (as I have upon many others) to my *late* ingenious Friend Dr. SEWEL, (whom Death has since robbed me of, tho' his Merit will long out-live these poor Sheets:) who gave me this Conjecture upon It.

----------- O World! World! World!
But that thy strange Mutations make us BATE *thee,*
Life would not yield to Age. ---

i. e. if the many Changes in Life did not induce us to *abate from*, and *make* Allowances for, Some of the bad Casualties, we should never endure to live to old Age.

This is excellent good Sense and Reasoning, and certainly comes very near to our Author's Meaning. I have since ventur'd to try my own Strength upon the Passage; and the *Doctor* was so complaisant to think my Conjecture less strain'd, and the more probable One. I suspect, the Poet wrote it thus;

---------- O World! World! World!
But that thy strange Mutations make us WAITE *Thee,*
Life would not yield to Age.

i. e. if the Number of Changes and Vicissitudes, which happen in Life, did not make us waite, and hope for some Turn of Fortune for the better, we could never support the Thought of living to be old, on any other Terms.

EMENDATION. LXII. *First Part of* K. HENRY IV. Page 223.

P. Hen. *Did'st thou never see* Titan *kiss a Dish of* butter? *pitifull-hearted* TITAN, *that melted at the sweet Tale of the* Sun? *if thou did'st, then behold that Compound.*

This absurd Reading possesses all the Copies that have ever fallen in my Way; and tho' it has pass'd thro' such a Number of Impressions, is Nonsense which we may pronounce to have arisen at first, from the Inadvertence and Blunder of the *Compositors* to the *Press*. 'Tis well known, *Titan* is one of the poetical Names of the Sun; but we have no Authority from Fable for *Titan*'s melting away at his own sweet Tale, as *Narcissus* did at the Reflection of his own sweet Form. The Poet's Meaning was certainly this: Sir *John Falstaffe* enters in a great Heat, after having been robb'd by the Prince and *Poines* in Disguise: And the Prince, seeing him in such a Sweat, makes the following Simile upon Him: " Do but " look upon that Compound of Grease; --- his Fat dripps away with the Violence of his " Motion, just as Butter does with the Heat of the Sun-Beams darting full upon it." Correct therefore, as common Sense requires.

P. Hen. *Did'st Thou never see* Titan *kiss a Dish of* Butter? *Pitiful-hearted* BUTTER, *that melted at the sweet Tale of the* Sun? ----- *If Thou did'st, then behold that Compound.*

EMENDATION. LXIII. LOVE'S LABOUR LOST, Page 117.

These are Complements, these are Humours, these betray nice Wenches that would be betray'd without these, and make THEM *men of Note: do you note* Men *that most are affected to these*?

The Speech here is a Description of the odd Altitudes and Affectations which Men in Love assume, and thereby seduce young Girls into that Passion. But do these Affectations make *Wenches* Men of Note too? This is a Transformation, which, I dare say, the Poet never thought

thought of. His Meaning is, as I conceive, that they not only inveigle the young Girls, but make the Men taken Notice of, who affect them. Correct therefore;

> --------- *and make* * THE MEN *Men of Note: Do you note Men, that are most affected to These.*
>
> * Or, the Men of Note.

This is not the only Passage of our Author, where, in the printed Copies, I have observ'd *them* thro' Error to have usurp'd the Place of *Men*.

COMEDY OF ERRORS, Page 432. *Occasional* EMENDATION.

> Ant. *Why is* Time *such a Niggard of Hair, being, as it is, so plentiful an Excrement?*
>
> S. Dro. *Because it is a Blessing that he bestows on Beasts; and what he hath scanted* THEM *in hair, he hath given them in Wit.*
>
> Ant. *Why, but there's many a Man hath more Hair than Wit.*

Sure, this is an evident Paradox, and Contradiction in Sense. Can *Hair* be supposed a Blessing that Time bestows on *Beasts* peculiarly, and yet that he hath *scanted* them of it too? Correct, as the Context plainly requires;

> S. Dro. *Because it is a Blessing that he bestows on* Beasts; *and what he hath scanted* MEN *in* Hair, *he hath given them in* Wit.
>
> Ant. *Why, but there's Many a* Man *hath more* Hair than Wit.

So there is a Passage in *Hamlet*, (tho' I have pass'd it over in my Examination of That Play,) where I have always suspected, on the other hand, that *Men* usurps the Place of *them*.

HAMLET, Page 405. *Occasional* EMENDATION.

> *Oh, there be Players, that I have seen play, and heard Others praise, and that highly, (not to speak it prophanely,) that neither having the Accent of Christian, Pagan, or Man, have so strutted and bellowed, that I have thought Some of Nature's Journeymen had made* MEN, *and not made them well, they imitated Humanity so abominably.*

What? Is *Hamlet* supposed to reason here, that, because he had seen a few very preposterous Players, therefore he should think Nature's Journeymen had made *all Mankind*? for so *Men* in this Place, without *Some* or *those* prefixed, must imply. No, those Players were so far from appearing human Creatures, that he could scarce imagine them the Handy-Work of Nature, but of Some of her clumsy Journeymen. If This be his Sense, might not the Poet more probably have wrote?

> -------------- *that I have thought Some of Nature's Journeymen had made* THEM, *and not made them well, they imitated Humanity so abominably.*

LXIV. *Ibid.* Page 173. EMENDATION.

> *An heavy Heart bears* NOT *an humble Tongue.*

From the whole Tenour of this Speech of the Princess, who is fresh in Sorrow on Account of her Father's Death, and who is making Apologies for any Thing that She may have said too freely to the King, 'tis plain, this Sentiment is the direct Opposite to the Poet's Meaning. Besides, it is true in Nature, that Heaviness of Heart, and any Oppression, always make us humble and submissive. Correct, without Scruple;

> *An heavy Heart bears* BUT *an humble Tongue.*

The Mistake is easy upon these *Monosyllables*, and may be found to have happen'd in several other Passages of our Author. I'll subjoin two or three Instances, in which I believe every Body will agree with Me, that the same Error possesses the printed Copies.

ALL'S

1st *Occasional* EMENDATION. ALL'S WELL THAT ENDS WELL, Page 439.

Men are to * *mell with, Boys are* NOT *to kiss.*

* *mell, from* meler, *to mingle,*

Here's a new Maxim obtruded upon Us, that *Boys are* not *to kiss.* The Poet's Thought, I am persuaded, goes further, *viz.* that Boys are fit only to kiss; Men to mingle with, and give more substantial Pleasures. Correct it;

Men are to mell with, Boys are BUT *to kiss.*

2d *Occasional* EMENDATION COMEDY OF ERRORS, Page 440.

Alas, poor Women, make us NOT *believe*
(Being compact of credit) that you love us;
Tho' others have the Arm, shew us the Sleeve,
We in your Motion turn, and you may move us.

Nothing can be more plain than the Poet's Sense in this Passage. Women, *says He*, are so easy of Faith, that only make them believe you love them, and they'll take the bare Profession for the Substance. Correct it;

Alas, poor Women! make us BUT *believe*, &c.

3d *Occasional* EMENDATION. CYMBELINE, Page 217.

Nay, do NOT wonder *at it; you are made*
Rather to wonder *at the Things you hear,*
Than to work *any.* ---

Surely, this is such a Mock-Reasoning that it cannot be SHAKESPEARE'S, but in its Corruption. What? because he was made *fitter to wonder* at great Actions, than to *perform* any, is he therefore *forbid* to *wonder*? I think it is evident, to Demonstration, that common Sense demands this Reading from the Poet.

Nay, do BUT wonder *at it; You are made*
Rather to wonder, *&c.*

EMENDATION. LXV. Ibid. Page 451.

A Fiend, a FAIRY, *pitiless and rough,*
A Wolf, nay, worse, &c.

Dromio here bringing Word in haste that his Master is arrested, describes the *Bailiff* by Names proper to raise Horror and Detestation of such a Creature, such as, a *Devil*, a *Fiend*, a *Wolf*, &c. But how does *Fairy* come up to these Ideas? Or with what Propriety can it be used here? Does he mean, that a Bailiff is like a *Fairy* in stealing away his Master? The truest Believers of those little Phantoms never pretended to think that they stole any thing but Children. Certainly, it will sort better in Sense with the other Names annexed, as well as with the Character of a Catch-Pole, to conclude that the Poet wrote;

A Fiend, a FURY, *pitiless and rough,*
A Wolf, &c.

EMENDATION. LXVI. MUCH ADO ABOUT NOTHING, Page 480.

He set up his Bills here in Messina, *and challeng'd* Cupid *at the flight; and my Uncle's Fool reading the Challenge, subscrib'd for* Cupid, *and challeng'd him at the* BURBOLT.

Thus

Thus the Copies, from the *Quarto*, publish'd in 1600, downwards, exhibit this Passage. The Editor certainly ought to have given us the *Gloss* of *Burbolt*, if there be any such Word; but I apprehend it to be a Corruption. I take the Author's Meaning to be no more than this; *Benedict* challenged *Cupid* to fly with him, and the Fool made *Cupid* challenge *Benedict* to shoot the Arrow with him. It must therefore be restored,

------ *and challenged Him at the* BIRD-BOLT; [*or*, BUT-BOLT.]

Arrows, being employ'd either to let fly at a *Bird*, or a *Mark*, were by our Author's Predecessors call'd both *Bird-Bolts*, and *But-Shafts*, or *Bolts*; and He himself employs the Words in other Passages of his Plays.

LOVE'S LABOUR LOST, Page 132.

King. *Ay me!*
Biron. *Shot, by Heaven.---Proceed, sweet* Cupid; *Thou hast thumpt him with thy* BIRD-BOLT *under the Left Pap.*

TWELFTH-NIGHT, Page 479.

To be generous, guiltless, and of free Disposition, is to take those Things for BIRD-BOLTS *that you deem Cannon-Bullets.*

ROMEO and JULIET, Page 279.

Alas, poor Romeo, *he is already dead! -- Stabb'd with a white Wench's Black Eye, run thro' the Ear with a Love-Song, the very Pin of his Heart cleft with the blind Bow-Boy's* BUT-SHAFT.

LXVII. Ibid. Page 494. EMENDATION.

Pedro. *My Visor is* Philemon's *Roof; within the House is* LOVE.
Hero. *Why then your Visor should be thatch'd.*

I must own, this Passage has appeared very obscure to me, and given me much Trouble in attempting to understand it. This is a Scene in which the Actors are Masqueraders; and *Pedro*, the Prince of *Arragon*, fixing his Discourse on *Hero*, asks her whether she will walk away with him? Yes, says She, when I like your Figure better; for, God forbid, the Lute should be like the Case: *i. e.* that your Face should be as homely and as coarse as your Masque. Upon This, *Pedro* compares his Visor to *Philemon*'s Roof. 'Tis plain, the Poet alludes to the Story of *Baucis* and *Philemon*, from OVID: And this old Couple, as that *Roman* Poet describes it, liv'd in a *thatch'd* Cottage;

---------- *Stipulis, & cannâ tecta palustri.*

But why, ---- *within the House is* Love? *Baucis* and *Philemon*, 'tis true, had liv'd to Old-Age together, in a comfortable State of Agreement: But Piety and Hospitality are the Top Parts of their Character. Our Poet, if I am not mistaken, goes a little deeper into the Story. Tho' this old Pair liv'd in a Cottage, this Cottage received two straggling * Gods under its Roof. So, *Pedro* is a Prince; and tho' his Visor is but ordinary, He would insinuate to *Hero*, that he has something *godlike* within: Alluding either to his Dignity, or the Qualities of his Person and Mind. By these Circumstances, I am sure, the Thought is mended: And I have no Doubt, but the Poet's Text ought to be so too. Read, therefore, with only cutting off the Tail of a single Letter;

* Jupiter *and* Mercury.

Pedro. *My Visor is* Philemon's *Roof, within the House is* JOVE.

EMENDATION. LXVIII ALL'S WELL THAT ENDS WELL. Page 422.

2d. Lord. ------ *He ſays, he has a Stratagem for't; when your Lordſhip ſees the Bottom of his Succeſs in it, and to what Metal this counterfeit Lump of* OURS *will be melted, if you give him not,* &c.

Why, *counterfeit Lump* of OURS? 'Tis true, *Parolles*, of whom they are ſpeaking, was of the ſame Side in the Wars as They; but yet thoſe Two *Monoſyllables* are of no Uſe, nor add a Grain of Elegance to the Sentence; ſo far from it, They rather clog than are neceſſary. I do not therefore think, they are to be blotted out: But let us ſee whether by a ſlight Change, they may not bear a Conſonancy with the other Terms accompanying them, (*viz. Metal, Lump*, and *melted*;) and help the Propriety of the Poet's Thought. I am perſuaded the Poet wrote, as it ought to be corrected;

----- *and to what Metal this counterfeit Lump of* OARE *will be melted,* &c.

For ſo one *Metaphor* is kept up, and all the Words are proper and ſuitable to it.

EMENDATION. LXIX. The TEMPEST, Page 68.

On the Bat's Back I do fly
After SUMMER *merrily*.

Why, *after* Summer? -- I have always ſuſpected this Word, though the Editions concur in the Reading. But is it true in Fact, that the *Bat* flies *after* Summer? * The *Houp* ſleeps during the Winter, ſay the *Naturaliſts*, and ſo does the BAT too. Again, † *Flies* and *Gnats* are the favourite Food of the BAT, which he procures by flying about in the Night. But this is a Diet, which, I preſume, he can only come at in the *Summer*-Seaſon. Another Obſervation has been made, that ‡ when BATS fly either earlier, or in greater Number, than uſual, *it is a Sign* the next Day will be *hot* and *ſerene*. This Prognoſtick likewiſe only ſuits with *Summer*. In ſhort, I am very apt to think the Paſſage is corrupt, and was not deſigned to have any Alluſion to the Seaſon of the *Year*, but rather the *Hour* at which *Bats* are accuſtom'd to fly. The *Bat* was call'd *Veſpertilio*, ſay the *Etymologiſts*, by the *Latines*; (as it was, νυκτερὶς, by the *Greeks*;) becauſe this Bird is not viſible by Day, but appears firſt about the Twilight of the Evening, and ſo continues to fly about during the dark Hours. From the Cuſtom and Nature of this Bird therefore, it ſeems to me that It ought to be corrected;

* *Upupa dormit Hyeme, ſicut &* Veſpertilio: Albert. Magn.

† *Cibus ejus ſunt Muſca & Culices; quem nocte volans inquirit.* Idem è Plinio.

‡ Veſpertiliones *ſi veſperè citiùs & plures ſolito volârint, Signum eſt Calorem & Serenitatem poſtridiè fore.* Gratarolus *apud* Geſner. *de Avibus.*

On the Bat's Back I do fly
After SUN-SET *merrily.*

EMENDATION. LXX. TAMING of the SHREW, Page 275.

Hoſt. *I know my Remedy; I muſt go fetch the* HEAD-BOROUGH.

Sly. *Third, or fourth, or fifth Borough, I'll anſwer him by Law; I'll not budge an Inch, Boy;* &c.

I think, I may with Modeſty affirm, either that Mr. POPE never reviſed this Paſſage; or, if he did, that He did not underſtand it. The Corruption has paſs'd down thro' all the Copies; and None of the Editors have pretended to gueſs at the Poet's Conceit. What a ſtrange, inſipid, unmeaning Reply does *Sly* make to his *Hoſteſs*! How do *third*, or *fourth*, or *fifth* Borough relate to *Headborough*? The Author intended but a poor Witticiſm; and even That is loſt. The *Hoſteſs* would ſay, that She'll fetch a *Conſtable*: But that *Headborough* was not SHAKESPEARE's Expreſſion, I dare warrant; and doubt not but the Readers will be of my Mind too. I am aſſur'd, the Paſſage came from our Poet's Pen thus;

Hoſt

Hoſt. *I know my Remedy; I muſt go fetch the* THIRD-BOROUGH.
Sly. Third, *or* fourth, *or* fifth *Borough, I'll anſwer him by Law*, &c.

Who does not perceive, at a ſingle Glance, ſome Conceit ſtarted by this certain Correction? There is an Attempt at Wit, tolerable enough for a Tinker, and one drunk too. But what is *Thirdborough*? * The GLOSSARIES tell us, that it was an old *Saxon* Term for *Conſtable*; and that *Head-Borough* was alſo call'd *Borough-Head, Burſholder, Third-Borough, Tything-Man*, &c. To This, if we look into our own *Statute-Books*, no farther back than the 28th Year of K. *Henry* VIII. (*Cap.* 10.) and not quite Thirty Years before the Birth of SHAKESPEARE, we ſhall there find *Third-Borough* uſed for a *Conſtable*.

I have no Doubt but the Uſe of the Word continued currently in People's Mouths in our Author's Time; and I have this Reaſon for thinking ſo, becauſe He uſes it himſelf in another of his Plays, which he would hardly have choſe to do, if it had been altogether antiquated and laid aſide.

LOVE'S LABOUR LOST, Page 99.

Dull. *I my ſelf* reprehend *his own Perſon, for I am his Grace's* THARBOROUGH.

We know very well that *Dull*, in this Play, repreſents the Character of a Conſtable: And there is no Queſtion but *Thirdborough* is the very Word intended here: 'Tis probable, indeed, that the Author humourouſly makes *Dull* knock the Word out of Joint, and purpoſely ſay *Tharborough* for *Thirdborough*, as he likewiſe makes him ſay *reprehend* for *repreſent*. Our Poet very frequently plays with this Cuſtom of the Vulgar, *of frighting* Engliſh *out of its Wits*, as he calls it in his MERRY WIVES of WINDSOR.

LXXI. K. LEAR, Page 12. EMENDATION.

Well, my Legitimate, if this Letter ſpeed,
And my Invention thrive, Edmund *the baſe*
Shall TO *th' legitimate* ------

I ſee no Reaſon in the World for the Break here, and leaving the Senſe imperfect. I rather think the Poet wrote it.

Shall BE *th' legitimate.*

i. e. ſhall quite ſupplant his Brother out of his Father's Affections, and ſtand himſelf in the Degree of his lawful Heir.

LXXII. *Ibid.* Page 73. EMENDATION.

---------- *Full oft 'tis ſeen*
Our MEAN SECURES *us, and our meer Defects*
Prove our Commodities.

I have already, in Page 37, quoted this Paſſage as one Authority of the Poet's making Uſe of *Adjectives ſubſtantively*: But, I muſt own, I ſuſpect the Reading not genuine. 'Tis certain, 'tis good Senſe to ſay that our *Mean Fortunes* may be a *Security* to us, and our *Wants* an *Advantage*; but, I am ſure, the Contraſt both in Senſe and Terms will be much ſtronger, and the Variation not ſo great to ſtartle us, if we may ſuppoſe, that our Author's Sentiment was This;

* Third-Borough, Thrid-Borough, Thrith-Borough, Thri-Borough, *or, more corruptedly*, Thra-Borough, *is a* Conſtable *or ſuch like Officer in the* Third *Part of any County, or Shire, ſo divided, or canton'd.* — Head-Borough *(quaſi Primus inter Pares) is the Foreman only of ſuch Conſtable*, &c. *See* LAMBERT'S *Explication* of *Saxon* Terms, and Dr. COWEL'S *Interpreter* of *Law Terms*, in *Conſtable, Head-Borough, Third-Borough*. &c.

-------- Full oft 'tis seen,
Our MEANS ENSNARE *us, and our meer Defects*
Prove our Commodities.

EMENDATION. LXXIII. K. RICHARD II. Page 128.

North. *And yet* OUR *fair Discourse has been as Sugar,*
Making the hard Way sweet and delectable.

By the whole Tenour of *Northumberland*'s Speech here, 'tis plain, that he is in no Part paying any Compliment to his own Discourse, but to the Pleasures and Advantages which he deriv'd from the Society and Conversation of *Bolingbroke*, which sweeten'd and made short the Fatigue of a very rough Road. I dare say therefore the Poet wrote;

And yet YOUR *fair Discourse hath been as Sugar,*
Making, &c.

EMENDATION. LXXIV. *The First Part of* K. HENRY IV. Page 266.

------------ suffer'd his Kinsman March
(Who is, if ev'ry Owner were right plac'd,
Indeed, his King;) to be ENGAG'D *in* Wales,
There, without Ransom, to lie forfeited.

I think the Term, *engaged*, is very much to be suspected here; for as it cannot signify *impawned*, it has no Consonancy, nor Agreement in Sense, with *lying forfeited without Ransom.* The Truth of the History was this, *Mortimer* Earl of *March* was taken Prisoner, and closely confin'd in *Wales* by *Owen Glendower:* Many Sollicitations were made to K. *Henry* for redeeming him, but he would never listen to it, suspecting *Mortimer* of Treason; and so he continued to be a close Prisoner, till he found his Releasement by the Means of the *Piercys* Rebellion. Correct therefore, to correspond both with Sense and History,

------------ to be ENCAG'D *in* Wales,
There without Ransom to lie forfeited.

EMENDATION. LXXV. K. HENRY V. Page 440.

High Dukes, great Princes, Barons, Lords and KINGS.

The *French* King is speaking here to the Great Lords of his Court, and Army, in all these pompous Titles. But why, *Kings*? There was not one King amongst them besides the Speaker. Tho' this Error runs thro' all the Copies, correct it,

High Dukes, great Princes, Barons, Lords, and KNIGHTS.

When the Battle is over, and we come to have an Account of the Loss on the *French* Side, we find that they had 500 Knights dubb'd but the Day before the Battle: And that in the 10000 Men, which they lost, there were but 1600 who fought for Pay. The rest, as the Poet tells us, Page 481. were

Princes, Barons, Lords, KNIGHTS, *Squires,*
And Gentlemen of Blood and Quality.

LXXVI

LXXVI. *The First Part of* K. HENRY VI. Page 66. EMENDATION.

I dare presume, sweet Prince, he thought no Harm.
York. *And if I* WISH *he did ---*

Here again a Break is made without Occasion, and the Text is likewise slightly corrupted. Correct it,

And if I WIS, *he did.*

i. e. if I think right, or know any Thing of the Matter, he did think Harm. To *wis*, and *wist*, (from the SAXON, *wistan, Cognoscere*) is a Word frequent both with CHAUCER and SPENSER.

LXXVII. *Second Part of* K. HENRY VI. Page 123. EMENDATION.

Come, come, my Lords,
These Oracles are HARDLY *attain'd,*
And hardly *understood.*

This is Part of a *degraded* Passage, which Mr. POPE thinks to be an unnecessary Repetition. I am very free to own, as it is here, and in all the preceding Editions, exhibited, it seems to have so little Meaning, that it is very unworthy of our Author. But if by a very slight, yet certain, Alteration, I can both give it a Meaning, and a fine Sentiment; it may be worth while to restore the Poet his own Text. The Case is this: *Eleanor*, Dutchess of *Gloucester*, resorting to Conjurers and Wizards to be resolv'd of the Fate of the King and several of the Court, is caught in the Fact by the Dukes of *York* and *Buckingham*; the Parties being apprehended, and their Papers seized, *York* says he'll see the Devil's Writ; and reading over the Answers which the Wizards had given, and finding 'em intricate and ambiguous, he makes this general Comment upon such Sort of Intelligence. But how are *These Oracles* hardly *attained*? 'Tis plain, they were *actually* attained, and taken down in Writing; or the Discoverers could never have come to the Knowledge of them. Not only the Sense, but the Verse, labours, with the Corruption of this Passage: And I have not the least Doubt but they are both to be restor'd thus with the greatest Certainty.

------------- *Come, come, my Lords,*
These Oracles are HARDILY *attain'd,*
And hardly *understood.*

i. e. A great Risque and Hazard is run to obtain them, *viz.* going to the Devil for them, as 'twas pretended and supposed: And likewise the incurring severe Penalties by the Statute-Law against such Practices: And yet after these *hardy* Steps taken, the Informations are so perplex'd that they are *hardly* to be understood.

LXXVIII. *The Third Part of* K. HENRY VI. Page 229, 30. EMENDATION.

---------- *That Face of his,*
The hungry Canibals would not have touch'd,
Would not have stain'd the Roses JUST *with Blood,* &c.

I cannot but suspect this to be a Corruption. What can the Word *just* import here? Does the Poet mean, that the Canibals would not have *just* stain'd the Roses in his Cheeks with Blood, *i. e.* would not so much as have fetch'd Blood of him? Besides, that the Position of the Words is forc'd, I believe, SHAKESPEARE had another Thought, and that we ought to read the Passage;

Would not have stain'd the Roses JUIC'D *with Blood.*

i. e. would not have ſpilt that Blood, whoſe Juices ſhone thro' his young Cheeks, bright as the Vermilion Dye in Roſes.

EMENDATION. LXXIX. K. RICHARD III. Page 366.

> *Death makes no Conqueſt of* HIS *Conqueror;*
> *For now he lives in Fame, tho' not in Life.*

The Poet is here ſpeaking of *Julius Cæſar*, of immortal Memory. But, methinks, it is no very notable Sentiment, that Death does not conquer *That* which conquers *Him:* It would be very extraordinary indeed, if He did. I can ſcarce think ſo exceptionable an Expreſſion dropt from our Poet, but rather that he wrote it thus;

> *Death makes no Conqueſt of* THIS *Conqueror;*
> *For now he lives in Fame, tho' not in Life.*

EMENDATION. LXXX. K. HENRY VIII. Page 458.

> *They've all new Legs, and lame ones; one would take it,*
> *(That never ſaw 'em pace before,) the Spavin*
> *And* SPRING-HALT *reign'd among 'em.* ----

The Editor has taken this Word upon Content from the preceding Editions, but it muſt be corrected;

> --------- *the Spavin*
> *And* STRING-HALT *reign'd among 'em.*

The *String-Halt* is a Diſtemper in Horſes, which by a ſudden Twitching up of the hinder Leg, makes them go lame.

EMENDATION. LXXXI. TIMON of ATHENS, Page 8.

> *Yet you do well*
> *To ſhew Lord* Timon, *that* MEAN *Eyes have ſeen*
> *The Foot above the Head.*

Why, *mean* Eyes, more than the Eyes of Perſons of *Figure*? The Painter, I preſume, here, had no Deſign of affronting the Poet by calling him either one of *mean* Rank, or *mean* Obſervation. It will, certainly, be more intelligible to write it thus;

> ---------- *Yet you do well*
> *To ſhew Lord* Timon, *that* MENS *Eyes have ſeen*
> *The Foot above the Head.*

EMENDATION. LXXXII. CORIOLANUS, Page 148.

> Coriol. ------- *Shall!*
> O GOD! ---- *but moſt unwiſe Patricians; why,*
> *You grave, but wreakleſs Senators, have you thus*
> *Given* Hydra *here to chuſe an Officer,* &c.

After this Exclamation, methinks, 'tis very odd to continue the Sentence with ſuch a disjunctive *But:* Beſides, as the Text now ſtands, there ſeems that Contraſt of Terms wanting, and broken off, which appears intended in this Paſſage by the next immediate Line. As the Addition of a ſingle Letter reſtores us this Beauty, I make no Doubt but the Paſſage ought to be reſtor'd;

Coriol.

Coriol. --------- *Shall!*

O GOOD, *but most* unwise, Patricians, *why*,
You grave, *but* wreakless, *Senators*, *have you thus*, &c.

LXXXIII. *Ibid.* Page 165. EMENDATION.

-------- *Consider further*,
That when he speaks *not like a Citizen*,
You find him like a Soldier; *do not take*
His rougher ACTIONS *for malicious Sounds*;
But, *as I say*, *such as become a Soldier*.

I have no Manner of Apprehension how a Man's *Actions* can be mistaken for *Words*. If I were to do a sawcy Thing in Company to any One, I should think it very extraordinary, if he told me, Sir, you give me very impudent Language. There seems to me a manifest Corruption in the Text, thro' all the Copies; and that, for the sake of common Sense, it ought to be corrected thus;

--------- *Do not take*
His rougher ACCENTS *for malicious Sounds*, &c.

LXXXIV. *Ibid.* Page 200. EMENDATION.

Coriol. --------- You Gods I PRAY,
And the most noble Mother of the World
Leave unsaluted.

I dare say, an old Corruption has possess'd this Passage, for two Reasons. In the *first* Place, whoever consults this Speech, will find, that he is talking fondly to his Wife, and not praying to the Gods at all: *Secondly*, if he were employ'd in his Devotions, no Apology would be wanting for leaving his Mother unsaluted. The Poet's Intention was certainly this; *Coriolanus*, having been lavish in his Tendernesses and Raptures to his Wife, bethinks himself on the sudden, that his Fondness to her had made him guilty of ill Manners in the Neglect of his Mother. Restore, as it certainly ought to be;

------------ You Gods! *I* PRATE,
And the most noble Mother of the World
Leave unsaluted.

Mr. DENNIS, (than whom, in my Opinion, no Man in *England* better understands SHAKESPEARE) in his Alteration of this Play, whether he made the same Correction which I now do, certainly understood the Passage exactly with me: An undeniable Proof of this, is an Appeal to the Change in Expression which he has put upon it.

But Oh! ye Gods, while fondly thus I talk,
See, the most noble Mother of the World
Stands unsaluted.

I question not, but his Reason for varying the Expression, was, because *prate* is a Term ill-sounding in it self, and mean in its Acceptation. Our Language was not so refin'd, tho' more masculine, in *Shakespeare*'s Days; and therefore (notwithstanding the κακοφωνία) when he is most serious, he frequently makes Use of the Word. But *four* Pages afterwards in this very Play we again meet with it.

--- *yet*

---------- *yet here he lets me* prate
Like one i'th' Stocks.

K. JOHN, Page 166.

If I talk to him, with his innocent Prate
He will awake my Mercy. -- -

HAMLET, Page 458.

And if Thou prate *of Mountains, let them throw*
Millions of Acres on Us.

Nor is it infrequent with him to employ the *Diminutive* of this Term.

The TEMPEST, Page 43.

Mir. --------- *But I* prattle
Something too wildly, and my Father's precepts
I do forget.

MEASURE for MEASURE, Page 401.

Duke. *Silence that fellow*; ------- *I would he had some Cause to* prattle *for himself.*

OTHELLO, Page 506.

-------- *O my Sweet,*
I prattle *out of Fashion, and I dote*
In mine own Comfort.

EMENDATION. LXXXV. *Ibid.* Page 210.

Auf. -------- *Serv'd his Designments*
In my own Person; HOP'D *to reap the Fame*
Which he did make all his; and took some Pride
To do my self this Wrong.

How could *Aufidius* hope to reap that Fame, which *Coriolanus* made all his own, if he took a Pride in doing himself that Wrong? This was never the Poet's Meaning. *Aufidius* is angry that *Coriolanus* over-top'd him so far, as to bear away the whole Glory, which the other reasonably expected to share in, having contributed all the Assistances in his Power towards acquiring it in Partnership. Suitable to the Complaint of *Aufidius*, notwithstanding all the Copies concur in the Error, I have no Doubt but the Text ought to be restor'd,

---------- *Serv'd his Designments*
In my own Person; * HOLPE *to reap the Fame*, &c.

* Or, *help'd.*

EMENDATION. LXXXVI. JULIUS CÆSAR, Page 249.

Cæsar *should be a Beast without a Heart,*
If he should stay at home to day for fear. *
No, Cæsar *shall not; Danger knows full well,*
That Cæsar *is more dangerous than He.*
WE HEARD *two Lions litter'd in one day,*
And I, the elder, and more terrible;
And Cæsar *shall go forth.* -----

All

All the Lines from the *Asterisk* are degraded by Mr. POPE; partly, I suppose, for the Reason which he gives in his Preface for these Degradations; but chiefly, I believe, because he did not understand them. The Copies, indeed, are all corrupt; and the Passage, of Course, Nonsense and unintelligible, till we look nearer, and see thro' the Disguise of the bad Text. But a slight Alteration will restore Sense to the Whole; and then the Sentiment will neither be unworthy of SHAKESPEARE, nor the Boast too absurd for *Cæsar* in a Vein of Vanity to utter. I dare warrant, This was the genuine Reading of our Author;

> ------ *Danger knows full well*
> *That* Cæsar *is more dangerous than He.*
> WE WERE *two Lions litter'd in one Day,*
> *And I the Elder and more terrible*; &c.

i. e. Cæsar and Danger were Twin-whelps of a Lion, and *Cæsar* the Elder, and more terrible of the Two.

LXXXVII. ANTONY and CLEOPATRA, Page 318. EMENDATION.

> ------- *My more Particular,*
> *And That which most with You should* SAVE *my Going,*
> *Is* Fulvia's *death.*

Antony is giving several Reasons to *Cleopatra*, which make his Departure from *Ægypt* absolutely necessary; most of them Reasons of State; but the Death of *Fulvia*, his Wife, was a particular and private Call, which demanded his Presence in *Italy*. But the Poet's Text, I find, in all the printed Copies, would rather make us believe that *Fulvia*'s Death should prevent, or save him the Trouble of going. The Text in this Respect, I dare engage, runs counter to its Master's Meaning. *Cleopatra* is jealous of *Antony*'s Absence, and suspicious that he is seeking Colours for his Going: *Antony* replies to her Doubts, with the Reasons that obliged him to be gone for a Time; and tells her that, as his Wife *Fulvia* is dead, and so She has no Rival to be jealous of, that Circumstance should be his best Plea and Excuse, and have the greatest Weight with her for his Going. Who does not see now, that it ought to be read?

> ----- *My more Particular,*
> *And that which most with you should* SALVE *my Going,*
> *Is* Fulvia's *Death.*

EMENDATION.

LXXXVIII. *Ibid.* Page 321.

> ----- *This common Body,*
> *Like to a vagabond Flag upon the Stream,*
> *Goes to, and back,* LASHING *the varying Tide,*
> *To rot it self with Motion.*

How can a Flag, or Rush, floating upon a Stream, and that has no Motion but what the Fluctuation of the Water gives it, be said to *lash* the Tide? This is making a Scourge of a weak ineffective Flag, and giving it an active Violence in its own Power. I don't know whether the *Editor* has adopted this Reading from any Authorities, or it be One of his own Conjecture; the Generality of the Editions have it LACKING: 'Tis true, there is no Sense in that Reading; and yet the Addition of a single Letter will not only give us good Sense, but, I dare promise, the genuine Word of our Author into the Bargain. Correct,

> *Goes to and back,* LACKYING *the varying Tide,*
> *To rot it self with Motion.*

i. e

i. e. floating backwards and forwards with the Variation of the Tide, like a Page, or *Lackey* at his Master's Heels. The Edition which I have above made mention of (in Page 138.) with Marginal Corrections in *Manuscript*, concurs with Me in this Reading: As I have had the Pleasure to find several more of my Emendations authoriz'd by the Conjectures there inserted.

EMENDATION. LXXXIX. *Ibid.* Page 327.

-------- *But let us rear*
The higher our Opinion, that our Stiring
Can from the Lap of Ægypt'*s Widow pluck*
The NEAR *lust-wearied* Antony.

Sextus Pompeius, upon Hearing that *Antony* is every Hour expected in *Rome*, does not much relish the News: He is twice the Soldier (*says He*) that *Octavius* and *Lepidus* are; and I did not think the petty War which I am raising would rouse him from his Amours in *Ægypt*. ---But why should *Pompey* hold a higher Opinion of his own Expedition, because it awak'd *Antony* to Arms, who was *almost* weary and surfeited of lascivious Pleasures? The Copies are all defective, and the Editor follows them implicitly. Correct it,

--------- *but let us rear*
The higher our Opinion, that our Stiring
Can from the Lap of Ægypt'*s Widow pluck*
The NE'ER-*lust-wearied* Antony.

i e. if *Antony*, tho' *never* tir'd of Luxury, yet mov'd from that Charm upon *Pompey*'s Stiring, it was Reason for *Pompey* to pride himself upon being of such Consequence.

EMENDATION. XC. *Ibid.* Page 394.

--------- *Behold this Man,*
Commend unto his Lips thy SAVOURING *Hand*;
Kiss it, my Warriour: he hath fought to day,
As if a God in Hate of Mankind had
Destroy'd in such a Shape.

Antony here recommends one of his Captains, who had fought valiantly, to *Cleopatra*; and desires he may have the Grace of kissing her Hand. But why, *savouring* hand? --- *Antony* did not want his Captain to grow in Love with his Mistress, on Account of the Flavour and Lusciousness of her Hand; but only to have a Reward of Honour from the Queen for his good Service. Tho' all the Copies join in this Reading, I much rather believe the Poet's Word was,

Commend unto his Lips thy FAVOURING *hand*;

EMENDATION. XCI. TITUS ANDRONICUS, Page 496.

How if that Fly had a Father, and Mother?
How would he hang his slender gilded Wings,
And buz lamenting DOINGS *in the Air?*

To buz *lamenting Doings* can certainly neither be *English*, nor an Expression of SHAKESPEARE; nor does it convey any satisfactory Image. It is one of the *Manuscript* Conjectures, (in the Margin of that Edition which I but a little above took Notice of,) that we ought to read here, as I think there is no Dispute but we ought.

And buz lamenting DRONINGS *in the Air.*

This Word representing that heavy, sleepy Noise, made by the *Fly*, *Chafer*, *Bee*, &c.

XCII.

XCII. *Ibid.* Page 485. EMENDATION.

Ye white-LIMB'D *Walls, ye Ale-house painted Signs,*

Thus the old *Quarto* in 1611, the second *Folio* Edition, and all the subsequent Copies that I have seen, read with Mr. POPE; but the Poet's Epithet is slightly corrupted. Restore it.

Ye white-LIMED *Walls,* -------

It carries a Reproach to a Man, who makes a fine Appearance outward, and has no Virtues, or Bravery, within to set him off;

Introrsùm turpem, speciosum pelle decorâ,

As HORACE calls it. The Term in our Author comes up exactly to the *Greek*, one used by St. *Paul* against *Ananias*, * τοῖχε κεκονιαμένε, *Dealbate Paries*; which our Translation has render'd, *Thou whited Wall.*

* Acts xxiii. 3.

XCIII. MACBETH, Page 554. EMENDATION.

We have SCORCH'D *the Snake, not kill'd it.* -----
She'll close, *and be herself;* ------

This is a Passage which has all along pass'd current thro' the Editions, and likewise upon the Stage; and yet, I dare affirm, is not our Author's Reading. What has a Snake, *closing* again, to do with its being *scorch'd*? Scorching would never either *separate*, or *dilate*, its Parts; but rather make them instantly *contract* and *shrivel*. SHAKESPEARE, I am very well persuaded, had this Notion in his Head, (which how true in Fact, I will not pretend to determine,) that if you cut a Serpent, or Worm asunder, in several Pieces, there is such an unctious Quality in their Blood, that the dismember'd Parts, being only plac'd near enough to touch one another, will cement and become as whole as before the Injury receiv'd. The Application of this Thought is to *Duncan*, the murther'd King, and his surviving Sons: *Macbeth* considers them so much as Members of the Father, that tho' he has cut off the old Man, he would say, he has not entirely kill'd him; but he'll cement and close again in the Lives of his Sons, to the Danger of *Macbeth*. If I am not deceiv'd therefore, our Poet certainly wrote thus;

We have SCOTCH'D *the Snake, not kill'd it.* -----
She'll close, and be her self; -----

To *scotch*, however the Generality of our *Dictionaries* happen to omit the Word, signifies to *notch, slash, cut* with Twigs, Sword, &c. and so SHAKESPEARE more than once has used it in his Works.

So CORIOLANUS, Page 182.

He was too hard for him directly, to say the Troth on't: Before Corioli, *he* SCOTCH'D *him, and notch'd him, like a Carbonado.*

And so again, ANTONY and CLEOPATRA, Page 393.

We'll beat them into Bench-Holes, I have yet
Room for six SCOTCHES *more.*

To shew how little we ought to trust *implicitly* to *Dictionaries* for *Etymologies*, we need no better Proof than from BAILY in his Explication of the Term, SCOTCH-Collops; he tells us,

that

that it means Slices of Veal fry'd after the *Scotch* Manner: But, besides that that Nation are not over famous for the Elegance of their Cookery, it is more natural, and I dare say more true, to allow that it ought to be wrote SCOTCHT-Collops, *i. e.* Collops, or Slices *slash'd* cross and cross, before they are put on the Coals. *Sed hæc obiter.*

EMENDATION. XCIV. *Ibid.* Page 561.

---------- Be alive again,
And dare me to the Desart with thy Sword;
If trembling I INHIBIT, *then protest me*
The Baby of a Girl.

All the Editions before Mr. POPE's, that I have seen, read, *If trembling I inhabit*, which is unsufferable Nonsense. I don't know whether the Editor's Reading be from any Authority, or his own Conjecture; but I am afraid it is not *English*. There cannot be brought a Passage to shew that *Inhibeo* is ever used by the *Latines* as a *Neuter* or *Deponent* Verb, but always *actively*: And so with us, to *inhibit*, always signifies, to *restrain*, *stop*, some Thing else; never, to *desist*, *renege*, &c. If therefore *inhibit*, be the Poet's Word here, (which I am not absolutely satisfied about,) we must correct his Text thus;

If Trembling ME *inhibit*, *then protest me ---*

i. e. If the Passion of Trembling, the Influence of Fear upon my Nerves, prevent me from following Thee, *&c.*

EMENDATION. XCV. *Ibid.* Page 562.

There is not ONE *of Them, but in his House*
I keep a Servant feed.

One of Whom? --- *Macbeth* has just said, that he heard *Macduff* meant to disobey his Summons, and not come to Court: And he would immediately subjoin, that there is not a Man of *Macduff*'s Quality in the Kingdom, but he has a Spy under his Roof. This is understood, not express'd, as the Text now stands. For this Reason, and because there's a various Reading in the second *Folio* Edition, I am apt to think there's a slight Corruption in this Passage. That Copy exhibits it to Us thus;

There's not a A ONE *of them.*

Here we again meet with a *Deprav'd* Reading; but it is such a One as will help us to the Poet's *true* Words. Correct, as it certainly ought to be restor'd,

There's not A THANE *of them,* ----

i. e. a *Nobleman:* And so the Peers of *Scotland* were all call'd, till *Earls* were created by *Malcolme* the Son of *Duncan*.

EMENDATION. XCVI. *Ibid.* Page 570.

Who can impress the Forest, bid the Tree
Unfix his earth-bound Root? ---- *Sweet Bodements! Good!*
Rebellious DEAD *rise never, till the Wood*
Of Birnam *rise,* ----

Thus all the Impressions, from the very Beginning, exhibit this Passage; but I cannot imagine what Notion the Editors could have of the *Dead* being *rebellious*. It looks to Me, as if they were content to believe the Poet *genuine*, wherever he was *mysterious* beyond being understood. The Emendation of one Letter will give us clear Sense, and the very Thing which *Macbeth* should be suppos'd to say here. Restore it.

* *Rebellious*

* *Rebellious* HEAD *rise never, till the Wood*
Of Birnam *rise,*

* Or, Rebellion's Head.

i. e. Let Rebellion never make Head against me, till a Forest move, and I shall reign long enough in Safety. *Shakespeare* very frequently uses the Word *Head* in this Manner, of which I'll subjoin an Example, or two.

First Part of K. HENRY IV. Page 249.

------ Douglas, *and the* English REBELS *met*
Th' Eleventh of this Month, at Shrewsbury.
A mighty and a fearful HEAD *they are*, &c.

Second Part of K. HENRY IV. Page 307.

For his Divisions, as the Times do brawl,
Are in three HEADS; *one Pow'r against the* French, &c.

CORIOLANUS, Page 132.

When Tarquin *made a* HEAD *for* Rome, *he fought*
Beyond the Mark of Others.

XCVII. *Prologue to* TROILUS and CRESSIDA. EMENDATION.

-------- Priam's *six-gated City,*
Dardan, *and* Timbria, Helias, Chetas, Troien,
And Antenoridas, *with massy Staples,*
And corresponsive and fulfilling Bolts,
STIR *up the Sons of* Troy. ---

I have no Notion, in what Sense a City, having six strong Gates, and those well barr'd and bolted, can be said to stir up its Inhabitants: Unless that they may be suppos'd to derive some Spirit from the Strength of their Fortifications. But I do not take this to be the Poet's Thought. The second *Folio* Edition reads it thus;

STIRRE *up the Sons of* Troy.

This odd Manner of Spelling the Word both gave me a Suspicion of the Place being corrupt, and administer'd to my Conjecture for restoring it. The Author, I take it, means no more than This; that the *Greeks* have pitch'd their Tents upon the Plains before *Troy*; and that the *Trojans* are securely barricaded within the Walls of their City. I have no Doubt therefore but we ought to read;

SPERRE *up the Sons of* Troy.

For, to *sperre*, or *spar*, (from the old *Teutonick* Word, **sperren**,) signifies to *shut up*, *defend by Bars*, &c. And in this very Sense I remember CHAUCER uses the Term in the fifth Book of his *Troilus* and *Cressida*.

For when he saw her Doores sperred *all,*
Well nigh for Sorrow 'adown he gan to fall.

 I little

Occasional EMENDATION

I little suspected, when I first quoted the above Passage, that it would have afforded Matter for further Correction: But I find that even in the Names of *Troy*'s Gates we meet with Some of them, that are no where else to be met with. I don't remember, indeed, that either *Didymus*, *Eustathius*, *Spondanus*, or any of the more modern Commentators upon *Homer*, furnish us with a List of their Names: If they had, I doubt not but the Editor would have set them right from those Authorities; Not even the laborious Commentator upon *Lycophron*, where we might have expected it, has touch'd this Matter. I am aware, that in *Homer* the *Scæan* and *Dardanian* Gates are said to be one and the same; and so the *six* Gates would be reduc'd to *five*. But notwithstanding This, they are enumerated as our Poet meant to set them out: The late Learned Sir *Edward Sherburn* in his Notes upon the *Troades* of SENECA, Page 324. tells us, *that* Troy *had six Gates, viz. the* Antenorian, *the* Dardanian, *the* Ilian, *the* Catumbrian, *the* Trojan, *and the* Scæan. He quotes us no Authority for this, but I believe I can trace him in the Account. For CERDA, upon the six hundred and twelfth Verse of the second *Æneid* of VIRGIL, informs us from *Dares Phrygius*; --- Trojanæ *urbis portas sex enumerat* Dares; Antenoriden, Dardaniam, Iliam, Scæam, Catumbriam, Trojanam. Here again, if I am not mistaken, we meet with fresh Corruption. *Catumbria* is a very odd Word; and, I am well satisfied, a deprav'd One. We are to know, there was near Old *Troy*, a Plain call'd *Thymbra*; a River, that run through it, call'd *Thymbrius*; and a Temple to *Apollo Thymbræus*. The Gate, that we are speaking of, was probably describ'd in the *Greek* Author to be κατὰ Θύμβριον, the Gate that fac'd the aforesaid Plain and River: And from thence, as I suspect, by the Negligence or Ignorance of the Transcriber, the Words were join'd and corrupted into *Catumbria*. The correcter Editions of *Dares Phrygius*, I know, neither read as Sir *Edward Sherburn*, nor as *Cerda* upon *Virgil* give us the Passage, but thus; Ilio *portas fecit* (*scil.* Priamus;) *quarum Nomina hæc sunt*, Antenoridæ, Dardaniæ, Iliæ, Scææ, Thymbrææ, Trojanæ. I doubt not but the Author ought to be corrected by this Authority;

----- Priam'*s Six Gates i'th' City*,
Dardania, THYMBRIA, Ilia, Scæa, Troien,
And Antenorides, *with massy Staples*
And corresponsive and fullfilling Bolts,
Sperre up the Sons of Troy.

EMENDATION.

XCVIII. TROILUS and CRESSIDA, Page 11.

And like as there were Husbandry in War,
Before the Sun rose, he was harnest LIGHT,
And to the Field goes He: ---

Why, harnest *light*? Does the Poet mean that *Hector* had put on *light* Armour? Or that he was *sprightly* in his Arms, even before Sunrise? Or is a *Conundrum* aim'd at in, *Sun* rose, and harnest *light*? A very slight Alteration makes all these Constructions unnecessary; and gives us the Poet's Meaning in the properest Terms imaginable. I am inclin'd to think he wrote;

Before the Sun rose, He was Harness-DIGHT, &c.

i. e. compleatly drest, accoutred in Arms. It is frequent with our Poet, from his Masters, CHAUCER and SPENSER, to say *dight* for *deck'd*, *pight* for *pitch'd*, &c.

EMENDATION.

XCIX. *Ibid.* Page 42.

* Paris, *and* Troilus, *You have Both said well*,
AND *on the Cause and Question now in Hand*
Have gloss'd, but superficially. ---

* *Vid. suprà ad* Pag. 134.

I can never think that the Poet express'd himself thus: 'Tis absurd to say, that People have talked *well*, and yet but *superficially* at the same Time. I am persuaded (as above in Page 66.) the *Copulative* is here mistakenly put for the *Disjunctive*; and that we ought to restore it;

Paris

Paris *and* Troilus, *you have Both said* well,
BUT *on the Cause and Question now in hand*
Have gloss'd but superficially.

i. e. You have argued very well in the *general,* but have gloss'd too superficially upon the *particular* Question in Debate.

C. CYMBELINE, Page 178.

------- *and I grieve Myself*
To think, when Thou shalt be DIS-EDG'D *by Her*
Whom now Thou tir'st on, &c.

Notwithstanding the *Antithesis* that there is betwixt *dis-edg'd* and *tirest on,* yet, methinks, too gross an Image is convey'd for so reserv'd and modest a Princess as *Imogen.* I would suppose that our Poet wrote, with a very small Variation;

------ *and I grieve Myself*
To think, when Thou shalt be DIS-SIEG'D *by her,* &c.

i. e. *displac'd, put out of her Favour.* Siege, it is well known, was the old Word used for *seat, place,* as also *rank, dignity,* &c. So the King, in HAMLET, Page 445.

------- *Your Summ of Parts*
Did not together pluck such Envy from Him,
As did That One, and That, in my, Regard,
Of the unworthiest SIEGE. ---

So, in OTHELLO, Page 482.

------- *I fetch Life and Being*
From Men of worthiest SIEGE. ---

And so, in MEASURE for MEASURE, Page 382.

Besides, upon the very SIEGE *of Justice*
Lord Angelo *hath to the publick Ear*
Profess'd the contrary.

'Tis certain, supposing my Conjecture to be right upon the Passage now in Question, SHAKESPEARE might as well have said *displac'd,* as *dissieg'd,* by her; but I appeal to all the nicer and more Critical Readers of our Poet, whether it is not his Custom, to love an unusual Term where a common one might serve his Turn. As I presume He has here chose *dissiege* to answer *displace,* so in his CORIOLANUS he has industriously adopted another Word to express the same Meaning. Page 132.

----- *Sir, I hope, my Words*
DIS-BENCH'D *you not.* ---

CI.

EMENDATION. CI *Ibid.* Page 162.

----- THIS IS HER HONOUR;
Let it be granted You have seen all this,
Praise be to your Remembrance, the Description
Of What is in her Chamber nothing saves
The Wager you have laid.

To be as brief as possible in my Reasons for suspecting this Passage. --- *Jachimo*, a Libertine in his Thoughts of Women, wagers with *Posthumus* that he will debauch his Wife, so that he can once get Access to her. *Posthumus* takes the Bett, and makes Way by Letters to his Wife for *Jachimo*'s Introduction. *Jachimo* impudently pretends to have carried his Point; and, in Confirmation, is very minute in describing to the Husband all the Furniture and Adornments of his Wife's Bedchamber. But how is fine Furniture any ways a Princess's Honour? It is an *Apparatus* suitable to her Dignity, but certainly makes no Part of her Character. I am persuaded the Poet intended his *Posthumus* should say, " This particular Description, that you make, can't convince me that I've lost my Wager; your Memory is good; " and Some of these Things you may have learn'd from a third Hand; I therefore expect " Proofs more direct and authentick. " If I do not deceive myself therefore, there is little Question but we ought to restore the Place thus:

----- WHAT'S THIS T'HER HONOUR?
Let it be granted, You have seen all This,
Praise be, &c.

EMENDATION. CII. *Ibid.* Page 216.

Our Britain's HEARTS *dye flying, not our Men:*
To Darkness fleet Souls that fly backwards!

I should have look'd upon This in the Rank of a mere *literal* Error, but that I find it is so faithfully Copied from the old Editions; which makes me believe the *Editor* did not attend to the *Poet*'s Sense in it. Correct, with the greatest Certainty;

Our Britain's HARTS *die flying, not our* Men; *&c.*

i. e. our *Harts*, or *Stags*, receive their Death as they fly; our Men stand boldly to it, and die fighting.

EMENDATION. CIII. ROMEO and JULIET, Page 250.

As is the Bud bit with an envious Worm,
E're he can spread his sweet Leaves to the Air,
Or dedicate his Beauty to the SAME.

Sure all the Lovers of *Shakespeare* and Poetry will agree with me that --- *to the same* --- is here a very idle, dragging *Parapleromatick*, as the Grammarians style it. I do not think the Author was any ways necessitated to it, since he might by an additional *Epithet* in the foregoing Verse have avoided the Fault objected, and express'd his Thought with more Elegance: As thus,

E're he can spread his sweet and infant *Leaves,*
Or dedicate his Beauty to the Air.

This

This would have been the Natural Way of conveying his Idea, without those unpleasing *Expletives*: But SHAKESPEARE generally in his *Similies* is accurate in the *Cloathing* of them; and therefore, I believe, would not have over-charg'd This so *insipidly*. When we come to consider that there is some Power else besides *balmy Air*, that brings forth, and makes the tender Buds spread Themselves, I do not think it improbable that the Poet wrote thus;

> *E're He can spread his sweet Leaves to the* Air,
> *Or dedicate his Beauty to the* SUN. *

* Or Sunne, *according to the old Spelling, which brings it nearer to the Traces of the corrupted Text.*

CIV. *Ibid.* Page 259. EMENDATION.

> *We'll have no* Cupid *hoodwink'd with a Scarf,*
> *Bearing a* Tartar'*s painted Bow of Lath,*
> *Scaring the Ladies like a* CROW-KEEPER.

If there ever was such a Thing as a *Crowkeeper*, in Nature, I must own it is an Employment quite out of my Acquaintance. And surely, the Poet cannot be supposed to intend by it, a Man arm'd to *keep off the Crows*? --- I would read it, cashiering only a single Letter;

> *Scaring the Ladies like a* COW-KEEPER.

The Herdsmen of Old were used to watch in the Field, with Bows and Arrows, to defend their Cattle either from Dogs, or any other Injuries: Objects very likely to scare the Ladies, both from the Size of their Bows, and their aukward Method of managing them. What gives me the Foundation for this Suspicion and Emendation is the following Passage in K. LEAR, Page 86.

> Lear. *There's your Press-mony. --- That Fellow handles his Bow like a* COW-KEEPER.

For so Mr. POPE has very rightly restor'd it; tho' the second *Folio* Edition, (as does also my *Quarto*, publish'd in 1655.) reads it here too absurdly --- *Crowkeeper.*

CV. HAMLET, Page 382. EMENDATION.

> *Mean time, we thank you for your Well-*TOOK *Labour.*

I have Nothing to object to the Sense of this Passage, which I forgot to take Notice of in my Examination of this Play. The second *Folio* Edition however has a various Reading, which gives some Room for suspecting the Text as it now stands. It is there,

> *Mean time, We thank You for your Well-*LOOK'D *Labour.*

It is probable the Poet might, therefore, have wrote,

> *Mean time, We thank you for your Well-*LUCK'D *Labour.*

To say, that their Labour had been *well-took*, is saying, methinks, only that they had not *labour'd in vain*: But to say it was *well-luck'd*, is passing a Sort of Complement on the *Address*, *Skill*, and *Good Fortune*, of the Persons employ'd in it.

This Conjecture is of no great Moment, but I embrac'd the Mention of it the more readily, because it lends me an Opportunity of correcting Myself upon Another Passage of the same Play. I should reckon it very disingenuous, as well as ridiculous, in a Work which I have profess'd to have undertaken for the Restoration of SHAKESPEARE, if I should be asham'd to own myself mistaken, and retract the Error. In my Eighty Ninth Remark upon *HAMLET, I have call'd in Question the Text upon two Passages, where the Poet has made Use of the Word

* *Pag.* 119. & *seq.*

Word UNBATED. To avoid Repitition and Prolixity, I shall beg Leave to refer the Readers back to that Note. Since my Beginning this Appendix, I have chang'd my Opinion, and begin to think the *Text* may rather be *explain'd*, than *disturb'd* or *alter'd*. The Poet is speaking of *Swords* and *Foils*, and by a Sword UNBATED, perhaps, he may mean a Sword *unabated*, or not robb'd of its Point, to distinguish it from a *Foyl*, which is *blunted* and charg'd at the End with a *Button*. If we are to suppose the Poet wrote *Imbaited*, or daub'd over with an Ointment, (as I there conjectured,) it is absurd for *Laertes* to reply to the King, who tells him he might easily chuse a Sword ready *baited*, that he would *anoint* his Sword for the Purpose: Nor can there be any Occasion in the *Second* Passage for the *Epithet* ENVENOM'D, as *imbaited* signifies the same Thing. But I submit Both Opinions to Judgment.

EMENDATION. CVI. OTHELLO, Page 484.

Judge Me the World, if 'tis not gross in Sense,
That Thou ha'st practis'd on Her with foul Charms,
Abus'd her delicate Youth with Drugs, or Minerals,
That weaken MOTION.

Desdemona having fall'n in Love and married with *Othello*, *Brabantio*, her Father, accuses *Othello* of having used some foul Play, and intoxicated her by Drugs and Potions to win her over to the Match. But why, *Drugs* to weaken *Motion*? How then could She have run away with him voluntarily from her Father's own House? Had she been averse to chusing *Othello*, tho' he had given her Medcines that took away the Use of her Limbs, might She not still have retained her Senses, and opposed the Marriage? Her Father, 'tis evident from several of his Speeches, is positive that She must have been *abused* in her *rational* Faculties, or She could not have made so preposterous a Choice as to wed with a *Moor*, a *Black*, and refuse the finest Young Gentlemen in *Venice*. What then have We to do with her *Motion* being weaken'd? If I understand any Thing of the Poet's Meaning here, I cannot but think he must have wrote,

Abus'd her delicate Youth with Drugs, or Minerals,
That weaken NOTION.

i. e. her *Apprehension*, right *Conception*, and *Idea* of Things, *Understanding*, *Judgment*, &c. 'Tis frequent with us to say, We have no Notion of such a Thing, when we would mean, We do not very clearly understand it. The *Classics*, I think, have employ'd the Word in the same Sense: And CICERO, I remember, to quote no worse an Author, has defin'd it thus for Us. NOTIONEM *appello*, *quod* Græci *tùm* ἔννοιαν, *tùm* πρόληψιν.

EMENDATION. CVII. *Ibid.* Page 555.

What if I said, I'ad seen him do you Wrong?
Or heard him say, as Knaves be such abroad,
Who having by their own importunate Suit,
Or voluntary Dotage of some Mistress,
Convinced, or SUPPLIED *them, cannot chuse*
But they must blab. ---

I could not have wish'd to conclude with a more remarkable Instance of *Corruption*, or One that fell more closely within the Method which I propos'd to my self of *amending*. All the Editions concur in the Reading, and yet I'll be bold to say, 'tis neither *Sense*, nor *intelligible*, nor conveys our Author's *Sentiment* as it stands: So that it may fairly be look'd upon to have been one of his *Loci desperati*. His Meaning is undoubtedly This; That there are some such long-tongued Knaves in the World, who, if they thro' the Force of Importunity obtain a Favour from their Mistress, or if thro' her own Fondness they make her pliant to their Desires, cannot help boasting of their Success. Restore it, without the least Scruple, thus;

Who

Who having by their own importunate Suit,
Or voluntary Dotage of some Mistress,
Convinc'd, *or* SUPPLED *them,* they *cannot chuse*
But They must blab.

I have already observ'd, in the Course of these Sheets, that it is usual with SHAKESPEARE, thro' Negligence or Licentiousness, to change his Numbers, as he does here: So no more need be said on that Head. To *supple*, 'tis well known, is to make *pliant* and *flexible*; and is particularly a Term in *Surgery*, when any Part, swoln and stiff, is by *Fomentations*, &c. *reduced*, and made *soft* and *pliable*. To *convince*, here, is peculiar in its Sense; it is not, as in the common Acceptation, to make sensible of the Truth of any Thing by Reasons and Arguments; but to *overcome*, *get the better of*, &c. As the Usage of the Term in this Sort is one of the Author's Singularities, I'll produce two or three Passages, in Support of This before us, where it bears the same Sense.

MACBETH, Page 580.

Ay, Sir, there are a Crew of wretched Souls
That stay his Cure; their Malady convinces
The great Assay of Art.

LOVE'S LABOUR LOST, Page 173.

And tho' the mourning Brow of Progeny
Forbid the smiling Courtesy of Love,
The holy Suit which fain it would convince, &c.

And so in * CYMBELINE, more aptly to the Place for which I bring these Authorities;

* *Page* 136.

Your Italy *containes None so accomplish'd a Courtier to* convince *the Honour of my Mistress.*

CONCLUSION.

At tandèm Manum dè Tabulâ. ---- I have endeavour'd to acquit my self of the Promises made in my *Introduction*, and produc'd, and corrected, *Errors* throughout the Poet, numerous, when we consider This as a SPECIMEN only; of no Number, when compar'd with that unequal Quantity, which remain behind in Store to make our Author perfect. I may, indeed, say with Mr. POPE, that I have gone thro' this Work *with more Labour than I can expect Thanks:* I have run a Risque, and must wait the Sentence of the *Publick*, whether I have gone upon a mistaken View of Reputation, or whether I have done any Thing to set SHAKESPEARE in a clearer Light than his *Editors* have hitherto done. It is upon this Issue I shall be determin'd, whether I have already written too much on the Subject; or, whether I may promise my self Encouragement in prosecuting a Design, that savours more of *publick Spirit* than *private Interest*.

I ought to be in some Pain for the Figure that these Sheets may make, this being the *first Essay* of *literal Criticism* upon any Author in the ENGLISH Tongue. The Alteration of a *Letter*, when it restores Sense to a corrupted Passage, in a *learned Language*, is an Atchievement that brings Honour to the *Critick* who advances it: And Dr. BENTLEY will be remember'd to Posterity for his Performances of this Sort, as long as the World shall have any Esteem for the Remains of *Menander* and *Philemon*. But I no more pretend to do Justice to that Great Man's Character, than I would be thought to set my own poor Merit, or the Nature of *this* Work, in Competition with *his*.

I must expect some Attacks of Wit, upon being engag'd in an Undertaking of so much *Novelty:* The Assaults that are meerly *idle*, or meerly *splenatick*, I shall have the Resolution to despise: And, I hope, I need be under no great Concern for Those, which can proceed from a *generous Antagonist*. Wherever I am mistaken, it will be a Pleasure to me to be *corrected*, since the Publick will at the same Time be *undeceiv'd:* And wherever I have the Luck to be right in any Observation, I flatter my self, Mr. POPE himself will be pleas'd, that SHAKESPEARE receives some Benefit.

But to pass from Apologies on Account of these Sheets, however they may be received; I have a Number of Pardons to beg of my SUBSCRIBERS, who have done me the Honour to wait so long for my *Translation* of ÆSCHYLUS. My best Plea will be, that I have, in this Interval, been at the Expence of Copper Plates to be prefix'd to each Play, that I may by Ornament, at least, make up in Part for the Defects of my own Power. And as the DISSERTATION, to be prefix'd to that Work, is design'd a compleat History of the *Ancient* STAGE in all its Branches, I hope it will be agreed in my Favour, that the *Materials* for such a Collection must be *inrich'd* by the Delay.

FINIS.